CPP STUDY GUIDE

13th Edition

Contributing Authors:

James R. Bomba, CPP

Philip S. Deming, CPP

Special Recognition:

Milton E. Moritz, CPP

Edward F. McDonough, CPP

George C. Moore, CPP

Thirteenth Edition, May 2008

IMPORTANT NOTE

THE QUESTIONS CONTAINED IN THIS STUDY GUIDE ARE "SAMPLE" QUES-
TIONS ONLY AND HAVE BEEN DESIGNED PRIMARILY TO EMPHASIZE THE
SECURITY CONCEPTS INVOLVED. IF ANY QUESTION IN THIS STUDY GUIDE
HAPPENS TO BE WORDED EXACTLY THE SAME AS A QUESTION ON THE CPP
EXAMINATION, IT IS ENTIRELY BY ACCIDENT AS THE EDITORS HAVE MADE
NO EFFORT TO OBTAIN A LIST OF THE ACTUAL QUESTIONS.

PREFACE

This study guide has been designed primarily to provide those who intend to take the Certified Protection Professional (CPP) examination with resource data as a foundation for a comprehensive study program.

The material in this study guide concerns the following subjects:

Part I   Emergency Practices
Part II   Investigations
Part III   Personnel Security
Part IV   Physical Security
Part V   Information Security
Part VI   Security Principles and Practices
Part VII   Business Principles and Practices
Part VIII   U.S. Legal Aspects

Please note that the material in each part is presented in the format of "Basic Facts" followed by a section consisting of "Study" questions composed in a multiple choice format. The questions are not known to be similar in wording to the actual questions on the CPP examination, but have been selected to assist you in learing the key concepts of each of the subjects.

Following the sample questions is a section of answers together with the source citation for the correct answer.

IMPORTANT NOTE

The material in this Study Guide is designed as an educational tool to review the general subject matter covered in the CPP examination. The question format merely serves as a convenient method for the reader to determine his/her knowledge of a specific topic area.

The authors of this guide are recognized security professionals who have developed this material based solely on their experience, knowledge, and reference material. They have no affiliation with the CPP Program or the Professional Certification Board, and they have no knowledge of the CPP examination process, structure, or content not available to the general public.

The only similarity between the questions in this guide and those contained in the actual exam are that they are multiple-choice with four answer options. The writers and editors of this guide have no access to actual CPP examination questions.

The material contained in this Study Guide and in its references includes, but is not limited to the official suggested reading list.

PLEASE CONTACT THE CERTIFICATION DEPARTMENT AT ASIS HEADQUARTERS FOR ALL OFFICIAL INFORMATION CONCERNING EXAM CONTENT, THE CPP READING LIST, THE APPLICATION PROCESS, THE EXAM SCORING PROCESS, OR ANY OTHER ISSUE RELATED TO THE EXAMINATION.

TABLE OF CONTENTS

PART I - EMERGENCY PRACTICES

Basic Facts 1
Sample Questions 17
Answers 25
Significant Notes 28
Content Outline 30
Study Planning Tips 31
References 32

PART II - INVESTIGATIONS

Basic Facts 1
Sample Questions 19
Answers 22
References 24

PART III - PERSONNEL SECURITY

Basic Facts 1
Sample Questions 10
Answers 12
References 13

PART IV - PHYSICAL SECURITY ✐

Basic Facts 1
Sample Questions 26
Answers 34
Significant Notes 37
Content Outline 39
Study Planning Tips 40
References 41

PART V - INFORMATION SECURITY

Basic Facts 1
Sample Questions 19
Answers 24
References 26

PART VI - SECURITY PRINCIPLES AND PRACTICES ○

Basic Facts 1
Sample Questions 21
Answers 29
Significant Notes 32
Content Outline 35
Study Planning Tips 36
References 38

PART VII - BUSINESS PRINCIPLES AND PRACTICES

Basic Facts 1
Sample Questions 12
Answers 16
Significant Notes 18
Content Outline 20
Study Planning Tips 21
References 22

PART VIII - U.S. LEGAL ASPECTS

Basic Facts 1
Sample Questions 35
Answers 40
References 42

REFERENCES

Reference A–Drugs of Abuse A-1
Reference B–Excerpts from the Emergency Management Guide for
    Business & Industry B-1
Reference C–Bomb Threats and Physical Security Planning. C-1
Reference D–Detecting Suspicious Packages/Letters. D-1

I. Plan Development

A. General Facts

1. The three primary goals of emergency planning are:
   a. Protection of lives
   b. Protection of property
   c. Restoration of normal activities and operation

2. Emergency plans should be in writing.

3. The plans should be precise and specific.

4. A separate emergency plan should be prepared for each type of disaster which has a probability of occurring.

5. The most serious hazards commonly threatening industrial facilities are:
   a. Fire
   b. Explosion

6. During the past decade, the most common emergencies have been:
   a. Fire
   b. Bomb threat
   c. Labor dispute

7. Some key items which appear in most emergency plans are:
   a. Policy
   b. Risk assessment as to the hazard involved
   c. Emergency organization structure
   d. Description and details regarding emergency facilities
   e. Listing of emergency equipment and supplies
   f. List of mutual aid agreements
   g. Shut down procedures
   h. Evacuation procedures

8. A new organization should not be developed to handle emergency situations. The existing organizations should be able to take care of emergency and crisis problems.

9. The first step in establishing an emergency capability within a facility is the appointment of an emergency coordinator.

10. One of the persons designated with authority to declare an emergency must be available or on call at all times.

11. The management succession list must include enough names to insure that there is always an appropriate executive available during an emergency.

12. Leadership and direction are critical elements in the successful conduct of emergency programs.

13. Specifically required in a plan for continuity of leadership are measures to:
    a. Assure a functioning board of directors
    b. Establish lines of succession for key officers
    c. Establish an alternate company headquarters
    d. Assure records preservation

14. A major problem in emergency planning pertains to the situation where a large number of the members of the board are dead or unable to establish the quorum legally necessary for board action.

15. The following methods have been suggested to make certain a quorum is present during emergencies:
    a. Reducing the quorum number
    b. Summary filling of board vacancies
    c. Establishing an emergency management committee
    d. Appointing alternate directors

16. The security director not only should be involved in emergency planning but often the emergency organization is built around the security force.

17. Some key characteristics of the director of the emergency plan are:
    a. Should be member of top level management
    b. Is responsible for liaison with outside agencies and cooperating companies
    c. Will have authority to declare a state of emergency

18. The responsibilities of the emergency plan director include:
    a. Classifying emergency and (starting action)
    b. Activating emergency forces
    c. Ordering shutdown
    d. Ordering evacuation
    e. Making emergency announcement
    f. Requesting mutual aid
    g. Coordinating emergency action

19. In providing for continuity of management during an emergency, plans should call for the establishment of alternate headquarters.

20. The purpose of a remote control center is to bring together during an emergency, the policy-making skills, executive decisions and communications necessary to maintain vital production in time of disaster.

21. Security responsibilities in emergency situations may include:
    a. Access control
    b. Traffic and pedestrian control
    c. Protection of lives
    d. Protection of property
    e. Prevention of theft
    f. Evacuation control
    g. Assistance in first aid and rescue
    h. Protection of vital information
    i. Control of hazardous areas
    j. Fire fighting
    k. Establishing communication with outside agencies

22. Security will have special protective responsibilities during shutdowns.

23. Responsibility for a shutdown in a firm should be assigned to persons familiar with the specific operations. Emergency shutdown procedures should be developed and tested by the department managers concerned. Maintenance employees on each shift should be assigned specific responsibilities for emergency shutdown.

24. A relocation plan should be tested at least one day per year.

25. Distinctive signals should be established to identify fire and other emergency situations.

26. One aspect of emergency planning which will be relatively uniform for almost all situations is **evacuation procedures**.

27. Some key points regarding evacuation procedures:
    a. Advance training is necessary to prevent panic
    b. Exit routes should be clearly marked
    c. Wardens should be utilized where firm is large
    d. Security sometimes functions as warden

28. Evacuation routes and exits should be same for bomb threat or a fire.

29. Since fire is the primary destroyer of property, an emergency fire protection group should be organized and trained.

30. A mutual assistance agreement with local governments, other plants and nearby government installations is the most important aspect of plans for coping with major plant fires.

31. A very important aspect of emergency planning consists of cooperation in the form of a "Mutual Aid Association."

32. A "Mutual Aid Association" is a cooperative organization of industrial firms, business firms and similar organizations united by a voluntary agreement to assist each other by providing material, equipment, and personnel to help in disaster control functions.

33. Duplicate records for storage at alternate headquarters may be in a variety of forms:
    a. Microform
    b. Data tapes and disks
    c. Photocopies
    d. Blueprints

34. Photographic coverage of a disaster area is desirable for two main reasons:
    a. Insurance copies
    b. To support legal claims

II. Implementation

A. General Facts

1. Every industrial firm, regardless of size, should establish an internal organization that will be able to protect life and property in time of any emergency.

2. The first step in establishing an emergency capability is the appointment of an emergency coordinator at the corporate level. The coordinator has the responsibility to:
   a. Develop emergency organization
   b. Develop emergency plans
   c. Take preparedness measures
   d. Supervise recruitment and training of personnel

3. "Emergency Readiness" means preparation has reached the point where you are prepared to react promptly to save life and protect property if the plant is threatened or hit by major emergency.

4. The one thing that distinguishes disasters or major emergencies from the emergencies plant personnel deal with each day is the need for coordinated emergency operations.

5. The essential first step in preparing for disaster operations is the establishment of an overall corporate disaster plan.

6. The basic emergency plan should be made up of three elements:
   a. Authority
   b. Types of emergencies
   c. Plan of execution

7. All plant emergency operations plans should be in writing.

8. All emergency plans must be tested after being formulated.

9. The plan should be supported by appropriate appendices which might be needed during an emergency. The following appendices are recommended:
   a. Maps
   b. Procedure charts
   c. Call-up lists
   d. Listing of local resources
   e. Mutual-aid agreements
   f. A glossary of terms

10. A community-based emergency control center must be established to coordinate all efforts in a major emergency.

11. The emergency plan should include the following emergency shutdown elements:
    a. A complete checklist for emergency shutdown and disaster control
    b. Training of personnel to implement the emergency shutdown procedures
    c. Damage assessment and control techniques to minimize property loss.

12. The value of an emergency plan is that it:
    a. Provides a written record and means of communicating information throughout an organization
    b. Assures all procedures fit into an integrated plan
    c. Promotes uniformity
    d. Assures a permanent record of decisions and acquired knowledge
    e. Provides a means of orientation of new employees into emergency responsibilities
    f. Permits management to delegate specific authorities
    g. Presents a public relations medium for communication to employees, customers and stockholders

13. The basic operating element of a Mutual Aid Association is an operating board. The duties of an operating board are:
    a. Resolving group operating problems
    b. Preparing effective emergency plans
    c. Establishing a method of pooling resources
    d. Developing training program
    e. Conducting test drills
    f. Standardizing protective equipment

14. It is vital that all executives, supervisors, managers, foremen, section heads, and trade union representatives, be thoroughly acquainted with the emergency plan and give it their full support.

15. New employees should be made aware of the existence of the disaster plan as soon as they begin their career with the company.

16. "Vital Records" are those necessary to insure the survival of business. Vital records usually constitute no more than **two percent** of a corporation's records.

17. The following records are considered to be fundamentally vital to any corporate organization:
    a. The incorporation certificate
    b. The bylaws
    c. Stock records
    d. Board of directors minutes
    e. Certain corporate finance records

18. A suggested procedure for analyzing a company's vital records is as follows:
    a. Classification of company operations into broad **functional** categories
    b. The determination of the role of each function in an emergency
    c. The identification of the minimum information that must be readily accessible during or after a disaster or emergency to assure vital functions perform properly.
    d. The identification of the particular record that contains this vital information and the departments.

19. Effective protection of Electronic Data Processing (EDP) vital information is more complicated than safeguarding paper vital records for the following reasons:
    a. Formerly dispersed information is consolidated which increases its exposure to possible destruction or compromise.
    b. Data processing medium is extremely vulnerable to a wide variety of perils such as fire and water.
    c. The computer and the physical area in which located must be protected along with the vital information which is so closely linked to it.
    d. The adequacy and validity of the programs used to process this information and related computer operations documentation must be safeguarded to assure the usefulness, currency and accuracy of the basic information.

20. Recommendations for improving the physical security of a computer:
    a. Make the facility as inconspicuous as possible.
    b. Institute strict controls over access to the computer facility.
    c. Review possible computer facility exposure to water and fire damage.
    d. Provide sufficient emergency power generation capacity to compensate for voltage surges and otherwise maintain uninterrupted power input to the computer.
    e. Insure that alternate facilities to be used in an emergency are compatible with the company's computer and the work performed on it.

21. Data processing tapes and disks must be protected by specially insulated records containers which have been approved for temperatures up to 150° F and 80 percent humidity protection.

22. The integrity of computer processed vital records is maintained by careful control over:
    a. Data input and file access
    b. Program content revisions
    c. Computer facility operating procedures

23. The Vital Records Protection Plan should be tested at least once a year

24. The tests of Vital Records Program should verify that vital records needed after a disaster are:
    a. Current
    b. Protected sufficiently against natural disasters, nuclear detonation and other perils
    c. Retrievable as needed in usable form

III. Types of Emergencies

A. Natural Disasters

1. In assessing the vulnerability of individual facilities, major factors considered are:
   a. Environment
   b. Indigenous
   c. Economic

2. The major natural disasters which must be planned for are:
   a. Forest fires
   b. Hurricanes
   c. Floods
   d. Tornadoes
   e. Winter storms
   f. Earthquakes

3. A hurricane "warning" is issued as soon as the forecaster determines that a particular section of the coast will encounter winds of 74 m.p.h. or higher.

4. The onset of most floods allows for adequate warning.

5. Tornadoes are violent local storms with whirling winds that can reach 200-400 m.p.h. The width of a tornado ranges from 200 yards to one mile and travels 5-30 miles along the ground at speeds of 30-70 m.p.h.

6. Earthquakes may last from a few seconds to as many as five minutes. Most casualties during an earthquake result from falling materials.

7. During the actual shaking of an earthquake, employees should be warned to:
   a. Stay indoors if already there
   b. Take cover under sturdy furniture
   c. Stay near the center of the building
   d. Stay away from glass windows and doors

8. Some key weather terms are:
   a. **Severe thunderstorm** indicates the possibility of frequent lightning and/or damaging winds of greater than 50 m.p.h., hail and heavy rain
   b. **Severe thunderstorm watch** indicates the possibility of tornadoes, thunderstorms, frequent lightning, hail and winds of greater than 75 m.p.h.
   c. **Tornado watch** means tornadoes are expected to develop
   d. **Tornado warning** means that a tornado has actually been sighted in the area
   e. A **heavy snow warning** usually means an expected snowfall of four inches or more in a 12-hour period or six inches or more in a 24-hour period
   f. A **blizzard** is the most dangerous of all winter storms. A **blizzard warning** is issued when considerable snow and winds of 35 miles per hour or more are expected.
   g. A **severe blizzard warning** means that a very heavy snowfall is expected with winds of at least 45 miles per hour and temperatures of 10 degrees or lower
   h. **Freezing rain or freezing drizzle** is forecast when expected rain is likely to freeze as soon as it strikes the ground

B. Man-Made Disasters

1. The principal man-made disasters are:
   a. Plant fires
   b. Chemical accidents
   c. Transportation accidents
   d. Public demonstrations - civil disturbances
   e. Bomb threats
   f. Sabotage
   g. Radiological accidents
   h. Labor disturbances/strikes

2. The most important aspect of plans for coping with major plant fires is the development of mutual assistance agreements.

3. The biggest single need to combat plant fires is not manpower or equipment but the ability to respond quickly and to confine the fire to manageable limits.

4. All hazardous chemicals being transported must be appropriately labeled as to identification and caution.

5. Regardless of the type of transportation accident, the first consideration should be to save lives.

6. Public demonstrations and civil disturbances can usually be watched and planned for in order to arrange for control measures.

7. No facility is immune to sabotage but reducing target accessibility and vulnerability will help prevent it.

8. Methods of sabotage may be classified as follows:
   a. Chemical
   b. Electric or electronic
   c. Explosive
   d. Incendiary devices
   e. Mechanical
   f. Psychological

9. A large proportion of energy in a nuclear explosion is emitted in the form of light and heat generally referred to as **thermal radiation**.

10. A nuclear detonation produces an electro-magnetic pulse (EMP) which is easily picked up by any conductive material, damaging any electrical or electronic equipment connected to this material

C. Bomb Threats

1. An essential part of planning for bomb threats is contact with explosive ordinance disposal personnel and with local police.

2. Experience shows that 98 percent of all written or telephoned bomb threats are hoaxes.

3. If a telephone threat is received, the following key procedures should be followed:
   a. Keep caller on line
   b. Request caller to furnish location of bomb and time it is to detonate
   c. Note peculiar characteristics of caller's voice
   d. Record exact time of conversation
   e. Notify the security department and:
      1) Persons responsible for evacuation and search
      2) Law enforcement agencies
      3) Fire Department
      4) Medical authorities

4. The decision to evacuate a building upon receipt of a bomb threat should be made by a senior member of management.

5. Two factors which play a key role in the decision to evacuate are:
   a. Whether suspected bomb actually is found, or
   b. There is other compelling evidence that the bomb threat is real.

6. In a search for a suspected bomb the following key points are worthy of note:
   a. The facility manager should make the decision as to who should search.
   b. A search is made after every bomb threat call.
   c. The search includes common areas, occupied areas, and unoccupied areas.
   d. The area can best be searched by employees who work in that area.

e. When a suspicious object is found, the object should not be touched except by those specially trained in bomb disposal procedures.

f. A clear zone with a radius of at least 300 feet should be established around a suspicious object including the floors **above** and **below**.

7. A "bomb blanket" should be used only by specially trained personnel.

8. Those assigned to search a specific area should report to the control center after the completion of search.

9. If evacuation is ordered, elevators should not be used and doors and windows should be left open to allow for venting of the explosive force.

10. Control over the entry of personnel and materials is the most important countermeasure to bombs.

D. Strikes

1. In a potential strike situation, one of the most important early decisions to be made by management is whether to shut down or to continue operations.

2. If the facility remains open during the strike, note that:
   a. The union and its members are protected by law.
   b. The company cannot engage in "strike-breaking" activities.
   c. The security officer must maintain a professional impartial posture during the strike.

3. One of the key functions of the security force is to assist in controlling violence.

4. The most frequent strike is the "economic strike," which must be preceded by at least 60 days notice.

5. The "unfair labor practice strike" can occur suddenly with little or no effective planning.

6. Security must be very careful during its function to avoid unfair practice charges.

7. Technically the law does not allow picketing which prevents non-striking employees from entering or leaving the premises.

8. To help avoid violence, the number of access points to the premises should be as few as possible.

9. Arrange to minimize the amount of movement past pickets.

10. A key strike tactic is the **lockout** which is the refusal by management to allow members of the bargaining unit on the premises.

11. During the strike the use of car pools should be encouraged for a number of reasons:
    a. Provides added security
    b. Provides witnesses to illegal action
    c. Affords shelter and protection
    d. Reduces number of vehicles entering premises

12. The most important outside contact will be with local police.

13. A sound policy with respect to police arrests would be not to attempt to influence the police against initiating prosecutions where police are complaining witnesses.

14. Documentary surveillance of workers engaged in legal and legitimate labor practices such as legal picketing during a strike could amount to an unfair labor practice.

15. The professional police policy during a strike is that the police will respond to a strike site in sufficient number to prevent violence and that the law will be enforced fairly and criminal violations will not be condoned.

E. Terrorism

1. Kidnapping is a classic act of terrorism.

2. In developing preventive measures, a "duress code" should be established. This is a word or phrase which would be a signal to the listener that the speaker is under duress.

3. For most effective personal protection of a possible kidnapping target, a minimum of two bodyguards is recommended.

4. A kidnapping victim should:
   a. Endeavor to remain calm
   b. Do what they are told by captors
   c. Try to remember everything possible including movement, noises, and smells.

5. In event of kidnapping, notify appropriate law enforcement agencies.

6. Remember that payment of ransom or complying with any criminal demand, **without company approval** could render the payer civilly liable.

7. Key points regarding letter bombs:
   a. Will usually be mailed to a named person.
   b. The addressee will usually be a key official who is well known publicly.
   c. The letter will be larger, heavier, or thicker than a typical first-class business letter.
   d. It will bear no return address or a fictitious return address.

8. The best way to determine if a hostage is alive is direct communication.

9. The most common of all terrorist tactics is bombing.

IV. Fire Protection
A. General Facts

1. There are fire-resistant buildings, but no fireproof buildings.

2. **Fire-loading** is the amount of combustible materials that occupy its interior spaces.

3. The four legs of a fire consist of heat, fuel, oxygen and a chemical reaction.

4. Several by-products accompany every fire:
   a. Smoke
   b. Gas
   c. Heat
   d. Expanded air

5. Fires are classified as follows:
   a. Class A - fire in ordinary combustibles (waste paper, rags, and furniture).
   b. Class B - fire fueled by gasoline, grease, oil or volatile fluids.
   c. Class C - electrical fires
   d. Class D - fires involving combustible metals (magnesium, sodium and potassium).

6. Extinguishing agents for the 4 classes of fires are:
   a. Class A - extinguished by water or water fog
   b. Class B - CO2 or water fog
   c. Class C - A non-conductive extinguishing agent
   d. Class D - extinguished by dry powder

7. Different types of extinguishers
   a. Soda and Acid - effective on Class A fires (Green Triangle)
   b. Dry chemical - generally used for Class B (Red Square)
   c. Dry powder - effective on Class D fires (Yellow Star)
   d. CO2 - generally used on Class C fires (Blue Circle)
   e. Water fog - very effective for Class A & B fires

8. Fire alarm systems consist of two main parts:
   a. Signaling device
   b. Sensor

9. A normal fire proceeds through 4 basic stages:
   a. The incipient stage - no smoke at this point
   b. Smoldering stage - smoke begins to appear
   c. Flame stage - at this point we see actual visible fire
   d. Heat stage - at this point the heat is intense and building up

10. The principal fire sensors are:
    a. Ionization detector - this sensor is useful in giving early warning
    b. Photoelectric smoke detector - when source of light is interrupted, unit alarms
    c. Infrared flame detector - it reacts to emissions from flame
    d. Thermal detectors - it operates on a significant change in temperature

11. Manual fire alarm stations are of two types:
    a. Local alarms which are for the purpose of alerting personnel in the building.
    b. Stations from which a signal is transmitted directly to a monitoring station.

12. The automatic sprinkler system is ordinarily activated by the melting of a metal seal and water then flows through the system when the head valves are released.

13. An ongoing fire safety program will reduce losses due to fire by eliminating the causes of most fires:
    a. Carelessness
    b. Ignorance

14. Some key educational fire prevention tips:
    a. Fire should be reported first and then attempt should be made to extinguish it
    b. Alarm system should be clearly explained
    c. Avoid panic
    d. Elevators are never to be used
    e. Never open a "hot" door
    f. If escape is cut off:
       1) Move as far from fire as possible
       2) Move into a perimeter area with a solid door
       3) Remove readily flammable material out of area
       4) Open top and bottom of windows
       5) Stay near floor
       6) Endeavor to alert fireman to plight by hanging material from window

15. As a general rule, industrial facilities can be evacuated in just a few minutes.

16. Most fires are **electrical** in origin.

17. More fire fatalities are caused by toxic gases than by the flames.

18. The major causes of death in a building fire are:
    a. Toxic gases
    b. Smoke
    c. High temperatures
    d. CO2
    e. Fear and resultant actions
    f. The fire itself

19. A sprinkler system consists of the following elements:
    a. Water supply
    b. Fire-activated sprinkler devices (heads)
    c. Water control valves
    d. Mechanism to activate the audible alarm system

20. Most sprinklers will operate at temperatures between 130° and 165° F.

21. Halogenated agents (1211,1302) are non-corrosive chemical agents used for extinguishing fires in areas containing computers and electrical equipment.

22. A **wet-pipe sprinkler** system is made up of sprinkler devices attached to pipes which are filled with water.

23. A **dry-pipe sprinkler** system contains air under pressure, when sprinkler is activated, the air which is released opens valves allowing a flow of water into the pipes.

24. A fire door is for the purpose of impeding the spread of the fire.

25. Automatic fire doors are held open until there is sufficient combustion to trigger the door closing devices.

26. Many industrial facilities prepare for fire emergencies by establishing "fire brigades" of qualified fire fighters.

V. CONCEPTS AND TERMS

A. General Facts

1. **Assets:** Products, processes, and/or personnel that are critical to the organization's operations. Identifying assets is the central feature of the risk analysis process. The risk analysis methodology should allow the analyst to define what is to be protected and their value. Assets may be categorized as tangible and intangible. Examples include: facilities, hardware, software, supplies, documentation, personnel, reputation, and morale.

2. **Annual Loss Exposure:** The projected loss (in dollars) that one can expect to lose in a year as a result of emergencies.

3. **Business Continuity (BC) and Continuity of Operations (COOP):** Plan that includes measures to keep an organization in operation in the face of an emergency and may include procedures that involve the temporary or permanent relocation of personnel and/or functions.

4. **Business Impact Analysis (BIA):** Integral part of the business continuity planning process (COOP). Used to identify critical functions, to assess the impact of a disaster or other emergency on those functions over time, to determine the other elements of the business on which those critical functions depend, and to help develop and prioritize recovery strategies.

5. **Business Recovery Planning:** The process of developing the capability to offset the effects of business disruption. The process involves arranging alternatives for critical business functions and planning for business or service survival.

6. **Comprehensive Emergency Management (CEM):** Four-pronged process developed and applied at the state and local government level and has been applied to business continuity. The four elements are mitigation, preparedness, response, and recovery.

7. **Consequence/Outcome:** The undesirable result of a threat's action against the asset, which results in measurable loss to the organization.

8. **Crisis:** A wide variety of events that cause significant disruption to the normal activities of an organization as a whole.

9. **Crisis Management:** A planned, systematic response that permits an organization to continue making its products or providing its services during an emergency. It allows the organization to capitalize on the expertise of personnel from various disciplines who plan for and manage the situation.

10. **Emergency Operations Center (EOC):** Location from which the emergency response can be directed.

11. **Emergency Preparedness:** Planning considerations that must be in place for a company to effectively respond to and manage an emergency event.

12. **Incident Command System (ICS):** A command and control mechanism used by many public safety agencies. ICS normally consists of five primary elements: Command, Operations, Planning, Logistics, Finance, and Administration.

13. **Likelihood of Occurrence:** A measure of the probability of a loss-causing event.

14. **Mitigation:** Actions involving lasting, often permanent, reduction of exposure to, probability of, or potential loss from hazard events.

15. **Preparedness:** Actions taken before an event to plan, organize, equip, train, and exercise in order to deal with emergencies that cannot be avoided or entirely mitigated.

16. **Recovery:** Involves near-term and long-term actions taken to return the organization to a pre-emergency level of operation or, in some cases, to a new level of operation. Recovery efforts may include implementation of continuity of operation or business resumption plans, activation of emergency relocation sites, and reconstitution or restoration at the original location or a new permanent location.

17. **Response:** Entails the implementation of the emergency plan to deal with the short-term effects of the event. Response may include incident identification, emergency notification, activation and deployment of emergency teams, and evacuation of personnel

18. **Risk:** The potential for causing losses due to the presence of a threat and vulnerability. A risk is derived from the analysis of the threat and corresponding vulnerabilities along with the probability of their interaction.

19. **Risk Analysis:** A procedure used to estimate potential losses that could result from various vulnerabilities and the damage from the action of certain threats. Risk analysis identifies both the critical assets that must be protected and the environment in which these assets are located.

20. **Risk Exposure:** The disclosure of high probability vulnerabilities.

21. **Safeguards:** Physical controls, mechanisms, policies, and procedures designed to protect assets from threats.

23. **Threat:** A person, thing, event, or idea that poses some danger to an asset. The actions of a threat may compromise the confidentiality, integrity, or availability of an asset by exploiting vulnerabilities or weaknesses in the safeguards system.

24. **Vulnerabilities:** Weaknesses in the safeguards system, or the absence of safeguards. Vulnerabilities can be clearly associated with threats: For example, the threat of fire is associated with the vulnerability of inadequate fire protection, and the threat of unauthorized access can be linked to inadequate access controls.

1. Searches made during work hours as a result of a bomb threat call should be made by:
   a. Local police department
   b. Military personnel
   c. Federal investigative personnel
   d. Employees familiar with work area where bomb is reportedly located

2. A cooperative organization of industrial firms, business firms, and similar organizations within an industrial community that are united by a voluntary agreement to assist each other by providing materials, equipment and personnel needed to ensure effective industrial disaster control during emergencies is called:
   a. Emergency squads
   b. Mutual aid association
   c. Community emergency cooperatives
   d. Disaster control squads

3. Which of the following procedures should not be advocated as part of emergency planning?
   a. Emergency plan should be in writing
   b. Emergency plan should be revised as needed
   c. Distribution should be limited to senior management
   d. Plan should be tested through practice

4. The greatest single destroyer of property is:
   a. Bombs
   b. Sabotage
   c. Fire
   d. Earthquakes

5. Responsibility for shutdown of machines in the plant as a result of disaster should be assigned to:
   a. The security officers on duty
   b. The maintenance persons on duty
   c. The persons familiar with the shutdown process
   d. The plant manager

6. In the event the media makes contact as a result of a crisis situation, they should:
   a. Be given "no comment"
   b. Be put in touch with person designated in the emergency plan for orderly release of information
   c. Be put in contact with the president of the company
   d. Be put in contact with the plant manager

7. Which of the following does not fit into good emergency planning?
   a. An individual should be appointed as coordinator
   b. Plan should be in writing
   c. Plan should be simple
   d. A new organization should be developed to handle emergency situations

8. The ionization fire detector warns of fire by responding to:
   a. Invisible products of combustion emitted by a fire at its earliest stages
   b. Infrared emissions from flames
   c. Light changes
   d. Smoke

9. The fire detector which responds to a predetermined temperature or to an increase in temperature is known as:
   a. Ionization detector
   b. Photoelectric smoke detector
   c. Infrared flame detector
   d. Thermal detector

10. The fire detector which responds to changes or interruption in the light source is known as:
    a. The ionization detector
    b. The photoelectric smoke detector
    c. The infrared flame detector
    d. Thermal detector

11. After a bomb threat is made and a suspicious object is found during search, it should be:
    a. Handled with great care
    b. Disarmed immediately
    c. Reported immediately to designated authorities
    d. Placed in a bucket of water

12. The removal of any suspected bomb should be done by:
    a. Proprietary guard force
    b. Office employees
    c. Professional bomb-disposal personnel
    d. The patrol office of the city police department

13. Which of the following is **not** suggested behavior for the victim of a kidnapping?
    a. Stay calm
    b. Do not cooperate with captors
    c. Do not try to escape unless good chance of success
    d. Try to remember events

Copyright © 2008 by ASIS International

14. In connection with corporate kidnapping by terrorists, the decision as to whether ransom is to be paid should be made by:
    a. Local police
    b. Spouse or blood relative of victim
    c. City government
    d. Highest corporate level

15. Which of the following should not be applicable to the development of an effective emergency disaster plan?
    a. Plan should be written
    b. It should involve the minimum number of people possible in the preparation of the plan
    c. It should contain an inventory of available resources
    d. It should list preventative measures

16. Earthquake emergency plans should stress that the safest place during a quake is:
    a. Within work area under preselected cover
    b. At work in open spaces away from building
    c. At home
    d. In a building made of concrete

17. In a strike, the refusal by management to allow members of the bargaining unit on the premises is called:
    a. A lockout
    b. Shutout
    c. Lock in
    d. Permissive picketing

18. At the time of a strike, if no guard force is available, the following action should be taken:
    a. Immediately hire one
    b. Mobilize supervisory personnel into a patrol group
    c. Have police come on property to act as security force
    d. Have maintenance employees trained to act as guards

19. In a labor dispute which of the following measures is **not** advisable?
    a. Change all perimeter gate padlocks
    b. Issue special passes to non-striking employees
    c. Notify employees who go to work to keep windows rolled up
    d. Armed guards

20. Usually the most difficult part of an Executive Protection Plan is:
    a. To secure trained personnel
    b. To initiate liaison with Federal Agencies
    c. To initiate liaison with local authorities
    d. To convince the executive being protected on the need for such protection

21. Which of the following is **not** recommended action with regard to survival of earthquakes?
    a. If outside, immediately go inside
    b. Keep calm
    c. Douse all fires
    d. Keep away from utility wires

22. Of all reported bomb threats, it is estimated that the percentage of real threats is:
    a. 2-5 percent
    b. 7-10 percent
    c. 15 percent
    d. Less than 1 percent

23. A full evacuation of a building should be ordered upon receipt of a bomb threat when:
    a. The caller is credible and a suspicious object is located
    b. Any threat is received
    c. Threat is received during working hours
    d. The caller has foreign accent

24. You are charged with the responsibility of formulating a disaster plan to handle emergencies which arise as a result of earthquakes. Which of the following warnings to be issued to employees as to their actions during the shaking should **not** be included in the plan?
    a. If employees are outside, proceed to the nearest building and head for the basement promptly.
    b. If employees are indoors at the time of shaking, they should stay there.
    c. If inside, take cover under sturdy furniture.
    d. If inside, stay near center of building.

25. Earthquakes constitute a definite concern to the emergency management responsibilities of security managers in certain areas of our country. Accordingly, it is incumbent upon our security professionals to have a clear understanding of the basic facts concerning earthquakes. Which of the following is an incorrect statement?
    a. Earthquakes are unpredictable and strike without warning.
    b. Earthquakes may last from a few seconds to as much as five minutes.
    c. The actual movement of the ground in an earthquake is usually the direct cause of injury or death.
    d. Quakes may also trigger landslides and generate tidal waves.

26. Potential disasters caused by man should be included when developing a firm's emergency plan. One of the most common man-made disasters is the plant fire. Which of the following is considered to be the most important aspect of plans for coping with major plant fires?

    a. To make certain that the plant's fire-fighting equipment is adequate and in good operating condition.

    b. To make certain plant personnel are well-trained in fire-fighting techniques.

    c. To make certain that there is a command center with excellent communications.

    d. To make certain that mutual assistance agreements have been developed with local governments, other plants, and nearby installations.

27. Compared with other plant emergencies, bomb threats present a highly complex problem for plant management and emergency service personnel. Which of the following actions should not be in the bomb threat emergency plan as it is incorrect?

    a. Planning to meet the threat should include contact with a nearby military explosive ordnance disposal detachment (EODD).

    b. Prior planning should include contact with the local police department.

    c. Training programs for plant specialists in handling improvised explosive devices should be utilized when available from the military explosive ordnance disposal control center.

    d. The chief of police must make the decision whether or not to evacuate a building after a bomb threat has been received.

28. The continuity of business and industrial leadership and direction are essential parts of all industrial emergency plans. The following specific measures should be included in the development of a plan for continuity of leadership except:

    a. Assure a functioning board of directors.

    b. Establish lines of succession for key officers and operating personnel.

    c. Establish an alternate company headquarters.

    d. Provide for special stockholder's meeting immediately after attack to provide for methods of operation.

29. In reviewing the emergency plans of the ZYX Corporation, the legal counsel of the firm notes that there is a definite possibility that a quorum of the board of directors cannot be readily assembled which will not allow action in accordance with law. Which of the following methods generally would not be acceptable to remedy this legal problem?

    a. Reduce the quorum number if allowed by state law.

    b. Summary filling of board vacancies if allowed by state law.

    c. Establishment of an emergency management committee, if allowed by state law.

    d. Utilizing chain of command, execute proper power of attorney papers for the top three officials so the most senior could execute legal affairs if board not functioning.

30. In devising plans to protect vital records during an emergency, a prime decision to make would be the identification of vital records. Whether such records are vital depends, to a large extent, upon the type of business conducted. However, as a general rule, all of the following would be considered vital to any corporate organization except:

    a. The incorporation certification.

    b. Personal identification fingerprints of employees.

    c. The by-laws of the corporation.

    d. The stock record books.

31. Which of the following statements is incorrect in selecting records to be included in a vital records program:

    a. Management should protect vital records by systematically determining what information is vital.

    b. The vital records protection program is an administrative device for preserving existing records.

    c. If a particular record does not contain vital information, it has no place in the company's vital records protection program - even though having other value to the company.

    d. Decision making in determining individual vital records should be rapid. A record either contains vital information or it does not.

32. Comprehensive emergency management (CEM) is the term for a four-pronged process used by the emergency management community throughout the United States. The four elements of CEM are:

    a. Mitigation, preparedness, response, and recovery

    b. Mitigation, containment, response, and recovery

    c. Mitigation, preparedness, containment, and recovery

    d. Preparedness, containment, response, and recovery

33. The president of the ZYX Company expresses concern relative to the company's ability to act in time of emergency to protect life and property. He instructs that you undertake the necessary action to establish the desired emergency capability within the facility. Which of the following should be the first step in initiating this action?

    a. Contact established guard companies to make bids to oversee the operations.

    b. An emergency coordinator should be appointed at the corporate level.

    c. Make a physical survey of the plant.

    d. Form a committee of key executives to operate out of the command center.

34. In establishing a disaster plan, provision should be incorporated which would permit you to be prepared for a variety of emergency situations. Which of the following probably would not have a key role in such plans?

    a. Employee welfare service.

    b. Rescue teams.

    c. The recreational coordinator.

    d. Radiological Defense Service.

35. Perhaps one of the most difficult tasks in planning for disasters and emergencies is the actual formulation of a basic disaster plan. Which of the following is an incorrect procedure in developing such a plan?

    a. The basic plan should provide for coordination of government and company actions before and during a disaster.

    b. A glossary of terms used should be included.

    c. There should be a listing of types of emergencies limited to those experienced by the company in the past.

    d. The plan should utilize appendices as needed such as maps, call-up lists and mutual aid agreements.

36. While protection of people is the first priority in emergency planning, shutdown procedures must be thorough and done by those who are trained to do so. Your disaster plans should have such shutdown procedures assigned to:

    a. The security force.

    b. The plant manager.

    c. Employees on each shift who handle these procedures on a regular basis.

    d. The fire brigade.

37. In order to adequately plan for emergencies, the security manager must make certain that this corporation has access to all necessary resources that will save lives, minimize damages, and insure the continued operation of rapid restoration of damaged member plants. Most plants assure access to such resources by:

    a. Providing for a budget which will supply all the resources needed to cope with a major emergency.

    b. Establishing appropriate liaison with the police, fire, rescue and medical forces of the community to provide services as needed.

    c. Relying upon their own self-help organization and equipment and joining hands with other plants in the community for mutual aid.

    d. Establishing appropriate contact with nearest military base.

38. In forming an industrial mutual aid association, a number of definitive plans must be made. Which of the following is not true and should not be relied upon in formulating these plans?

    a. Each member firm must be willing to defray Industrial Mutual Aid Association expenses.

    b. Capital outlay and operating costs are usually modest.

    c. The basic operating element of a mutual aid association is an operating board.

    d. Any industrial mutual aid association should be established in advance of emergencies.

39. A key role in any emergency will be played by the plant manager or in his place, such authorized official as emergency coordinator or security chief. Which of the following should not be done personally by this official?

    a. Take personal charge of all operations at the disaster scene.

    b. Activate the plant control center.

    c. Alert and inform head of local government emergency coordinator.

    d. Brief plant control center staff on the emergency situation.

40. The keys to the success of any emergency organization and plan are training and testing. In designing effective testing procedures, the following are all valid observations except:

    a. Records should be maintained so deficiencies can be corrected following the test.

    b. The testing exercise should be as realistic as possible.

    c. Plenty of advance notice should be given so all possible preparations can be made.

    d. One of the best times to test the plant emergency plan is in coordination with your local government periodic test exercises.

1. d. Employees familiar with work area where bomb is reportedly located
   Source: *Protection of Assets Manual*

2. b. Mutual Aid Association
   Source: *Protection of Assets Manual*

3. c. Distribution should be limited to senior management
   Source: *Protection of Assets Manual*

4. c. Fire
   Source: *Protection of Assets Manual*

5. c. The persons familiar with the shutdown process
   Source: *Protection of Assets Manual*

6. b. Be put in touch with person designated in the emergency plan for orderly release of information
   Source: *Protection of Assets Manual*

7. d. A new organization should be developed to handle emergency situations
   Source: *Protection of Assets Manual*

8. a. Invisible products of combustion emitted by a fire at its earliest stages
   Source: *Protection of Assets Manual*

9. d. Thermal detector
   Source: *Protection of Assets Manual*

10. b. The photoelectric smoke detector
    Source: *Protection of Assets Manual*

11. c. Reported immediately to designated authorities
    Source: *Protection of Assets Manual*

12. c. Professional bomb-disposal personnel
    Source: *Protection of Assets Manual*

13. b. Do not cooperate with captors
    Source: *Protection of Assets Manual*

14. d. Highest corporate level
    Source: *Protection of Assets Manual*

15. b. It should involve the minimum number of people possible in the preparation of the plan
    Source: *Protection of Assets Manual*

16. a. Within work area under preselected cover
    Source: *Protection of Assets Manual*

17. a. A lockout
    Source: *Protection of Assets Manual*

18. b. Mobilize supervisory personnel into a patrol group
    Source: *Protection of Assets Manual*

19. d. Armed guards
    Source: *Protection of Assets Manual*

20. d. To convince the executive being protected on the need for such protection
    Source: *Handbook of Loss Prevention and Crime Prevention*

21. a. If outside, immediately go inside
    Source: *Protection of Assets Manual*

22. a. 2-5 percent
    Source: *Security & Loss Prevention*

23. a. The caller is credible and a suspicious object is located.
    Source: *Handbook of Loss Prevention and Crime Prevention*

24. a. If employees are outside, proceed to the nearest building and head for the basement
    promptly.
    Source: *Protection of Assets Manual*

25. c. The actual movement of the ground in an earthquake is usually the direct cause of injury
    or death.
    Source: *Protection of Assets Manual*

26. d. To make certain that mutual assistance agreements have been developed with local
    governments, other plants and nearby federal installations.
    Source: *Protection of Assets Manual*

27. d. The chief of police must make the decision whether or not to evacuate the building after a
    bomb threat has been received.
    Source: *Protection of Assets Manual*

28. d. Provide for a special stockholder's meeting immediately after attack to provide for
    methods of operation.
    Source: *Protection of Assets Manual*

29. d. Utilizing chain of command, execute proper power of attorney papers for the top three
    officials so the most senior could execute legal affairs if board not functioning.
    Source: *Protection of Assets Manual*

30. b. Personal identification. Fingerprints of employees.
    Source: *Protection of Assets Manual*

31. b. The vital records protection program is an administrative device for preserving existing
    records.
    Source: *Protection of Assets Manual*

32. a. Mitigation, preparedness, response, and recovery.
    Source: *Protection of Assets Manual*

33. b. An emergency coordinator should be appointed at the corporate level.
    Source: *Protection of Assets Manual*

34. c. The recreational coordinator
    Source: *Protection of Assets Manual*

35. c. There should be a listing of types of emergencies limited to those experienced by the
    company in the past.
    Source: *Protection of Assets Manual*

36. c. Employees on each shift who handle these procedures on a regular basis.
    Source: *Protection of Assets Manual*

37. c. Relying upon their own self-help organization and equipment and joining hands with
    other plants in the community for mutual aid.
    Source: *Protection of Assets Manual*

38. b. Capital outlay and operating costs are usually modest.
    Source: *Protection of Assets Manual*

39. a. Take personal charge of all operations at the disaster scene.
    Source: *Protection of Assets Manual*

40. c. Plenty of advance notice should be given so all possible preparations can be made.
    Source: *Protection of Assets Manual*

1. The most significant hazard threatening industrial facilities is fire.

2. A new organization should not be developed to handle emergency situations, but the existing organizations should be prepared to take care of the situations.

3. A search is made after every bomb threat call.

4. The search includes common areas, occupied areas, and unoccupied areas.

5. Control over the entry of personnel and materials is the most important countermeasure to bombs.

6. The emergency plan is tested at least annually.

7. Data media must be protected in specially insulated records containers which protect the contents against temperatures up to 150° F and 80 percent humidity.

8. The automatic sprinkler system is ordinarily activated by the melting of a metal seal and water then flows through the system when the head valves are released.

9. Government and industry share the responsibility for emergency and disaster planning.

10. The emergency plan must be distributed to all personnel with responsibility for action.

11. A "bomb blanket" is used only by specially trained personnel.

12. "Vital Records" are those necessary to insure the survival of business. Vital records usually constitute no more than **two percent** of a corporation's records.

13. Responsibility for a shutdown should be assigned to persons familiar with the process.

14. The emergency plan is activated by the facility manager, the president, or the CEO.

15. The emergency plan should be directive in nature.

16. In a fire, the facility must have "the capability to respond quickly with well trained personnel to contain and extinguish the fire".

17. In a high rise building, partial evacuation includes the floor above and the floor below.

18. The most common of all terrorist tactics is bombing.

19. The purposes of emergency planning are to:
    a. Anticipate the emergency;
    b. Provide action during the emergency; and,
    c. Return to normal operations.

20. In dealing with plant fires, mutual assistance and prior coordination with the fire department is essential. The critical element is the ability to respond quickly with well trained personnel to contain and extinguish the fire.

21. A tidal wave (**Tsunami**) is caused by underwater disturbances.

22. The focus of disaster control planning is on solutions to major problems and to prevent a disaster from becoming a tragedy.

23. The three principles of disaster control planning are:
    a. Coordinated planning;
    b. Mutual assistance; and,
    c. Community resources.

24. When a bomb threat is received, the following are notified, in order:
    a. Persons responsible for search and evacuation;
    b. Local authorities;
    c. Explosive demolition teams; and,
    d. Medical facilities.

CPP Study Guide

1. Implementation

2. Plan development

3. Types of emergency

Formulate a study plan of the following specific concepts:

1. Natural and man-made disasters

2. Emergency lines of executive succession

3. Plant emergency operations planning

4. Planning for management continuity

5. Mutual aid association for emergencies

6. Emergency service operations

7. Bomb threats

8. Emergency shut-down procedures

9. Alternate headquarters

10. Protection of vital records

11. Development of basic disaster planning

12. Public relations

13. Disaster recovery

14. Warning and alert systems

15. Corporate disaster plan manual

16. Security/fire protection

17. Executive protection/terrorism

18. Testing/evaluation of plan

ASIS International. (2008). *Protection of Assets Manual.* Alexandria, VA: ASIS International.

— Alarm Sensors

— Emergency Management

— Strikes and Labor Disturbances

— Bombs and Bomb Threats

— Executive Protection

Fennelly, Lawrence J. (2004). *Handbook of Loss Prevention and Crime Prevention*, (4th ed.), Elsevier/Butterworth-Heinemann, Burlington, MA.

Fischer, Robert J., Halibozek, Edward, and Green, Gion (2008). *Introduction to Security*, (8th ed.), Elsevier/Butterworth-Heinemann, Burlington, MA.

I. The Investigative Process

When we speak of an investigation, we are talking about a fact-finding activity that involves searching, examining, observing, collecting data, and studying this information in order to respond to a particular inquiry or address a complaint.

The investigative process evolves thorough several stages: (i) from deciding whether to investigate the matter; (ii) to selecting an investigator; (iii) to planning, articulating the objectives and developing the methodology for the investigation; (iv) to obtaining information; (v) preparing the investigative reporting; and (vi) managerial decision-making based on the investigative fact-finding.

A. Key Qualities of an Effective Investigation:

Essentially, most investigations can be characterized by five (5) key components which are:

1. Objectivity:
   a. Any fact, regardless of its significance to preconceived ideas, is accepted.

2. Thoroughness:
   a. All investigative leads are verified in order to achieve consistency in the results; and
   b. Information should be corroborated through differing sources as a means to achieve thoughtfulness and fairness.

3. Relevance:
   a. Any information developed must pertain to the focus of the investigation; and
   b. Unrelated information should not askew the quality of the information pertaining to the subject of the investigation.

4. Accuracy:
   a. Data that can be verified and quantified should be scientifically measured;
   b. Confidential sources should be tested on the quality of information provided; and
   c. All information must be examined for inherent contradictions.

5. Timeliness:
   a. The ability to complete an investigation within a reasonable period of time. However, these efforts must not be made in haste as to jeopardize the quality of the inquiry.

B. Goals of an Investigation:

1. Identify parties involved;

2. Identify sources that can provide information; and

3. Present evidentiary factors to support investigative findings.

C. Objectives of an Investigation:

To attempt to answer the "six (6) basic questions:"

1. Who?

2. What happened?

3. Where?

4. When?

5. How?

6. Why?

D. Tools of the Investigator (i.e., the three "I's"):

1. Information:, the knowledge which the investigator obtains from other persons;

2. Interrogation: which includes the skillful questioning of witnesses as well as suspects; and

3. Instrumentation: methods of physical science used to detect crime (e.g., physics, biology and pathology[1]).

E. Types of Investigations: [Three Main Categories]

1. Applicant and background investigations;

2. Incident investigations; and

3. Administrative inquiries.

II. Applicant and Background Investigations:

Typically, an employer, when hiring a new employee or promoting an employee to a new position, wants to be able to judge whether that individual has the appropriate background necessary for the position.

In order to assess an applicant for employment, this investigation is commonly referred to as a pre-employment background investigation. The preemployment background investigation is intended to determine *skills, knowledge, and abilities.*

In the case of a current employee, the employer will conduct a post-employment background investigation in order to seek relevant information for determining if promotion or transfer is

---

[1]Pathology is the scientific study of the nature of disease, its causes, processes, development, and consequences.

appropriate. Each of these types of investigations is governed by industry practices, statutory rules and regulations, and common law.[2]

Within the context of workplace violence, the preemployment and post-employment background investigations can serve as an opportunity for an organization to reduce the potential risk exposure.

A. Preemployment Background Investigation:

1. A statement of release should be executed by the applicant prior to initiating any investigative activities.

   [**Note:** Do not accept the résumé as the form of authorization. However, for EEO purposes, a résumé must be treated like an application.]

2. Verify the accuracy and competency of the representations made by the applicant;

3. Develop additional relevant information;

4. Determine if applicant's character, experience, and past practices are suitable for employment consideration; and

5. When conducting a background investigation, the interviewee should be informed that the "inquiry is in connection with a position of trust."

6. The employer background investigation should be completed prior to the applicant being offered a position of employment.

7. Once the offer has been extended and accepted, the hiring process is not complete until the employee has been verified as eligible for employment

B. Post-Employment Background Investigation:

1. The seeking of any information should be obtained in accordance with statutory requirements; and

2. Any adverse information should be verified by additional sources.

3. Unfavorable information should be retained for not less than three years.

III. Incident Investigations:

Incident investigations are precipitated by an event occurring or a complaint made by someone concerning the alleged conduct of another. As in all investigations, the activities are governed by industry practices, statutory rules and regulations, and common law.

---

[2]Common law identifies with and consists of judicial opinions and decisions of courts.

A. Claims Investigations:

Key components for such investigations:

1. All serious, significant, and/or sensitive claim investigations should be handled through personal contact.

2. The scope of these investigations will be determined by the nature and extent of the claim.

3. Certain information should be obtained such as:
   a. Notice of the claim by the reporting party.
   b. Coverage information, including and not limited to identification of vehicles, premise, product, and value of item covered under the claim.
   c. Statements of:
      (1) Material witnesses.
      (2) Claimants.
      (3) Independent witnesses (i.e., insurance producer, claims adjuster, appraiser).
   d. Official agency reports (i.e., police, rescue, hospital, fire department, weather, etc.)
   e. Newspaper, periodicals, and other media reportings (i.e., television, electronic).
   f. Reports from experts (i.e., appraisers, physicians, laboratory analysis, and forensic analysis).
   g. Visual aids (i.e., diagrams, photographs, videos, x-rays, models).
   h. Documentary evidence (i.e., deeds, mortgages, leases, contracts, liens, and other claims).

4. Interviews should be carefully documented. If interviews are designed in a statement fashion, there are two (2) types of statements:
   a. Narrative; and
   b. Question and answer.

   [**Note:** Any recordings, notes or other documentation should be maintained.]

B. Employee Misconduct Investigations:

1. These investigations are designed to determine if the employee has:
   a. Violated any company rules, policies; and/or
   b. Violated any state or federal laws.

2. Discretion is essential in this type of investigation.

3. Investigative techniques utilized during an internal investigation may include:
   a. Interviews on a selected basis;
   b. Searches to locate and preserve physical evidence;
   c. Conducting surveillances;
   d. Using confidential sources;
   e. Preparing photographic aids; and
   f. Checking permanent records.

4. Substance Usage:
   a. Abuse of substances is generally considered an indication of psychological or physiological need;
   b. Substance abusers have common characteristics of a feeling they need the psychological or physiological support of the substance;
   c. Substance abusers commonly have a history of maladjustment;
   d. Substance abuse is usually learned by:
      (1) Absenteeism;
      (2) Accidents;
      (3) Arrests; or
      (4) Reports from others.

5. Conflict of interest – is created when an employee: (i) engages in personal business transactions that arise from or are based on an employee's position of authority; (ii) owns a financial interest in a business that does business with a company; and/or; (iii) participates in an opportunity discovered from information provided by competitor, customer or supplier.

6. Workplace violence – are acts or threats of violence including conduct which is sufficiently severe, offensive, or intimidating to alter the employment conditions at the organization or to create a hostile, abusive, or intimidating work environment for one or more of its employees, visitors or others.

7. Embezzlement – key factors which contribute to employee embezzlement are:
   a. Extravagance;
   b. Heavy or chronic dependency on wagering or substance abuse;
   c. Living beyond income; and/or
   d. Undesirable associates.

8. One of the most effective countermeasures against embezzlement is a disciplined environment with appropriate audits and other safeguards.

9. Fraud – acts of fraud usually occur in a variety of forms such as:
   a. Falsification of employee timecards;
   b. Falsification of employment application;
   c. Falsification of accident/injury claims; and
   d. Falsification of expense reportings.

10. The most difficult type of fraud to deal with is the fraudulent accident/injury claim, because no preventative measure can be effectively instituted.

C. Compliance Investigations

In essence are investigations relating to the determination of ensuring that the organization and its employees have complied with all laws, regulations, and policies. These investigations may include: equal employment opportunity, harassment, workplace safety, confidential and proprietary information, conflict of interest, antitrust violations, securities requirements, and regulatory violations.

D. Explosion, Bombing and Arson Investigations:

1. An explosion is defined as a sudden, violent and noisy eruption, outburst or discharge of material acting upon a force such as fire, shock, or electrical charge which causes the material, either solid or liquid, to convert into a gaseous state and violently expand or burst.

2. There are three (3) basic rates of explosion and they are:
   a. Flash fire - an immediate reaction in which its fuel is consumed upon ignition;
   b. Explosion - a sudden outburst or discharge of material upon force or other material; and
   c. Detonation - a strong shock wave set up by a primary and secondary high explosive.

3. Detonations are multiple or compound explosions.

4. Flash fires usually occur in the open; if confined within a building, an explosion occurs.

5. Three (3) basic types of explosions are:
   a. Mechanical (e.g., steam building up in a boiler with a defective safety device will cause a sudden rupture and a mechanical explosion will occur);
   b. Chemical (e.g., resulting from an extremely rapid conversion of a solid or liquid explosive compound into gases); and
   c. Nuclear (e.g., an explosion is accomplished when the nucleus of an atom is split releasing tremendous energy).

6. There are two (2) general types of substances having detonation capabilities:
   a. **Low explosives.** Common examples of low explosives would be black powder, smokeless powder, and nitrocellulose.
   b. **High explosives.** Common examples of high explosives would be nitroglycerin, dynamite, nitro starch, TNT, picric acid, mercury fulminate, tetryl, lead azide nitromannite.

7. An implosion is a sudden bursting inward while an explosion is a sudden bursting outward.

8. Some of the key motives of the crime of arson are:
   a. Economic gain;
   b. Personal satisfaction;
   c. Sabotage;
   d. Pyromania; or
   e. Diversionary tactic to conceal the commission of other crimes.

9. Every fire, regardless of size, should be investigated.

10. Who investigates fires for determining cause and origin and responsibility?
    a. Fire department;
    b. Local police;
    c. Federal agencies (i.e., ATF, FBI);
    d. Insurance representatives; and
    e. Private organizations.

E. Sabotage Investigations:

1. A willful act designed to hinder or obstruct the purposes for which an organization operates.

2. Some motives for sabotage:
   a. Disgruntled employee;
   b. Union conflict;
   c. Dissatisfied outside contractor;
   d. Organized crime element;
   e. Foreign manipulation; or
   f. Rioting.

3. It is difficult to identify and prove acts of sabotage.

4. If sabotage is strongly suspected, the following action should be taken:
   a. Notify law enforcement authorities; and
   b. Preserve evidence.

5. A common type of sabotage, arson, is generally effective and tends to destroy evidence because evidence is consumed in the fire itself.

F. Theft Investigations:

1. An effective "loss control program" will do much to prevent internal theft.

2. Key elements in an effective loss control program:
   a. Carefully designed safeguard measures and preventive aids;
   b. Prompt reporting of missing items;
   c. Taking of immediate steps towards apprehension and recovery;
   d. Prosecution; and
   e. Remedial action.

3. Some commonly recognized key vulnerable areas are:
   a. Shipping and receiving;
   b. Warehouses and other storage areas;
   c. Stock rooms;
   d. Tool storage; and
   e. Parking lots.

4. Key points in conducting theft investigations:
   a. A complete description of missing items including:
      (1) Serial, model, and other identifying numbers;
      (2) Distinctive marks; and
      (3) Monetary value.
   b. Shipping/transfer/inventory documents;
   c. Ownership data;

d. Date and time loss noted;

e. To whom loss reported;

f. Exact location in which loss occurred;

g. Circumstances such as forced entry;

h. Extent of search; and

i. Internal control/security measures contributing to theft.

G. Traffic Accident Investigations:

1. In the emergency (first) phase of an accident:
   a. Care for the injured;
   b. Get any fire or other hazards under control;
   c. Locate drivers and possible witnesses;
   d. Determine any existing traffic hazards; and
   e. Locate and safeguard physical evidence.

2. After emergency phase is under control:
   a. Determine condition of drivers and conduct interviews regarding licensing, registration, and their explanations of what happened;
   b. Gather evidence for identifying any hit and run vehicles;
   c. Interview other witnesses;
   d. Determine and report position and condition of vehicles involved;
   e. Photograph vehicles and debris at the scene;
   f. Determine and report where injured persons and damaged vehicles were taken;
   g. Determine weather, visibility, and road surface conditions at time of accident;
   h. Determine traffic control devices at the scene;
   i. Ascertain any illegal conditions of equipment ownership, registration, etc.
   j. Determine how, if any, actions of drivers contributed to accident; and
   k. Thoroughly examine tire marks, skid marks, and tire imprints.

3. Other investigative steps which can be done away from the scene after the accident:
   a. Obtain medical records;
   b. Complete interviews of drivers and/or witnesses;
   c. Notify relatives of deceased or injured;
   d. Notify owners of vehicles;
   e. Determine vehicle damage and condition for contributing factors;
   f. Prepare investigative report; and
   g. Inform interested agencies of conditions at scene of accident requiring attention.

4. Measurements and maps important in accident investigations are usually of three (3) kinds:
   a. Urgent measurements to locate things at the scene;
   b. Measurements of location to make scale maps and diagrams; and
   c. Drawing a map from the measurements made and locating on it objects or marks at the scene.

Copyright © 2008 by ASIS International

5. Written statements should be taken, if possible, from all witnesses and drivers.

6. Photographs of an accident scene are most important to show:
   a. Position of vehicles at time of accident;
   b. Damage;
   c. Angles of collision;
   d. Marks on road;
   e. Paths of vehicles before, during and after collision; and
   f. Overall condition of scene as viewed by driver.

7. Reconstruction of an accident is usually necessary only when the cause of an accident cannot be satisfactorily determined by available evidence.

H. Undercover Investigations:

This is the placement of an operative in a situation in which the parties do not know the operative's true identity or purpose. The intent is to develop information for prosecution (either civil or criminal), for recovery, or limitation of asset losses.

1. Objectives:
   a. Obtain evidence of a past act or future crime;
   b. In asset diversion, identify persons engaged, methods used, and/or the destination of diverted materials;
   c. Identify parties involved in the activity; and
   d. Establish that certain employees engaged in activities for which disciplinary action can be taken.

2. Potential Problems:
   a. Injury: Employees may react violently to prevent discovery.
   b. Exposure: Employee morale, customer/supplier relationships, labor availability, distribution of goods may suffer.
   c. Unfair Labor Practices: Interference, restraint or coercion of employees in the exercise of the collective bargaining rights.
   d. Civil Actions for Damage: The accuser must show an intrusion at the time and place where there was an expectation of privacy, or public disclosure of private facts. The investigative techniques must stop short of any actual invasion of privacy.
   e. New Bargaining Issue: Disciplinary action might cause a grievance and an allegation that the investigation was a contractual violation.

3. Requirements for the Undercover Investigation:
   a. Investigator: Must not be known to the target population and must be a "logical" fit in the assignment. The investigator must know:
      (1) The identity of the control person;
      (2) Means of contact with the control person;
      (3) Actions forbidden;

(4) The general purpose of the assignment;

(5) Cover story; and

(6) Work environment.

b. Cover Story: Explains qualifications of the job, how he/she got the job and his/her past life. Routine documents are provided to support the cover. No document of actual identity is carried by the undercover operative.

c. Placement Technique: The method to place the undercover operative in the undercover assignment. The job must cover the area involved, have few controls and allow the operative to appear ordinary. The "tailor-made job" should be avoided.

d. Control Scheme: There are two (2) essentials, a control person and a control plan.

(1) The control person provides instructions, evaluates reports, and redirects efforts as needed. There should be an alternate to the control person who possesses the same information as the control person.

(2) The control plan includes:

➢ Control person(s) authorized to contact the operative;

➢ Means and frequency of communication contact;

➢ Contingencies (i.e., illness of the undercover operative, injury to the undercover operative, investigation is compromised);

➢ Law enforcement relations;

➢ Support resources (surveillance) and

➢ Termination of the investigation.

e. Communications:

(1) The contact telephones must be answered whenever called;

(2) Normal contact is made by the operative;

(3) All communications are recorded electronically if permitted by statute; and

(4) Communication is made daily.

f. A "drop" must be:

(1) Reasonably accessible;

(2) Not likely to be disturbed; and

(3) Where material will not be affected by weather.

g. Law enforcement relations: If criminal charges are secondary in importance, it may be better to proceed without law enforcement. Once law enforcement has been invited to participate in the investigation, due process requirements apply.

(1) Civil Liability: Private undercover operatives are not afforded the same protection as police officers who are protected by statute from crimes the officer commits when performing his duty in connection with an undercover operation. If a private undercover operative knows that he or she may be subject to committing illegal acts or engaging in a conspiracy to commit illegal acts, law enforcement authorities should be contacted or consulted.

h. Within the organization:

(1) Ideally, the undercover operative <u>should not</u> come from within the employer's organization.

       (2) No persons are informed or involved of the undercover operation unless it is essential to the plan;

       (3) No routine briefings are conducted; and

       (4) When other management personnel are required, these individuals should be informed of the investigation on a selected basis only.

  i. Terminating the investigation:

       (1) Planning the termination considerations:

          ➢ If the investigation will ever be disclosed;

          ➢ How to withdraw the undercover operative without creating questions; and

          ➢ How to use the results without exposing the undercover operative and/or the investigation.

       (2) If the investigation is compromised, the objectives are:

          ➢ Withdraw the undercover operative immediately and safely;

          ➢ Salvage as much from the investigation as possible; and

          ➢ Prepare explanation, defenses, or positions needed to offer if necessary.

       (3) If compromised, the true identity of the undercover operative must not be revealed. Discontinue the investigative activity and wait for (or create) an opportunity for a natural withdrawal from the undercover investigation.

4. Analysis:

The control person of the undercover investigation prepares reportings of all useful information developed during the course of the investigation. Analysis should be conducted to determine issues relating to the investigation.

5. Costs:

Include the prevailing wage paid to the undercover operative, payroll taxes, and the fee paid to the undercover operative and/or his/her agency. The expense is the reason for the daily reporting and information control.

6. Summary:

  a. Use undercover investigations when there is no alternative method available;

  b. Define the purpose and objectives clearly in advance of the investigation;

  c. Anticipate problems and difficulties clearly;

  d. Select a qualified resourceful operative;

  e. Prepare a plausible cover story;

  f. Devise an appropriate penetration;

  g. Have an effective control person and control plan;

  h. Budget sufficient funds to facilitate the investigation;

  i. Have a careful and well thought out placement and withdrawal plan; and

  j. Review all legal aspects, including licensing and requirements for the undercover operative.

V. Administrative Inquiries:

Such investigations are undertaken to ensure that an organization has complied with all laws, regulations, and policies. However, these investigations are not precipitated by any event occurring or any compliant being made by a party.

VI. Methods of Investigations:

A. Evidence:

In a board sense, those tangible objects (which show) or intangible things (which tell, such a witness statement) are the two (2) main categories of evidence, which are developed during the course of an investigation.

1. Real evidence is that which speaks for itself (i.e., fingerprints, gun, tire print).

2. Handling Evidence - Basic Rules:
   a. Photograph and sketch crime scene before moving articles; and
   b. Restrict handling to absolute minimum number of persons to shorten chain of evidence.

3. Marking Evidence:
   a. Avoid obliterating evidence while marking;
   b. Use a distinctive mark where possible;
   c. Should include date evidence secured and location from where taken; and
   d. Mark should be on item itself where possible.

4. Preserving evidence - key points:
   a. Allow blood stains to dry before packing for shipment to faraway lab.
   b. Submit all suspected body fluid stains to laboratory.
   c. Do not allow articles of suspect and victim to contact each other.
   d. In obtaining known specimens of hair from victim and/or suspect, submit at least 50 hairs from various areas of head.
   e. Never place loose fibers in a mailing envelope since they are difficult to locate and paper from which most envelopes are made contains fiber.
   f. If soil is firmly attached to some object, send object itself to laboratory.
   g. In case of glass headlights, all glass remaining in the shell should be recovered.
   h. Scrape paint samples off using a clean knife blade.
   i. Volatile liquids should be poured into clean glass bottle and sealed tightly.
   j. Bullets should be marked on the base.
   k. Cartridge cases should be marked on the inside of the open end.
   l. Unfired ammunition should be marked on the side of the cartridge case near the end of the bullet.

m. A questioned document should be sealed in a plastic or cellophane envelope.

n. Charred documents are placed on top of loose cotton in a box and hand delivered to the lab.

B. Interviews and Interrogations (i.e., Confrontational Interviews):

Interviews and interrogations are methods of gathering information from people. We differentiate between the two (2) methods in the following manner:

1. An interview is the questioning of a person who has or is believed to have information of relevant interest to the investigation.

2. Conversely, an interrogation or confrontational interview is the questioning of a person suspected of having committed an offense, or of a person who is reluctant to fully disclose information pertaining to the investigation.

The circumstances of each of these particular methods of interview are indicative of the characteristics of the investigative functions. Specifically, the investigator may initially start the investigation by interviewing a subject and then subsequently shift into a confrontational interview.

3. The key elements in conducting an investigative interview:
   a. To gain information to establish the facts of an incident or reporting;
   b. To verify information received from other sources;
   c. To identify additional witnesses;
   d. To identify persons responsible for the event and/or accomplices;
   e. To secure additional evidence;
   f. To develop background information on the specifics of the event or offense;
   g. To eliminate suspects; and
   h. To discover details of other offenses.

4. Procedural considerations when conducting an interview are as follows:
   a. Subject's statements must be **free** and **voluntary**;
   b. Interview be conducted in a manner in which an objective third party to the interview is there;
   c. Party is not restricted from personal movement and is free to leave;
   d. Position the interviewee within the confines of the interview area;
   e. Number of persons conducting the interview should be kept to no more than two (2) persons, so as not to intimidate the interviewee; and
   f. Consideration of the interviewee's background, intelligence, education, biases, emotional state, medical condition (i.e., physical health, substance usage).

5. Communicate with the interviewee on a level that he/she can understand;

6. Be observant for physical activities (i.e., fidgeting, nail biting, foot or finger tapping) or physiological activities (i.e., eye blinking, dry mouth, perspiration);

7. Be mindful of interviewee who is reluctant to talk. This may offer an indication of the need to protect himself/herself or others.

8. Responsiveness to certain questions may offer an indication of interviewee's need to relieve himself/herself of guilt. It may offer other motives for providing information.

9. Techniques of the Investigator:
   a. Establish a good rapport;
   b. Maintain eye contact;
   c. Do not jump to conclusions, maintain an open-mindedness;
   d. Listen attentively (i.e., be an active listener);
   e. Be perceptive to every comment; and
   f. Maintain control of the interview.

10. Strategies for the Investigator:
    a. Ask open-ended questions. Ask questions that require the interviewee to offer a more detailed response.
    b. Use silence as a method of soliciting a response from the interviewee.
    c. Have the interviewee offer a chronology of events starting from the beginning of the incident;
    d. Test the voracity of the truthfulness of the interviewee's responses by asking questions to which you know the answers;
    e. Discuss the seriousness or gravity of the incident or inquiry;
    f. Request the interviewee to repeat his/her version of the events;
    g. Identify any inconsistencies in the interviewee's statement and review the same with the interviewee;
    h. Appeal to the emotions of the interviewee;
    i. When appropriate, confront the interviewee with certain information that you have gathered during the course of your investigation;
    j. Maintain control, be aggressive, and be fair.

11. The form of a written statement may be:
    a. Narrative;
    b. Question and answer; or
    c. Combination.

12. The techniques most commonly used during an interrogation are:
    a. Sympathetic; and/or
    b. Logic and reasoning.

13. There are two (2) main approaches used with regard to interrogation:
    a. Indirect approach - exploratory in nature; or
    b. Direct approach - normally used to interrogate a suspect whose guilt is reasonably certain.

C. Devices to Detect Deception:

1. The best known types of devices to detect deception are:
   a. Polygraph, also known as a lie detector; or
   b. Psychological stress evaluation.

2. The polygraph records changes in respiration, blood pressure, pulse, and skin's sensitivity to electricity.
   a. The Employee Polygraph Protection Act of 1988 describes situations in which the polygraph examination may be conducted in the workplace:
      (1) An employer may use polygraphs to assist in their "ongoing investigation" of certain kinds of workplace crimes.
      (2) An employer who engages in providing certain kinds of security services may use polygraphs for preemployment screening of certain prospective employee candidates.
      (3) An employer who engages in manufacturing, distribution or dispensing certain controlled drugs may use polygraphs for some preemployment screening of certain prospective employee candidates and for investigation of certain incident-specific losses.

   A polygraph examination is only as good as the examiner.

3. Key points with regard to the psychological stress evaluation are:
   a. Does not require body attachment;
   b. It records and analyzes stress-related components of the human voice; and
   c. It may be used with or without the knowledge of the individual being tested.

D. Surveillance:

1. Surveillance is the process of observing persons, places, or activities during the course of an investigation.

2. A surveillance can be either covert or overt.

3. Results of a surveillance may be admitted into evidence in accordance with regular rules or evidence.

4. There are two basic forms of surveillance:
   a. Physical surveillance—done by humans; and
   b. Technical surveillance—done by technical and electronic equipment.

5. The most difficult type of surveillance is the "moving surveillance."

6. There are three (3) kinds of "moving surveillance:"
   a. Keep subject under observation regardless of whether you are "made";
   b. Discreet surveillance (discontinued as needed to keep from being "made"); and
   c. Keep subject under observation at all times and do not get "made."

7. Surveillance logs should be maintained and may be introduced into evidence.

8. Surveillance is expensive.

9. An electronic surveillance is also known as "bugging" or "wiretapping."

V. Results and Reports of Investigation:

A. Report Writing:

Investigative reports vary among organizations. However, in general, the report must be complete and readily understood by its reader.

There are key components that should be in this report such as:

1. Administrative Information

2. Summary

3. Narrative

4. Conclusion

5. Enclosures

B. Some key points regarding report writing are as follows:

1. Use short sentences;

2. Use short paragraphs;

3. Use simple words;

4. Be accurate;

5. Be clear;

6. Conceal confidential information; and

7. Be a fact-finder.

C. Statements and Confessions:

1. Confessions and statements must be voluntary;

2. There is no prescribed format for confessions or statements;

3. A person giving a statement must be appropriately advised of his/her rights;

4. A waiver of rights should be in writing;

5. It is preferable to have a statement typed, because many handwritten statements are difficult to read; and

6. An unsigned statement is not as good as one that is signed, but may be of value.

D. Distribution of Reports:

Sensitive information will usually be contained in the report of investigation, and it is important that copies be distributed only on a need-to-know basis. There is a possibility that a report of investigation or other documentation will be subject to discovery by means of a subpoena during litigation. The mere labeling of a document as "company sensitive" or "confidential" will not prevent discovery under certain circumstances. Consultation with legal counsel on how to safeguard documents in connection with the investigation is appropriate.

VI. Investigative Resources:

A. General:

1. Sources which are private or confidential should be identified in the file by a symbol or a code name. The actual identity should be recorded in a separate and secure place.

2. Reports of investigation and investigators under appropriate circumstances can be reached by subpoena.

B. Informants:

1. The term "informant" can be applied to any source which reveals information not readily available to the general public.

2. An informant is a very valuable resource to private investigators.

3. Endeavor to ascertain the real motivation of a source in furnishing information and constantly check out the reliability of the source.

4. The eight typical classifications of informants are:
   a. One-time Informant—is a person who has specific information and desires for the information to be acted upon.
   b. Occasional Informant—is a person who provides information from time to time.
   c. Employee Informant—is a person who may be considered a one-time or occasional informant and can be a source for intelligence within the organization.
   d. Anonymous Informant—is a person who does not disclose his/her identity.
   e. Criminal Informant—is a person who provides information on a *quid pro quo* [Latin: "something for something"], such as a release from criminal charges or reduced imprisonment. However, money is the key motive for providing the information.
   f. Personal Informant—is a person who provides information exclusively to one party (i.e., the investigator) and will only interact with this person.

g. Mentally Disturbed Informant—is a person with a mental defect who provides information.

h. Controlled Informant—is a person who possesses direct knowledge or is directly involved in the activities under investigation.

C. Proprietary Resources:

1. It is better to staff a proprietary investigative unit with personnel who have acquired investigative experience before joining the proprietary security organization.

2. The investigator's job should be regarded as an "exempt"[3] job because it is considered to be "professional" to the extent it requires special preparation.

3. The two (2) most important expense items in the budget of an investigations unit are:
   a. Personnel costs; and
   b. Communication costs.

---

[3]Under the Fair Labor Standards Act, employees are defined as either "exempt" or "non-exempt" for purposes of overtime pay consideration. "Exempt" employees are not required to be paid overtime by the employer.

1. There are several stages in an investigative process. Which of the following is **not** considered a stage?
   a. Whether to investigate
   b. Legal evaluation
   c. Gathering information
   d. Managerial decision-making

2. Which of the following is **not** a requirement for a successful undercover investigation?
   a. A qualified investigator
   b. A plausible cover story
   c. An effective control scheme
   d. Developing necessary evidence for prosecution

3. If necessary to terminate an undercover investigation which one of the following should **not** be done:
   a. Withdraw agent safely
   b. Withdraw agent immediately
   c. Salvage as much of the result of data
   d. Reveal identity of the agent

4. The principal item of expense in an investigations budget will be:
   a. Office supplies
   b. Equipment
   c. Maintenance
   d. Personnel costs

5. The single most important administrative control in handling investigations is:
   a. Indexing
   b. Case assignment
   c. Case review
   d. Documentation of status

6. As a general rule, the number of consecutive years employment or non-employment that should be verified preceding the date of investigation are:
   a. 5 years
   b. 7 years
   c. 3 years
   d. 2 years

7. Any investigation containing unfavorable information should be retained in file for a period not less than:
   a. 1 year
   b. 5 years
   c. 3 years
   d. 2 years

8. The rule that states that approximately one in ten applications will have major omissions which will require going back to the applicant is called:
   a. The Rule of Ten
   b. The Rule of Nine
   c. The 1-10 Rule
   d. The Verification Rule

9. Which of the following should be interviewed last or near the end of an investigation under usual circumstances:
   a. Those with extensive information
   b. Those preparing to take a trip out of area
   c. Those likely to be hostile
   d. Those with less than extensive information

10. If interviewee during investigations is hostile, it is preferable to conduct the interview at:
    a. The security office
    b. Home of interviewee
    c. A neutral location
    d. An automobile

11. Which of the following characterization regarding investigative surveillance is **not** true?
    a. They are expensive
    b. They are time-consuming
    c. They are often non-productive
    d. They are illegal in most jurisdictions

12. The process whereby communications are intercepted or recorded is known as:
    a. Physical surveillance
    b. Technical surveillance
    c. Surreptitious surveillance
    d. Black bag operations

13. It is becoming increasingly more difficult to do a good preemployment background investigation because:
    a. Expense
    b. Lack of skilled investigators
    c. Various laws and court decisions which inhibit the use of techniques and/or instruments available.
    d. Uncooperative attitude of persons interviewed

14. Interviews should be conducted:
    a. In the company of suspect's attorney
    b. In an area where distractions are minimal
    c. In a comfortable room which is well furnished like home
    d. In an area where light is focused in suspect's face

15. An undercover operator should be:
    a. A member of the investigative staff of the organization
    b. A trusted employee in the department under investigation
    c. Unknown by anyone likely to be in the target population
    d. An off duty law enforcement officer

16. One of the objectives of an undercover investigation is **not** to:
    a. Establish a method of diversion of goods
    b. Ascertain the level of organized labor activity in the work force
    c. Provide information for personnel action
    d. Obtain evidence of past or future crime

17. In an incident investigation, the general rule is to first interview persons who:
    a. Are not likely to be available for later interview
    b. Are likely to be hostile
    c. Have the most extensive information about the incident
    d. Are familiar with some part of the subject matter

18. Which of the following is **not** true regarding communications with an undercover agent:
    a. Normal contact is initiated by the agent
    b. The contact telephone should be answered with the name of the company
    c. An alternate contact telephone number should be established
    d. The telephones should be reserved exclusively for investigations

1. b. Legal evaluation
   Source: *Security and Loss Prevention,* p. 224

2. d. Developing necessary evidence for prosecution
   Source: *Protection of Assets Manual*

3. d. Reveal identity of the agent
   Source: *Protection of Assets Manual*

4. d. Personnel costs
   Source: *Protection of Assets Manual*

5. a. Indexing
   Source: *Protection of Assets Manual*

6. a. 5 years
   Source: *Protection of Assets Manual*

7. c. 3 years
   Source: *Protection of Assets Manual*

8. a. The Rule of Ten
   Source: *Protection of Assets Manual*

9. c. Those likely to be hostile
   Source: *Protection of Assets Manual*

10. a. The Security Office
    Source: *Protection of Assets Manual*

11. d. They are illegal in most jurisdictions
    Source: *Protection of Assets Manual*

12. b. Technical surveillance
    Source: *Protection of Assets Manual*

13. c. Various law and court decisions which inhibit the use of techniques and/or instruments available
    Source: *Protection of Assets Manual*

14. b. In an area where distractions are minimal
    Source: *Protection of Assets Manual*

15. c. Unknown by anyone likely to be in the target population
    Source: *Protection of Assets Manual*

16. b. Ascertain the level of organized labor activity in the work force
    Source: *Protection of Assets Manual*

17. a. Are not likely to be available for later interview
        Source: *Protection of Assets Manual*

18. b. The contact telephone should be answered with the name of the company
        Source: *Protection of Assets Manual*

ASIS International. (2008). *Protection of Assets Manual,* Alexandria, VA: ASIS International.

Fischer, Robert J., Halibozek, Edward, and Green, Gion (2004). *Introduction to Security,* (8th ed.). Burlington: Butterworth-Heinemann.

Purpura, Philip P. (2008). *Security and Loss Prevention: An Introduction,* (5th ed.). Burlington: Butterworth-Heinemann.

Sennewald, Charles A. (2003). *Effective Security Management,* (4th ed.). Burlington: Butterworth-Heinemann.

Whitman, Michael E. and Mattord, Herbert J. (2008). *Management of Information Security,* (2nd ed.). Boston: Thomson Course Technology.

I. Purpose and Functions:

A. Personnel security's primary purpose is to ensure that an organization hires those candidates best suited to assist the organization in achieving its desired goals. After the individual is hired, this employee now serves to augment the security program by protecting the organization's assets (e.g., people, property and information).

B. Vulnerability to losses caused by employees is measured in part by the character of the employees, their awareness of asset protection requirements and their motivation to cooperate.

C. Personnel security is one of the three major security processes utilized in providing the total protection of an organization. The two other components are:

1. Information security

2. Physical security

D. Personnel security is the most critical security process, because the potential risk (e.g., theft, embezzlement, release of sensitive information) could be perpetrated by an employee.

E. The key functions of the personnel security process are:

1. Screening

2. Background investigations

3. Investigation of current employees suspected in violation of organization's rules and regulations

4. Security awareness and educational programs

5. Protection of employees from discriminatory practices

F. A comprehensive personnel security program should include the following elements:

1. Adequate job specifications[1] which are documented in the form of a job description

2. Appropriate applicant screening procedures and standards

   [***Note:*** A well constructed application form serves as a pre-screening device.]

3. Background investigative standards

4. Criteria for employee conduct and performance standards[2]

---

[1]Job specifications provide information to determine the worth of the job. For example, it identifies the *knowledge* and *skill* required.
[2]Performance standards describe the results that should exist upon the completion of a specific assignment or activity.

CPP Study Guide

5. Investigation process for questionable workplace conduct

6. Disciplinary or corrective action procedures (i.e., progress discipline)

7. Procedures for employee discharge

   [*Note:* A comprehensive personnel security program must be non-discriminative and in accordance with federal and state employment laws.]

II. Job Analysis and Job Description:

Prior to an organization engaging in the recruitment for employment, the organization must define the job specifications. The key tools in this process are the job analysis and the job description.

A. Job Analysis - the procedure by which jobs are researched to determine the activities and responsibilities. This includes:

1. The relationship the job has with other jobs within the organization;

2. The personal qualifications necessary to perform the job; and

3. The condition under which the work or tasks are performed.

B. Job Description - one of the important outputs of the job analysis is the job description. Based on the job analysis, a written job description can be prepared for the position within the organization.

Key elements within the job description:

1. General purpose of the job

2. Duties and responsibilities

3. Knowledge, skills, and abilities

4. Education and/or training

The job description can be used for:

1. Recruiting and screening

2. Test design (in relation to the job)

3. Hiring and placement

4. Orientation

5. Developing procedures

6. Training and development

III. Applicant Screening:

A. Verifies accuracy and completeness of applicant's statements and develops additional relevant information.

B. The key to an effective personnel security program is to endeavor to screen out the candidates who might pose a risk to the organization (e.g., not qualified for the position).

C. Deliberate misstatements or material omissions in any segment of the process should be considered major disqualifying features.

D. All relevant aspects of the candidate's background are weighed using the "whole man" rule.[3]

E. The governing standards should be the needs of the organization and fairness to the applicant.

F. Rejection should be on the basis of standards which have been clearly defined:

  1. The standards must be strictly adhered to

  2. The standards should be updated on a regular basis to ensure legal Compliance

G. Under federal law, there are certain criteria relating to the type of questions that candidates for employment may be asked. The following are federal laws that prohibit employment discrimination:

  1. Civil Rights Act of 1964 (hereafter referred to as "Civil Rights Act"), which prohibits employment discrimination based on race, color, religion, sex, or national origin. This law is applicable to those organizations that employ 15 or more employees.

  2. Age Discrimination Employment Act of 1967 (hereafter referred to as "ADEA"), which protects individuals who are 40 years of age or older. This law is applicable to those organizations that employ 20 or more employees.

  3. Americans Disability Act of 1990 (hereafter referred to as "ADA"), which prohibits employment discrimination against qualified individuals with disabilities.

     [**Note:** This statute is designed to protect qualified individuals with knowledge, skills, and abilities who can perform essential job functions and be able to perform these job functions with or without reasonable accommodation.] This law is applicable to those organizations that employ 15 or more employees.

  4. Equal Pay Act of 1963 (hereafter referred to as "EPA"), which protects men and women from performing essentially equal work in the same establishment from sexual-based wage discrimination.

---

[3]"Whole man" rule gives consideration for the totality of the person.

The Equal Employment Opportunity Commission (hereafter referred to as "EEOC") enforces all of the aforementioned laws. The EEOC also provides oversight and coordination of all Equal Employment Opportunity regulations, practices, and policies.

H. Focal Issues in a Screening Process:

1. Signs of instability in job/career

2. Candidate under or overqualified for position

3. Declining salary history

4. No referencing of former supervisors

5. Gaps in residences or unexplained moves

6. Inadequate or no personal references

I. Common Omissions and Falsifications:

1. Applicant's signature - The applicant does not sign the application.

2. Application date - The applicant is only responsible for the information listed as of the date of the application.

3. Education - Approximately 5 percent of all professional applicants falsify some aspect of their educational background.
   a. List schools, but omit dates of attendance or degrees
   b. List "diploma mills"
   c. List fictitious schools, omitting geographical location
   d. List recognized schools where applicant never attended
   e. Claim graduation from schools which applicant attended for a relatively short period of time
   f. Assume the name and degree of a bona fide graduate

4. Criminal records - They leave the question unanswered

5. Employment gaps - Applicants simply omit information

6. Former employers - The organization may have been owned/operated by the applicant or close relative.

7. There are virtually no restrictions on what can be asked of an individual once an offer of employment has been made.

8. Résumé (advertising promotional device) - Never accept a résumé in lieu of an application. It should, however, always be reviewed as part of the investigation.

J. Focus of the Background Investigation:

1. The purpose of the background investigation is to:
   a. Verify accuracy and completeness of candidate's statements
   b. Develop relevant information concerning the candidate
   c. Determine the candidate's suitability for employment

2. As a general rule, the background investigation should be completed prior to allowing the applicant to commence employment.

3. The most important information-gathering tool in a background investigation is the completed application form.

4. Application forms reveal substantial information pertinent to the investigation. Some key examples are:
   a. Name and variations
   b. Citizenship
   c. Military record
   d. References
   e. Any security clearances
   f. Previous education
   g. Employment history
   h. Convictions
   i. Organizational affiliations
   j. Previous residences

5. Investigative coverage should include all or part of the following depending upon job requirements and funds available:
   a. Check any available local security indices and police files to ascertain derogatory information
      [**Note:** Such information must be publicly available and lawfully obtained.]
   b. Criminal history - If a candidate indicates a conviction record, the details should be verified
   c. At least five consecutive immediately preceding years of employment and/or non-employment should be verified
   d. Any gaps in employment more than 30 days should be explained and be fully explored
   e. Claimed residence for the period covered in employment and education inquiries should be verified
   f. Criminal court records should be checked
   g. Listed and developed personal references are interviewed
   h. All education required for the position should be verified
   i. Interviews of former employees and work associates

6. Personal contact rather than telephone or mail queries is by far the most desirable method of investigation.

K. Investigative Standards - Information sought or developed must be:

1. Relevant to the hiring decision

2. Reliable (i.e., have a good probability of being correct)

3. If unfavorable, be confirmed by at least one other source

L. Investigative Review - All completed investigations are reviewed by a responsible supervisory employee.

M. Contract Investigative Agency - Should be advised in writing:

1. The reason for the reports, the nature of the investigations, the basis for pricing reports, and the time service periods.

2. That the agency is not to represent itself as the organization.

3. The identity, telephone number, and mailing address of organization personnel to whom reports should be made.

N. Government Background Investigation - Usually covers 4 stages:

1. Personal history statement

2. Evaluation of personal history statement

3. A national agency check

4. A full field investigation

O. Employment Tests:

The use of certain employment testing such as psychological assessment must be a valid, reliable, job-related predictor. Importantly, these assessment instruments must comply with ADA and related state statutes relative to employment tests.

Types of Assessment Instruments:

1. Performance or work sample tests

2. Ability tests (e.g., typing test)

3. Aptitude tests (i.e., ability to learn)

4. Personality inventories tests (e.g., MMP II, Myers-Briggs Test)

5. Honesty/integrity tests

6. Medical examinations

   [***Note:*** Under the ADA, the medical exam cannot be performed until after the job offer has been made to the candidate.]

7. Drug testing

8. Polygraph testing

   [***Note:*** The Employee Polygraph Protection Act prohibits most private employers from using polygraph tests to screen job candidates. However, there are exceptions, such as employees in certain security services or organizations involved with the lawful manufacturing and distribution of controlled substances.]

P. Orientation for New Employees:

The orientation program should be designed to familiarize the new employee with the organization's culture, goals, objectives, procedures, and rules. This process also identifies requirements for employees to protect assets and to play a role in loss prevention.

Q. Financial and Lifestyle Inquiry:

1. To gather basic information on income and mode of living

2. All employees are advised of the organization's policy

3. Considered:
   a. On promotion to a significantly more responsible position
   b. On assignment to significantly more sensitive duties
   c. On a cyclical basis for persons in sensitive positions

4. Subject selection:
   a. Select specific position titles
   b. Ask senior executive management to submit a confidential list
   c. Schedule on specific events (i.e., a garnishment notice)

5. Sources to be checked:
   a. Security/law enforcement agency files
   b. Civil litigation
   c. Personnel/payroll department records
   d. Bank/credit agency files/sources
   e. Inspection of residence
   f. Real property records

6. Any anomalies found should be investigated fully, including interviewing the subject of the inquiry

7. Re-investigations usually occur every 18 months

R. Security Awareness:

Security awareness is a state of mind. The purposes of security awareness are:

1. To understand the relationship between security and a successful operation

2. To know one's personal obligation under the security program

3. To comply with legal and regulatory requirements

4. To comply with any contractual obligations

S. Exit Interview:

An exit interview is a valuable tool for the following reasons:

1. Gives the employee an opportunity to list grievances and/or issues

2. Management often learns of problems not previously known

3. Helps to reduce loss when a checklist is used to have organization's property returned

4. Is used to remind departing employee of legal obligation to protect trade secrets or confidential records, non-compete agreements, and non-disclosure agreements.

T. Workplace Violence:

A protection method is to have a "Threat Management" approach which involves:

1. Preemployment screening;

2. Access control and other physical security measures;

3. A fully disseminated written policy statement and reporting procedures;

4. In Incident Management Team ("IMT"); and

5. Guidelines for threat and incident management.

U. Executive Protection

Key business persons have become focal targets for kidnapping, extortion, assassinations, bombings, and sabotage. The perpetrator(s) of these criminal acts utilize these acts as a vehicle to obtain money, influence business or government decision making, or develop public recognition for their organization and/or cause.

Prevention and defense are the common elements to mitigate terrorist acts and risk to potential targets. With this understanding, there are certain efforts that perpetrators of such criminal acts have to undertake:

1. Identify probable targets and venues for attack

2. Develop a plan

3. Gather intelligence

To respond to terrorists, an executive protection program should be developed with an emphasis on a crisis management plan and team. The primary objectives are to reduce vulnerabilities and develop contingencies. The crisis management plan may entail threat assessments, countermeasures, policies, procedures, protocols, lines of authority, and the responsibility for control in the event of an attack.

In the planning stages, the activities are separated into: (i) *"Contingency Event"* which is a potential act (e.g., terrorism); and (ii) *"Crisis"* which is the specific situation that arises from the act (e.g., kidnapping, assassination, sabotage). The focus of any planning should include:

1. Threat assessment

2. Resources allocation (i.e., interdisciplinary group of experts)

3. Education and training (i.e., understanding early warning signals of an attempted kidnapping, how to respond, and if abducted, how to survive)

Potential targets of terrorists' interest should maintain a low profile and avoid public communication of their address, telephone number, personal worth, or any data that might be utilized by a terrorist organization. Certain general protection strategies include:

1. Defensive plan and reaction (objective is to develop defensive actions to avoid predictable patterns and efforts to discourage attempts)

2. Be alert

3. Recognition of terrorist methods and operations (including use of pretexts)

4. Protection at residence (having a total security plan)

5. Protection at the office (select location to mitigate risks and have appropriate security measures)

6. Avoidance of attacks while traveling (alternate routes; never travel alone; use traveling vehicle as a "shield" or means to escape).

Corporations sometimes purchase "Kidnap-Ransom" insurance products for protection against such perils and, in turn, have available certain expertise for assistance in a crisis and funds for any exchange in the kidnapping.

If an abduction occurs, professionals (i.e., law enforcement, loss prevention personnel) should manage the situation regardless of the kidnappers' demands. The emphasis should be on the safety of the hostage first and the capture of the offenders second.

1. Of all security processes, the most critical is:
   a. Information
   b. Personnel
   c. Physical
   d. Perimeter

2. The concept that an individual should be aware of the security program and persuaded that the program is relevant to his or her own behavior is known as:
   a. Security consciousness
   b. Security awareness
   c. Security motivation
   d. Motivation analysis

3. An important task that faces every organization is the hiring of personnel. The purpose of applicant screening is:
   a. Workplace diversity
   b. Prohibiting discrimination in the hiring process
   c. Testing candidates on their honesty
   d. To identify the most appropriate person

4. Which of the following laws would **not** serve as a legal guide in the hiring of personnel?
   a. Civil Rights Act
   b. Age Discrimination in Employment Act
   c. Lanham Act
   d. Americans with Disabilities Act

5. Which is **not** a strategy for managing violence in the workplace:
   a. Establish a committee to plan violence prevention
   b. Consider OSHA guidelines to curb workplace violence
   c. Have professionally trained and armed security officers
   d. Establish policies and procedures and communicate the problems of threats and violence to all employees

6. When interviewing an applicant for employment, the interviewer may ask which questions:
   a. Have you ever been arrested?
   b. How old are you?
   c. Are you married?
   d. Can you meet the attendance requirements of this job?

7. Under federal law, the use of the polygraph for preemployment is permissible, except in which industry:
   a. Drug manufacturing
   b. Nuclear power
   c. Banking
   d. Alcohol manufacturing

8. When conducting an interview during a background investigation, the investigator should advise the party being interviewed that the applicant/employee is:
   a. Being considered for a promotion
   b. Suspected of wrongdoing
   c. Being investigated in connection with a position of trust
   d. Tell the interviewee nothing

9. The frequency of a reinvestigation of the "financial life style" inquiry should generally be:
   a. Never
   b. Every 6 months
   c. Every year
   d. Every 18 months

10. Any investigation which includes unfavorable information, or which results in an adverse employment decision, should be:
    a. Retained in file for a minimum of three years
    b. Retained in file for a minimum of five years
    c. Retained in file for one year
    d. Destroyed when the employment decision is made

11. Which of the following is **not** true with regard to a résumé?
    a. It does not provide the information which the company requires
    b. It is never accepted in lieu of a completed application form
    c. It is always accepted and is reviewed as part of the investigation
    d. It is an acceptable form of information for a professional position

12. The persons who find integrity tests offensive are:
    a. Twice as likely to admit to criminal or drug abuse behavior
    b. No more likely than anyone else to admit to criminal or drug abuse behavior
    c. Sensitive persons who should not be required to take the test
    d. Usually found to have a violent criminal past

1. b. Personnel
   Source: *Protection of Assets Manual*

2. b. Security awareness
   Source: *Protection of Assets Manual*

3. d. To identify the most appropriate person
   Source: *Security and Loss Prevention,* p. 110

4. c. Lanham Act
   Source: *Security and Loss Prevention,* pp. 110-111

5. c. Having professional trained and armed security officers
   Source: *Security and Loss Prevention,* pp. 471-472

6. d. Can you meet the attendance requirement of this job?
   Source: *Introduction to Security,* pp. 330-333

7. d. Alcohol manufacturing
   Source: *The Process of Investigation,* p. 93

8. c. Being investigated in connection with a position of trust
   Source: *Protection of Assets Manual*

9. d. Every 18 months
   Source: *Protection of Assets Manual*

10. a. Retained in file for a minimum of three years.
    Source: *Protection of Assets Manual*

11. d. It is an acceptable form of information for a professional position
    Source: *Protection of Assets Manual*

12. a. Twice as likely to admit to criminal or drug abuse behavior
    Source: *Protection of Assets Manual*

ASIS International. (2008). *Protection of Assets Manual,* Alexandria, VA: ASIS International.

Fischer, Robert J., Halibozek, Edward, and Green, Gion, (2008). *Introduction to Security,* (8th ed.). Burlington, MA: Elsevier/Butterworth-Heinemann.

Purpura, Philip P. (2008). *Security and Loss Prevention: An Introduction,* (5th ed.). Burlington, MA: Elsevier/Butterworth-Heinemann.

Sennewald, Charles A., (2003). *Effective Security Management,* (4th ed.). Burlington, MA: Elsevier/Butterworth-Heinemann

Whitman, Michael E. and Mattord, Herbert J. (2008). *Management of Information Security,* (2nd ed.). Boston: Thomson Course Technology.

I. Barriers

A. Protective barriers are divided into two major categories:

1. Structural.

2. Natural.

B. Barriers serve three basic purposes:

1. Deter/delay.

2. Psychological deterrent.

3. Supplement and/or complement security personnel needs.

C. Positive barriers should be established for:

1. Controlling vehicular and pedestrian traffic flow.

2. Checking identification of personnel entering or departing.

3. Defining a buffer zone for more highly classified areas.

D. When the greatest degree of security is essential, two lines of structural barriers should be installed on the perimeter. These barriers should be separated by not less than 15 feet and not more than 150 feet for best protection and control

E. Four types of fencing authorized for use in protecting restricted areas are:

1. Chain-link.

2. Barbed wire.

3. Concertina.

4. Barbed tape.

F. Specifications regarding use of chain-link fences are as follows:

1. Must be constructed of seven foot material excluding top guard.

2. Must be of 9 gauge or heavier.

3. Mesh openings are not to be larger than two inches per side.

4. Should be a twisted and barbed salvage at top and bottom.

5. Must be securely fastened to rigid metal or reinforced concrete posts set in concrete.

6. Must reach within two inches of hard ground or paving.

7. On soft ground must reach below surface deep enough to compensate for shifting soil or sand.

G. Specifications regarding barbed wire.

1. Standard barbed wire is twisted, double-strand, 12 gauge wire, with 4 point barbs spaced an equal distance apart.

2. Barbed wire fencing should not be less than seven feet high, **excluding top guard**.

3. Barbed wire fencing must be firmly affixed to posts not more than 6 feet apart.

4. The distance between strands will not exceed 6 inches and at least one wire will be interlaced vertically and midway between posts.

H. Specifications for concertina wire are:

1. Standard concertina barbed wire is a commercially manufactured wire coil of high-strength-steel barbed wire clipped together at intervals to form a cylinder.

2. Opened concertina wire is 50 feet long and 3 feet in diameter.

I. Specifications of barbed tape are:

1. The barbed tape system is composed of 3 things:
   a. Barbed wire
   b. Barbed tape dispenser
   c. Concertina tape

2. Barbed tape is fabricated from a steel strip with a minimum breaking system of 500 pounds.

3. The overall width is 3/4 of an inch.

4. The tape has 7/16 inch barbs spaced at 1/2 inch intervals along each side.

J. The top guard:

1. A top guard is an overhang of barbed wire or barbed tape along the top of the fence, facing outward and upward at approximately a 45-degree angle.

2. Top guard supporting arms will be permanently affixed to the top of fence posts to increase the overall height of the fence at least one foot.

3. Three strands of barbed wire, spaced 6 inches apart, must be installed on the supporting arms.

K. Utility openings - key points:

1. Manhole covers, 10 inches or more in diameter, must be secured to prevent unauthorized opening.

2. Unavoidable drainage ditches, culverts, vents, ducts, and **other openings** having a cross-sectional area greater than 96 square inches should be protected by securely fastened welded bar grills.

L. Clear zones:

1. A clear zone of 20 feet or more should exist between the perimeter barrier and exterior structures, parking areas and natural or manmade features.

2. A clear zone of 50 feet or more should exist between the perimeter barrier and structures within the protected areas **except** when a building wall constitutes part of the perimeter barrier.

M. It is practically impossible to build a protective barrier that cannot be penetrated by a human or heavy armor.

N. The three main lines of defense for physical security are:

1. Perimeter barriers—located at outer edge of property—first line of defense.

2. Exterior walls, ceilings, roofs, and floors of buildings themselves, considered the second line of defense.

3. Interior areas within the building.

O. The most frequently used fencing for security purposes is chain-link fencing.

P. A major advantage of chain-link security fencing is that it affords visibility on both sides of the perimeter barrier to police and security officer.

Q. A major disadvantage to chain-link security fencing is that it creates an "institution-like atmosphere."

R. All bolts and nuts holding hardware attachments on a chain-link fence should be welded.

S. As a general rule, the gate in a security perimeter barrier should be as high as the adjoining barrier (fence). Top guards on gates may be vertical.

T. Signs are advisable at not more than 100 ft. intervals along the perimeter stating that the property is not open to the public and intruders will be prosecuted. (This acts as deterrent.)

U. If possible, all doors except one should be locked from the inside and the remaining door should be located on a well-lighted, police-patrolled street. It should be used by all employees coming and leaving work.

V. Doors - special features:

1. Fire exit doors, required by building codes, are undesirable for security but necessary for safety.

2. As a general rule, fire exit doors are operable by pushing against a panic bar on the inside.

3. Security of a fire exit door is enhanced by use of audible alarms.

4. Unusually long warehouse doors should be padlocked on the inside at both ends.

5. Door hinge pins exposed to the outside can be protected in a number of ways:
   a. By spot welding
   b. By inserting a headless machine screw in a pre-drilled hole through a leaf of the hinge

6. Hollow core doors are a definite security risk.

W. Windows - key points:

1. Experts advise that windows with a ledge 18 feet or more above ground level are seldom used by intruders.

2. As a general rule, windows less than 18 feet from the ground or less than 14 feet from trees, poles, or adjoining buildings should be protected **if they** are larger than 96 square inches in area.

3. Types of protective coverings for windows are:
   a. Burglary-resistant glass
   b. Protective iron or steel bars
   c. A good grade of heavy steel mesh
   d. Chain-link fencing

4. Over 50% of all break-ins are through window glass.

5. Types of burglary-resistant glass:
   a. Underwriter's Laboratories "safety glass"
   b. Plastic glazing sold under trade names of TUFFAK (Rohm and Haas) or LEXAN (General Electric)
   c. Acrylic-glazing material sold as Plexiglas (Rohm and Haas)

X. Miscellaneous. Some special security problems are created by the following conditions which breach the perimeter barrier:

1. Sidewalk elevators.

2. Utility tunnels.

3. Operational tunnels.

4. Storm sewers.

5. Storm doors.

6. Piers, docks, and wharves.

II. Alarms

A. Key definitions and terms used in intrusion detection systems:

1. **Actuator** - The button, magnetic switch or thermostat that will cause system to alarm.

2. **Annunciator** - This is the monitor. Technically, it is the visual or audible signaling device that indicates conditions of the associated circuits.

3. **Capacitance** - The property of two or more objects which enables them to store electrical energy in an electrostatic field between them.

4. **Capacitance Proximity Sensor** - Records a change in capacitance or electrostatic fields to detect penetration through windows, ventilators, and other openings and can be used to detect attempted penetration into safes or storage cabinets.

5. **Conductor** - Material which transmits electric current - examples are wire and cable.

6. **Control Unit** - The terminal box for all sensors.

7. **Fail-Safe** - A term applied to a system designed so that if a component fails to function properly the system will, by a signal or otherwise, indicate its incapacity.

8. **Duress Sensor** - Used to call for assistance; consists of a hand or foot operated switch.

9. **False Alarm** - Activation of sensors for which no cause can be determined.

10. **Intrusion Detection System** - The combination of components including sensors, control units, transmission lines and monitor units integrated to operate in a specified manner.

11. **Intrusion Detection Sensors** - Devices that initiate alarm signals by sensing the stimulus, change, or condition for which designed.

12. **Local Audible Alarm** - An electronic bell for outdoor or indoor use in the vicinity of the protected area.

13. **Microwave Sensor** - A radio/radar frequency (RF) transceiver having a frequency range of GHz (billion cycles per second) which detects motion.

14. **Monitor** - A device that senses and reports on the condition of a system.

15. **Motion Sensor** - Detects movement inside the area to be protected.

16. **Passive Ultrasonic Sensor** - Detects the sounds of forced entry throughout walls, ceilings, and doors.

17. **Penetration Sensor** - Detects entry through doors, windows, walls, or any other openings into the protected area.

18. **Photoelectric System** - Consists of two separate units—a transmitter and receiver. An interruption of a light bean transmitted to the receiver causes an alarm.

19. **Ultrasonic** - The frequency range of sound that is above the capabilities of normal human hearing. In intrusion detection systems, it usually varies between 21,500 and 26,000 Hz (cycles per second).

20. **Ultrasonic Motion Sensor** - Detects by frequency shift the motion of an intruder inside the protected area.

21. **Vibration Sensor** - Detects forced entry through metal barriers placed over windows and ventilators or attempts to drill, saw, or cut through walls, ceilings, floors, or doors.

B. Purposes of intrusion detection alarm systems are:

1. To economize on people.

2. To substitute in place of other security measures.

3. To supplement by providing additional controls.

C. The basic principles of operation of intrusion detection systems are:

1. Breaking an electrical circuit.

2. Interrupting a light beam.

3. Detecting sound.

4. Detecting vibration.

5. Detecting a change in capacitance due to penetration of an electrostatic field.

D. Types of alarm systems:

1. Electro-mechanical
   a.   Metallic Foil
   b.   Magnetic Switches
   c.   Wire Service Detection
   d.   Pressure Mats, Ribbons, or Wafers

2. Volumetric
   a.   Capacitance
   b.   Vibration
   c.   Microwave
   d.   Ultrasonic
   e.   Passive Infrared
   f.   Photo Electric

E. Types of alarm detection systems are:

1. **Local alarm system** - The protective circuits activate a visual or audible signal in the immediate vicinity of the object of protection.

2. **Auxiliary system** - This system is one in which the installation-owned system is a direct extension of the police and/or fire alarm systems. (This is least effective system.)

3. **Central station system** - In this system, alarms are transmitted to a central station outside the installation from which appropriate action is taken such as notifying local police or fire departments.

4. **Proprietary system** - It is similar to the central station system except is owned by, and located on the installation. (Response to alarm is by the installation's own security or firefighting personnel.)

F. The three basic parts of an alarm system:

1. Sensor or triggering device.

2. Circuit which carries message to the signaling apparatus.

3. A signaling system or device, sometimes called the annunciator.

G. The functions of an alarm system could be one or more of the following:

1. Detection of fire.

2. Detection of intrusion.

3. Emergency notification.

4. Monitoring of equipment or facility conditions.

H. It has been estimated that 90-98 percent of all alarms are false.

I. The most common causes of false alarms are:

1. User negligence.

2. Poor installation or servicing.

3. Faulty equipment.

J. Monitoring systems. The closed circuit television (CCTV) system consists of the following:

1. Television camera.

2. A monitor.

3. Connecting circuits.

4. Power source.

III. Protective Lighting

A. General matters:

1. Protective lighting provides a means of continuing, during hours of darkness, a degree of protection approaching that maintained during daylight hours.

2. Importance of protective lighting is threefold:
    a.   Serves as deterrent to violators
    b.   Assists security force
    c.   Serves as an essential element of an integrated physical security program

B. General characteristics of protective lighting.

1. It is relatively inexpensive to maintain.

2. It will probably reduce need for security forces.

3. It may provide personal protection for security forces by reducing the element of surprise by the intruder.

4. It requires less intensity than working light.

C. Planning considerations for installation and maintenance of protective lighting.

1. Effect of local weather conditions.

2. Fluctuating voltages in power source.

3. Establishment of a ledger to maintain a burning time record based on life-expectancy of the lamp.

4. Limited and exclusion areas requirements:
   a. All limited and exclusion areas must have protective lighting on a permanent basis at both perimeter and access control points
   b. The lighting must be positioned to:
      1) Prevent glare to security force
      2) Avoid silhouetting security force
   c. Lighting in these areas must be under control of the responsible security force
   d. The perimeter band of lighting must provide a minimum intensity of 0.2 foot candles, measured horizontally 6 inches above ground, at least 30 feet outside the exclusion area barrier
   e. Lighting inside exclusion areas or on structures containing nuclear weapons must be of sufficient intensity to enable detection of persons in the area or at structure entrances
   f. Lighting at entrance control points must be of sufficient intensity to enable guards to compare and identify bearers and badges
   g. Protective lighting systems must be operated during hours of darkness
   h. Failure of one or more lights should not affect the operation of remaining lights
   i. The stand-by power source should be adequate to sustain the protective lighting of all vital areas and structures
   j. The cone of illumination from light source should be directed downward and away from the structure or area protected and away from security personnel assigned to such protection
   k. Light source for perimeter fence lighting should be located sufficiently within the protected area and above the fence so the light pattern will cover a ground area
   l. An effective light system must provide means of convenient control and maintenance
   m. Protective lighting should never be relied on alone but should be used with other security measures

D. General principles of protective lighting:

1. Protective lighting should enable security force personnel to observe without being seen.

2. Good protective lighting should consist of the following:
   a. Adequate and even light upon bordering areas
   b. Glaring lights in eyes of intruder
   c. Little light on security patrol routes

3. Two basic systems may be used to provide effective protective lighting:
   a. Light boundaries and approaches
   b. Light area and structures within general boundaries of property

4. To be effective, protective lighting should:
   a. Act as deterrent
   b. Make detection likely

E. Types of lighting.

1. There are 4 general types of protective lighting systems:
   a. Continuous
   b. Standby
   c. Movable
   d. Emergency

2. Key points of "Continuous Lighting:"
   a. It is the most common protective lighting system
   b. It consists of stationary luminaries
   c. Two primary methods of employing continuous lighting are:
      1) Glare projection
      2) Controlled lighting

3. Key points of "standby lighting:"
   a. The luminaries are stationary
   b. Luminaries are not continuously lighted

4. Key points of "Movable Lighting:"
   a. It consists of manually operated movable searchlights which may be either lighted during darkness or only as needed
   b. It is usually used to supplement continuous or standby lighting

5. Key points of "Emergency Lighting:"
   a. This system may duplicate the other three systems in whole or in part
   b. Its use is limited to times of power failure or other emergencies
   c. It depends on alternative power sources such as portable generators or batteries

F. Piers and docks - key points:

1. They should be safeguarded by illuminating both water approaches and the pier area.

2. Decks on open piers should be illuminated to at least 1.0 foot candles.

3. Water approaches, extending to a distance of 100 feet from the pier should be illuminated to at least 0.5 foot candles.

G. Wiring systems:

1. Circuit should be arranged so failure of any one lamp will not leave a critical or vulnerable position in darkness.

2. Feeder lines should be located underground (or sufficiently inside the perimeter in case of overhead wiring) to minimize sabotage or vandalism from outside the perimeter.

H. Maintenance. Periodic inspections should be made of all electrical circuits to replace or repair worn parts.

I. The following lighting values are recommended:

Location	Foot-candles on horizontal plane at ground level
Perimeter of outer area	0.15
Perimeter of restricted area	0.4
Vehicular entrances	1.0
Pedestrian entrances	2.0
Sensitive inner area	0.15
Sensitive inner structure	1.0
Entrances	0.1
Open yards	0.2
Decks on open piers	1.0

J. Lighting terminology and definitions:

1. Candle power - One candle power is the amount of light emitted by one standard candle.

2. Lumen - One lumen is the amount of light required to light an area of one square foot to one candle power.

3. Foot candle - One foot candle equals one lumen of light per square foot of space. The intensity of illumination is measured in foot candles.

K. Types of lighting used for protective purposes:

1. Incandescent - Example is the common light bulb. Advantages:
   a. Provide instant illumination
   b. Can be manufactured in a manner whereby light is reflected or diffused

2. Gaseous discharge lamps - there are two major types
   a. Mercury vapor lamps - give out soft blue light
   b. Sodium vapor lamps - give out soft yellow light
   c. Disadvantage of gaseous discharge lamp - Requires 2-5 minutes to light when cold and longer periods to relight when hot

d. Advantages of gaseous discharge lamps:
      1) More efficient than incandescent
      2) Widely used where fog is problem
      3) Frequently found on bridges and highways

3. Quartz lamps:
    a. They emit very bright white light and snap in rapidly
    b. Advantages:
      1) Excellent for use along perimeters and in critical areas
      2) Frequently used at very high wattage

L. Types of equipment

1. There are four basic types with security applications:
    a. Floodlights: Directional, with some diffusion to light specific areas
    b. Searchlights: Lights which project light in a concentrated beam; they are appropriate for use in instances calling for illumination of boundaries
    c. Fresnels: Wide beam units used to extend the illumination in long, horizontal strips; they protect a narrow beam approximately 180° in the horizontal and from 15-30° in the vertical plane; an appropriate application is to light parameters since little lights is lost vertically
    d. Street lights: Produce a diffused light widely used in parking areas

IV. Safes and Vaults

A. Safes

1. Safes are designated in two categories to describe their measure of protection:
    a. Fire resistive
    b. Burglary and robbery resistive

2. Rating safes in the area of fire protection is done through:
    a. Safe Manufacturers National Association (SMNA is no longer in existence. Their labels may be encountered on older safes)
    b. Underwriter's Laboratories

3. UL ceased use of letter classifications after 1972 and at that time began to show the type of container and the level of protection on labels.

4. UL labels indicate hours of protection and internal temperature a container can withstand.

5. Fire resistive safes give very little protection against the safecracker.

6. Once exposed to a fire, a fire-resistive safe does not have the degree of protection for which originally rated.

7. **FIRE-RESISTANT CONTAINERS**
   UL RECORD SAFE CLASSIFICATIONS

CLASSIFICATION	TEMPERATURE	TIME	IMPACT	OLD LABEL
350-4	2000° F	4 hrs	Yes	A
350-2	1850° F	2 hrs	Yes	B
350-1	1700° F	1 hr	Yes	C

INSULATED RECORD CONTAINER

350-1	1700° F	1 hr	No	D
350-1/2	1550° F	1/2 hr	No	E

UL COMPUTER MEDIA STORAGE CLASSIFICATION

150-4	2000° F	4 hrs	Yes	
150-2	1850° F	2 hrs	Yes	
150-1	1700° F	1 hr	Yes	

8. Burglary and robbery-resistive mercantile safes are classified by SMNA specifications, by UL ratings and by design features of door, wall and lock.
   A classification table in this regard is set out as follows:

UL MONEY SAFE CLASSIFICATION:

TL-15 - Tool resistant

Weight: At least 750 lbs or anchored. Body: At least one-inch thick steel or equal.

Attack: Door and front face must resist attack with common hand and electric tools for 15 minutes.

TL-30 - Tool resistant

Weight: At least 750 lbs or anchored. Body: At least one-inch thick steel or equal.

Attack: Door and front face must resist attack with common hand and electric tools plus abrasive cutting wheels and power saws for 30 minutes.

***TRTL-30** - Tool and torch resistant

Weight: At least 750 lbs.

Attack: Door and front face must resist attack with tools listed above, and oxy-fuel gas cutting or welding torches for 30 minutes.

*As of January 31, 1980, UL stopped issuing the TRTL-30 label, replacing it with the TRTL-30X6 label which requires equal protection on all six sides of the safe. Some manufacturers, however, continue to produce safes meeting TRTL-30 standards in order to supply lower priced containers, which provide moderate protection against tool and torch attack.

TRTL-30x6 - Tool and torch resistant

Weight: At least 750 lbs.

Attack: Door and entire body must resist attack with tools and torches listed above, plus electric impact hammers and oxy-fuel gas cutting or welding torches for 30 minutes.

TXTL-60 - Tool, torch and explosive resistant

Weight: At least 1000 lbs.

Attack: Door and entire safe body must resist attack with tools and torches listed above, plus eight ounces of nitroglycerin or its equal for 60 minutes.

9. The design features of a burglary-resistive safe, as a general rule, require the door be made of steel and at least 1-1/2 inches thick.

10. Following are some of the safecracking methods used:
    a. Drilling or punching - accomplished by knocking off combination dial and drilling hole to expose locking device
    b. Burning - The process of using high temperature oxyacetylene torches or "burning bars" to cut an opening in the wall or door of the safe
    c. Peeling - Is process of attacking the seams of metal plates with pry bars and other tools to peel back layers of metal and thus exposing either locking mechanism or interior
    d. Ripping - Similar to peeling except ripping can be accomplished against a solid, metal-walled container with a thin wall
    e. X-ray - Utilized to reveal position of the combination and mechanism necessary to open safe
    f. Explosives - Nitroglycerin and plastic explosives are still used but not as much as in the past
    g. Power tools - Examples: rotary devices, hydraulic tools and power drills
    h. Manipulation - Very few safe crackers have skill to use this technique

11. No safe is impenetrable.

12. Any safe that weighs less than 750 pounds should be anchored to building structure.

B. Vaults

1. Vaults are defined as enlarged safes.

2. Vaults, except for door, are usually made of high quality reinforced concrete.

3. They are usually located at or below ground level because of heavy weight.

4. Doors of a vault are normally 6 inches thick.

5. Walls, ceiling and floor, as a rule, should be twice as thick as the door but never less than 12 inches.

6. Vaults should be supported by alarm systems of the following types:
   a. Capacitance
   b. Vibration

7. Ratings for vaults are established by the Insurance Services Office (ISO).

V. Lock and Key Systems

A. The most accepted and widely-used security device is the lock.

B. Regardless of their quality or cost, locks should be considered **delay devices** only and not bars to entry.

C. Types of locking devices are as follows:

1. Key locks - Features are:
   a. May be picked by expert
   b. Possibility of loss
   c. Possibility of compromise

2. Conventional combination locks - May be opened by skillful manipulator.

3. Manipulation-resistant combination locks - Furnishes a high degree of protection for highly-classified or important material.

4. Combination locks with 4 or more tumblers which are desirable for containers of highly-important items.

5. Relocking devices - Attached to a safe or vault door, an added degree of security against forcible entry is furnished.

6. Interchangeable cores - Features:
   a. Cores may be quickly replaced
   b. All locks can be keyed into an overall complete locking system
   c. Economical
   d. System is flexible
   e. Simplified record keeping

7. Cypher locks - It is a digital combination door locking device.

D. Types of "key locks:"

1. Warded locks - Offer no security; the worst selection for security.

2. Disc tumbler locks, often called wafer locks:
   a. More secure than warded locks
   b. Used on most automobiles, desks and cabinets

3. Pin tumbler locks - Features:
   a. Used extensively in commercial, military and residential security
   b. It is more secure than warded or wafer

4. Lever locks - Used in safe deposit boxes and are difficult to pick.

E. "Other" locks:

1. Code-operated locks - Features:
   a. Opened by pressing a series of numbered buttons in proper sequence
   b. These are high security locking devices

2. Card operated locks - Features:
   a. They are either electrical or electromagnetic
   b. Coded cards which are etched, embossed or containing a pattern or copper flecks are used to operate the locks

3. Electromagnetic locks - These devices operate by holding a door closed by magnetism.

4. Padlocks - Features:
   a. Should be hardened and strong enough to resist prying
   b. All padlocks should be locked at **all** times even when **not** securing an area

F. Keying systems - 4 major types:

1. Change key - A key to a single lock within a master key system.

2. Sub-master key - a key which will open all the locks within a particular area in a facility.

3. Master key - A key which will open all the locks when two or more sub-master systems exist.

4. Grand-master key - A key that will open everything in a system involving two or more master key groups.

G. Key control - Main principles of system:

1. Keys should be accessible only to those whose official duties require access.

2. Combination to safe locks and padlocks securing containers for classified information should be changed at least once each 12-month period and at earliest if:
   a. Loss or possible compromise
   b. Discharge, suspension or reassignment of any person having knowledge of combination

3. More frequent rotation of key padlocks may be required in certain instances.

4. In selecting combination numbers, multiples and simple ascending or descending arithmetical series should be avoided.

5. Records containing combinations should be placed in the same security classification as the highest classification of the material authorized for storage in the container which the lock secures.

6. Use of keys must be based on the same general concept as applied to safe combinations.

7. Inventories of key systems should be conducted at least annually.

8. When key is issued the following should be recorded:
   a. Key number
   b. Name of person
   c. His position
   d. Date of issuance
   e. Any other relevant data

H. When a key is lost, circumstances should be investigated and set forth in writing.

I. Master keys should be kept at a minimum.

VI. Traffic Control

A. Traffic control includes the following:

1. Identification of employees and visitors.

2. Directing movements of employees and visitors.

3. Package control.

4. Control of trucks and private cars.

B. All visitors must be required to identify themselves.

C. Visitors should be limited to predetermined unrestricted areas.

D. The most practical system of identification is the use of badges or identification cards.

E. To be effective, identification badges should meet the following requirements:

1. Tamper-resistant.

2. Clear and recent photo of bearer.

3. Photo must be at least 1-inch square.

4. Photo must be up-dated every 2-3 years, and when facial appearance changes.

5. Must contain vital statistics such as date of birth, height, weight, color of hair and eyes, sex, and both thumbprints.

6. Should be laminated.

7. Sturdy construction.

8. Color-coded when necessary.

9. Signature.

F. A badge system is only as effective as its enforcement.

G. Every facility should have a package control policy relative to packages both entering or leaving the premises.

1. Packages brought in should be inspected.

2. In most cases, spot-checking will suffice.

3. Any policy relative to package control must be widely-publicized in advance.

H. Where possible, the parking area should be separated from all other areas of the facility.

1. Parking area should be protected from intruders.

2. Employees and visitors going to and from cars should pass through pedestrian gates manned by security personnel.

VII. Guards

A. In comparison to other security elements, security guards are expensive.

B. Proprietary guards usually receive higher hourly wages than contract-guard personnel.

C. Advantages of proprietary guards:

1. Less turnover.

2. Are more familiar with facilities they protect.

3. Tend to be more loyal to the company.

D. Disadvantages of proprietary guards:

1. Costs are higher.

2. May be required to join a guard union.

3. Problem of ensuring availability of back-up personnel.

E. Advantages of contract guards:

1. Less expensive.

2. Fewer administrative and payroll-related responsibilities.

3. Contractor has responsibility for scheduling and supervision.

4. Is able to obtain extra guards when needed.

5. Security firm usually accepts liability in civil suits.

F. Disadvantages of contract guards:

1. Lack of training.

2. Less loyalty to company.

3. Large turnover.

4. Not familiar with plant.

G. Training programs for private security personnel are generally inadequate.

H. A survey by the private security task force has recommended the following training for unarmed guards:

1. 8 hours formal pre-assignment training.

2. 32 additional hours within 3 months of assignment.

I. The task force report recommended the following minimum pre-employment screening qualifications for private security personnel:

1. Minimum age of 18 years.

2. High school diploma or equivalent written examination.

3. Written examination to determine ability to understand and perform duties assigned.

4. No record of conviction.

5. Armed personnel must have vision correctable to 20/20 in each eye and capable of hearing ordinary conversation at a distance of 10 feet with each ear. Other security personnel should have no physical defects that would hinder job performance.

J. The task force report recommended the following with regard to training by armed private security personnel:

1. Be required to successfully complete a 24-hour firearms course that includes legal and policy requirements or submit evidence of competency and proficiency prior to assignment to a job that requires a firearm.

2. Be required to qualify at least once every 12 months with the firearm carried while performing private security duties.

K. The task force set forth the following recommended qualifications for non-armed security personnel:

1. Be at least 18 years of age.

2. Be physically and mentally competent and capable of performing the specific job function being registered for.

3. Be morally responsible in the judgment of the regulatory board.

4. Successfully complete training requirements as recommended by the task force.

L. The task force set forth the following recommended qualifications for armed security personnel:

1. Be at least 18 years of age.

2. Have a high school diploma or pass an equivalent written examination.

3. Be mentally competent and capable of performing in an armed capacity.

4. Be morally responsible in the judgment of the regulatory board.

5. Have no felony convictions involving the use of a weapon.

6. Have no felony or misdemeanor convictions that reflect the applicant's ability to perform a security function in an armed capacity.

7. Have no physical defects that would hinder job performance.

8. Have successfully completed the training requirements for armed personnel as recommended by the task force.

M. Arguments in favor of seeking "peace officer" status for the security force.

1. A peace officer is generally allowed a wider discretion than a private citizen in making arrests or apprehensions.

2. Reputation often carries with it the right to carry deadly weapons.

3. Status of peace officer may open channels of communication not otherwise available.

4. There is a psychological advantage to an officer's being known as a peace officer.

N. Arguments against "peace officer" status are:

1. The constitutional requirements of due process will operate upon industrial officers if they are also agents of government.

2. The officer may be subject to emergency draft or mobilization orders of local authorities.

O. The number of personnel required to cover a single post around the clock providing coverage for three eight-hour shifts is 4-1/2 (5 actual persons). This allows for vacations, sick leave, etc.

VIII. Security Surveys

A. A security survey is the process of conducting an exhaustive physical examination and thorough inspection of all operational systems and procedures of a facility for the following purposes:

1. To determine existing state of security.

2. To locate weakness in defenses.

3. To determine degree of protection required.

4. To produce recommendations establishing a total security program.

B. Who should conduct a security survey?

1. Staff security personnel

2. Qualified security specialists (both of whom should have had training in the field).

C. No checklist exists that could be universally applied for survey purposes as no two facilities are alike.

D. A Security survey is known by a number of different terms such as:

1. Risk analysis.

2. Risk assessment.

E. Key steps in a risk assessment process:

1. To determine value, impact and cost of any asset should it be lost due to natural or man-made forces.

2. To determine the degree of vulnerability of the facility to damage or attack by natural or man-made forces.

3. To determine the degree of probability that natural or man-made forces will strike any given facility.

F. The "vulnerability of a facility" to damage or attack may be determined by a number of ways:

1. An inspection of the facility by the experienced inspector.

2. Examination of the facility's record of losses.

3. A determination whether the high-value property or items are properly safeguarded from theft by insiders.

G. Security surveys as a general rule cover one or more of the following objectives:

1. To determine existing vulnerabilities to injury, death, damage, or destruction by natural causes.

2. To determine existing vulnerabilities of corporate assets due to outside criminal activity.

3. To determine existing vulnerabilities of corporate assets due to criminal activity within organizations.

4. To determine existing conditions of physical security of corporate property.

5. To measure effectiveness of current security police.

6. To measure compliance of employees to security rules.

7. To conduct internal audit to determine fraud.

8. To inspect overall condition within facility which cause security problems.

9. To investigate environmental conditions in the community from a standpoint of interaction within the facility.

H. There is a similarity between physical security surveys and crime prevention surveys, but one of the differences is that physical security measures are oriented more toward the security of property and facilities whereas crime prevention measures focus on the deterrence of criminal activity regardless of the physical safeguards available.

I. Some key points relative to conducting a security survey are:

1. Written authority to conduct the survey should be obtained.

2. Any previous surveys should be reviewed.

3. An orientation tour should be made.

4. Photographs should be taken of objects or situations that are difficult to describe.

5. There should be a review with local plant supervisors of all deficiencies noted during survey so immediate corrective action can be taken.

6. Follow-up survey should be conducted to ascertain if deficiencies have been corrected.

7. A cost-benefit analysis should be prepared.

8. A cost-benefit analysis is a direct comparison of the costs of the operation of the security unit and all security measures with the amount of corporate property saved or recovered as well as reduction of losses caused by injuries and lost production time.

9. No security measure should be recommended which is not cost effective.

IX. SYSTEM DESIGN AND SPECIFICATION

A. System Design Process:

1. Planning Phase: Collecting information on security needs, objectives, and constraints and formulating concepts for security countermeasures. Includes development of the business and economic justification.

2. Design Phase: Documentation that is clear and complete to ensure consistent and accurate interpretation by vendors for procurement and implementation.

B. System: In security context is defined as a combination of equipment, personnel, and procedures design, coordinated in such a way as to assure optimum achievement of the system's stated security objectives.

C. Integration: Logical and symbiotic combination of the technology, supported by the staffing and procedural elements.

D. Requirements Definition: Used to develop countermeasure solutions to the problems identified by a vulnerability assessment.

1. Mission or objectives of the integrated security system (ISS) must reflect and support the overall mission.

2. Level of confidence factor for each requirement must focus on preventing, delaying or modifying the consequences.

E. Design Criteria: Are the ground rules for the design and selection of subsystems and components. Also known as functional requirements. The criteria fall into a number of categories based on expected performance, operational and financial considerations, on style and design and codes and standards.

1. Codes and standards: National and local building codes, safety codes and laws.

2. Quality: Sensible levels are needs to ensure costs are kept in check.

3. Capacity: Size and space requirements affect the design solutions and impact anticipated expansion.

4. Performance: Detailed in the system specification and include interface, reliability and maintainability.

5. Features: Major system features should be defined.

6. Cost: Most common constraint and should be defined in a budget.

7. Operations: Need to have minimum negative impact on productivity.

8. Culture and image: Greatly factors into the implementation of security programs in the corporate environment and the acceptance of change.

9. Monitoring and response: Proprietary vs. off site monitoring.

F. Minimum Security Specifications should include the following:

1. Instructions to bidders: List of all documents included in the contact.

2. Functional description: Intended operation and installation schedule.

3. List of all products and services included in the contract.

4. List of all products and services required but part of another contract.

5. List of applicable codes and standards.

6. Support services: Drawings, submittal, testing, training, warranty, maintenance.

7. Technical descriptions of all major subsystems and components.

8. General site conditions.

G. Procurement

1. Sole source: Used for smaller projects and usually involves a pre-qualified contactor.

2. Request for proposal: Commonly used by non-government organization. Specifications can be generic and performance based.

3. Invitation for bid: Used by government when a competitive bid is required and the award be given to the lowest *qualified* bidder.

CPP Study Guide

1. The degree of protection desired in any installation is predicated upon an analysis of the following two factors:
   a. Cost and environmental conditions
   b. Criticality and vulnerability
   c. Cost and vulnerability
   d. Cost and criticality

2. The process used by the security manager in establishing priorities of protection of assets is known as:
   a. Security survey
   b. Vulnerability study
   c. Risk analysis
   d. Inspection review

3. The type of fencing generally used for protection of permanent limited and exclusion areas is:
   a. Chain link
   b. Concertina
   c. Barbed wire
   d. Barbed tape

4. Which of the following characteristic of protective lighting is incorrect?
   a. Lighting is expensive to maintain
   b. It usually requires less intensity than working light
   c. It may also provide personal protection by reducing advantages of concealment
   d. It should not be used as a psychological deterrent only

5. Lighting units of 4 general types are used for protective lighting systems. Which of the following is not used:
   a. Continuous
   b. Intermittent
   c. Standby
   d. Moveable

6. A series of fixed luminaries arranged to flood a given area continuously during the hours of darkness with overlapping cones of light. It is called:
   a. Continuous lighting
   b. Intermittent lighting
   c. Standby lighting
   d. Moveable lighting

7. Piers and docks located on an installation should be safeguarded by illuminating both water approaches and the pier area. Decks on open piers should be illuminated to at least:
   a. 1.5 foot candles
   b. 2.0 foot candles
   c. 0.5 foot candles
   d. 1.0 foot candles

8. The intrusion detection system in which a pattern of radio waves is transmitted and partially reflected back to the antenna is known as:
   a. Ultrasonic system
   b. Microwave system
   c. Electrostatic system
   d. Capacitance system

9. The intrusion detection system which is used on a safe, wall and openings therein in an effort to establish an electrostatic field around the object to be protected is known as a:
   a. Ultrasonic system
   b. Microwave system
   c. Capacitance system
   d. Electro-mechanical system

10. A sentry dog can normally not operate at full effectiveness at:
   a. Ammunition storage areas
   b. Gasoline storage areas
   c. Radar sites
   d. Warehouses

11. Non-insulated security containers must satisfactorily pass a drop test of:
   a. 15 feet
   b. 20 feet
   c. 22 feet
   d. 30 feet

12. Which of the following is not an approved UL record safe classification:
   a. 350-4
   b. 350-3
   c. 350-2
   d. 350-1

13. The acceptable vault construction of insulated doors is a minimum reinforced thickness of:
   a. 12 inches
   b. 10 inches
   c. 8 inches
   d. 6 inches

14. Which of the following would be an acceptable computer media storage classification?
    a. 350-4
    b. 450-4
    c. 250-4
    d. 150-4

15. UL classified safes must be anchored to the floor or weigh at least:
    a. 750 lbs.
    b. 1,000 lbs.
    c. 1,250 lbs.
    d. 1,500 lbs.

16. A "relock" on a vault automatically stops the bolt mechanism from operating when:
    a. A switch is flipped
    b. A timer is used
    c. When there is an attack on the door or combination lock
    d. Locked by remote control

17. Security vaults differ from safes in that:
    a. They are tested by Underwriters Laboratories for burglary resistance
    b. They do not have both fire and burglary resisting properties
    c. Steel is used
    d. They are permanently affixed to building

18. The weakness of the burning bar as a burglar tool is:
    a. It will not burn through concrete
    b. Produces large volumes of smoke
    c. Actual heat is not intense enough
    d. It requires tanks of hydrogen

19. Which of the following is **not** correct with regard to safes?
    a. UL classification labels are removed from all safes exposed to fires
    b. Record safes are designed to resist fires only
    c. Money safes have accredited fire resistance
    d. Quality equipment should be purchased only from reputable dealers

20. The symbol "TRTL" indicates:
    a. Safe is resistant to torches
    b. Safe is resistant to tools
    c. Safe is resistant to both torches and tools
    d. Nothing pertaining to torches or tools

21. Illumination intensity minimums for lighting of the perimeter of restricted area is:
    a. 0.15 foot candles
    b. 0.40 foot candles
    c. 1.00 foot candles
    d. 2.00 foot candles

22. The temperature at which paper may be destroyed is:
    a. 200° F
    b. 250° F
    c. 300° F
    d. 350° F

23. Electronic process media can begin to deteriorate at:
    a. 100° F
    b. 125° F
    c. 150° F
    d. 200° F

24. The interior height of a vault should not exceed:
    a. 8 feet
    b. 9 feet
    c. 10 feet
    d. 12 feet

25. A system using inaudible sound waves to detect the presence of an intruder or other disturbance of the inaudible sound system is known as:
    a. Motion detection system
    b. Sonic motion detection
    c. Ultrasonic motion detection
    d. Radio frequency motion detection

26. The weakest area in a window is usually:
    a. The sash
    b. Frames
    c. Glass
    d. The putty

27. Which of the following is considered to be the most resistant to blast from explosion?
    a. Thick brick or concrete walls
    b. Thick earthen barricades
    c. Steel-frame building walls
    d. Thick, reinforced concrete walls

28. A type of glass used in street-level windows or displays where security is necessary and which is composed of two sheets of ordinary glass bonded to an intervening layer of plastic material is known as:
    a. Tempered glass
    b. Plastic coated glass
    c. Vinyl coated glass
    d. Laminated glass

29. The type of glass which is often utilized for both safety and security purposes because it is 3 to 5 times stronger than regular glass and 5 times as resistant to heat is:
    a. Tempered glass
    b. Coated glass
    c. Plastic coated glass
    d. Reflected glass

30. The mechanical lock longest in use and which has practically no security value is:
    a. The lever lock
    b. The warded lock
    c. The wafer tumbler lock
    d. The pin tumbler lock

31. Probably the most widely-used lock for both exterior building doors and interior room doors is the:
    a. Warded lock
    b. Pin tumbler lock
    c. Disc tumbler lock
    d. Lever lock

32. Which of the following is not an authentic characteristic of the guard operation:
    a. Guards are costly
    b. Guards are generally recognized as an essential element in the protection of assets and personnel
    c. Guards are the only element of protection which can be depended upon to give complete security
    d. Guards can also perform as a public relations representative when properly trained

33. Each guard post that is manned 24 hours a day, 7 days a week requires:
    a. 3 guards
    b. 6 guards
    c. 2 guards
    d. 4.5 guards

34. Usually in facilities where visitors are to be escorted, this is done by:
    a. Guards
    b. Individuals being visited
    c. Special escort service
    d. Supervisor of unit visited

35. One of the main reasons for not arming private security guards is:
    a. The cost of extra equipment
    b. The extra salary costs
    c. Very few are qualified to handle them
    d. The typical business or government facility is not customarily a place where violent crime occurs

36. The argument usually used by contract guard representatives as a selling point in their service is:
    a. Better trained
    b. Non-union
    c. No administrative problems
    d. Reduction in cost

37. The most important written instructions for the guard force are known as:
    a. Memoranda
    b. Post orders
    c. High policy
    d. Operational orders

38. Which of the following should be a required criteria of post orders?
    a. Each order should deal with multiple subjects
    b. The order should be detailed
    c. The order should be written at the lowest level possible
    d. Orders should be indexed sparingly

39. The guard's primary record of significant events affecting facility protection is called:
    a. The guard log
    b. Ingress log
    c. Egress log
    d. Daily record manual

40. The sensor which is used when air turbulence is present in the protected room and when there are no potential false alarm sources outside the room and in the field of the detector is:
    a. Acoustic detector
    b. Vibration detector
    c. Microwave motion detector
    d. Ultrasonic motion detector

41. The sensor which is used when light air turbulence, vibration, and motion outside the room are present is:
    a. Acoustic detector
    b. Vibration detector
    c. Microwave motion detector
    d. Ultrasonic motion detector

42. Foil used as a detector on a glass window to signal a surreptitious or forcible penetration is an example of:
    a. Microwave sensor
    b. Capacitance sensor
    c. Vibrator sensor
    d. Electro-mechanical sensor

43. The type of sensor designed to place a current-carrying conductor between an intruder and an area to be protected is known as:
    a. Electro-mechanical sensor
    b. Microwave sensor
    c. Capacitance sensor
    d. Audio sensor

44. The kind of sensor which is based on the Doppler Principle (named after the Austrian scientist who originated the concept) is:
    a. Electro-mechanical sensor
    b. Microwave sensor
    c. Capacitance sensor
    d. Audio sensor

45. The sound wave sensor is commonly referred to as:
    a. Proximity detector
    b. Radar
    c. Vibration detector
    d. Ultrasonic detector

46. The type of sensor which is not influenced by exterior noise; which reacts only to movement within a protected area; and which can be adjusted so the movement of air caused by fire will activate an alarm is known as:
    a. Proximity detector
    b. Ultrasonic sensor
    c. Electro-mechanical sensor
    d. Audio sensor

47. A personal identification method based on the length of each finger of one hand from base to tip and the width of the hand inside the thumb is called the:
    a. Henry fingerprint system
    b. Hand geometry identification
    c. The Bertillion method
    d. Basch-Lomb method

48. A visual indicator that shows from which of several zones or buildings an alarm signal has originated is called:
    a. An annunciator
    b. Contact device
    c. Break alarm
    d. Cross alarm

49. A specially constructed microphone attached directly to an object or surface to be protected and which responds only when the protected object or surface is disturbed is known as:
    a. Parabolic microphone
    b. Special audio device
    c. Contact microphone
    d. Surreptitious microphone

1. b. Criticality and vulnerability
   Source: *Protection of Assets Manual*

2. b. Vulnerability Study
   Source: *Protection of Assets Manual*

3. a. Chain link
   Source: *Protection of Assets Manual*

4. a. Lighting is expensive to maintain
   Source: *Protection of Assets Manual*

5. b. Intermittent
   Source: *Protection of Assets Manual*

6. a. Continuous lighting
   Source: *Protection of Assets Manual*

7. d. 1.0 foot candles
   Source: *Protection of Assets Manual*

8. b. Microwave system
   Source: *Protection of Assets Manual*

9. c. Capacitance system
   Source: *Protection of Assets Manual*

10. b. Gasoline storage area
    Source: *Protection of Assets Manual*

11. d. 30 feet
    Source: *Protection of Assets Manual*

12. b. 350-3
    Source: *Protection of Assets Manual*

13. d. 6 inches
    Source: *Protection of Assets Manual*

14. d. 150-4
    Source: *Protection of Assets Manual*

15. a. 750 lbs.
    Source: *Protection of Assets Manual*

16. c. When there is an attack on the door or combination lock
    Source: *Protection of Assets Manual*

17. d. They are permanently affixed to building
    Source: *Protection of Assets Manual*

18. b. Produces large volumes of smoke
    Source: *Protection of Assets Manual*

19. c. Money safes have accredited fire resistance
    Source: *Protection of Assets Manual*

20. c. Safe is resistant to both torches and tools
    Source: *Protection of Assets Manual*

21. b. 0.40 foot candles
    Source: *Protection of Assets Manual*

22. d. 350° F
    Source: *Protection of Assets Manual*

23. c. 150° F
    Source: *Protection of Assets Manual*

24. d. 12 feet
    Source: *Protection of Assets Manual*

25. c. Ultrasonic motion detection
    Source: *Protection of Assets Manual*

26. c. Glass
    Source: *Protection of Assets Manual*

27. d. Thick, reinforced concrete walls
    Source: *Protection of Assets Manual*

28. d. Laminated glass
    Source: *Protection of Assets Manual*

29. a. Tempered glass
    Source: *Protection of Assets Manual*

30. b. The warded lock
    Source: *Protection of Assets Manual*

31. b. The pin tumbler lock
    Source: *Protection of Assets Manual*

32. c. Guards are the only element of protection which can be depended upon to give complete security
    Source: *Protection of Assets Manual*

33. d. 4.5 guards
    Source: *Protection of Assets Manual*

34. b. Individual being visited
    Source: P*rotection of Assets Manual*

35. d. The typical business or government facility is not customarily a place where violent crime occurs
     Source: *Protection of Assets Manual*

36. d. Reduction in cost
     Source: *Protection of Assets Manual*

37. b. Post orders
     Source: *Protection of Assets Manual*

38. c. The order should be written at the lowest level
     Source: *Protection of Assets Manual*

39. a. The guard log
     Source: *Protection of Assets Manual*

40. c. Microwave motion detector
     Source: *Protection of Assets Manual*

41. a. Acoustic detector
     Source: *Protection of Assets Manual*

42. d. Electro-mechanical sensor
     Source: *Protection of Assets Manual*

43. a. Electro-mechanical sensor
     Source: *Protection of Assets Manual*

44. b. Microwave sensor
     Source: *Protection of Assets Manual*

45. d. Ultrasonic detector
     Source: *Protection of Assets Manual*

46. b. Ultrasonic sensor
     Source: *Protection of Assets Manual*

47. b. Hand geometry identification
     Source: *Protection of Assets Manual*

48. a. An annunciator
     Source: *Protection of Assets Manual*

49. c. Contact microphone
     Source: *Protection of Assets Manual*

1. A cost-benefit analysis is a direct comparison of the costs of the operation of the security unit and all security measures with the amount of corporate property saved or recovered as well as reduction of losses caused by injuries and lost production time.

2. No security measure should be recommended which is not cost effective.

3. The perimeter band of lighting must provide a minimum intensity of 0.2 foot candles, measured horizontally 6 inches above ground, at least 30 feet outside the exclusion area barrier.

4. The basic principles of operation of intrusion detection systems are:
   a. Breaking an electrical circuit
   b. Interrupting a light beam
   c. Detecting sound
   d. Detecting vibration
   e. Detecting a change in capacitance due to penetration of an electrostatic field

5. The three main lines of defense for physical security are:
   a. Perimeter barriers - located at outer edge of property - first line of defense
   b. Exterior walls, ceilings, roofs and floors of buildings themselves, considered the second line of defense
   c. Interim areas within the building

6. The most frequently used fencing for security purposes is chain-link fencing.

7. An advantage of chain-link fencing is that it affords visibility on both sides of the perimeter barrier to police and security officer.

8. The cone of illumination from light source should be directed downward and away from the structure or area protected and away from security personnel assigned to such protection.

9. Specifications regarding use of chain-link fences are as follows:
   a. Must be constructed of 7 foot material excluding top guard
   b. Must be of 9 gauge or heavier
   c. Mesh openings are not to be larger than 2 inches per side
   d. Should be a twisted and barbed salvage at top and bottom
   e. Must be securely fastened to rigid metal or reinforced concrete posts set in concrete
   f. Must reach within 2 inches of hard ground or paving
   g. On soft ground must reach below surface deep enough to compensate for shifting soil or sand

10. Any safe that weighs less than 750 pounds should be anchored to building structure.

11. Combination to safe locks and padlocks should be changed at least once each 12 month period and on the loss or possible compromise of the combination, or on the discharge, suspension or reassignment of any person having knowledge of combination.

12. Inventories of key systems should be conducted at least annually.

13. There is a similarity between physical security surveys and crime prevention surveys, but one of the differences is that physical security measures are oriented more toward the security of property and facilities whereas crime prevention measures focus on the deterrence of criminal activity regardless of the physical safeguards available.

14. The number of personnel required to cover a single post around the clock providing coverage for three eight-hour shifts is 4-1/2 (5 actual persons). This allows for vacations, sick leave, etc.

15. Where possible, the parking area should be separated from all other areas of the facility.

16. A vibration sensor detects forced entry through metal barriers placed over windows and ventilators or attempts to drill, saw or cut through walls, ceilings, floors or doors.

17. As a general rule, windows less than 18 feet from the ground or less than 14 feet from trees, poles or adjoining buildings should be protected **if they** are larger than 96 square inches in area.

18. Signs are advisable at not more than 100° intervals along the perimeter stating that the property is not open to the public and intruders will be prosecuted.

19. A clear zone of 50 feet or more should exist between the perimeter barrier and structures within the protected areas **except** when a building wall constitutes part of the perimeter barrier.

20. Gaseous discharge lamps are mercury vapor lamps (soft blue light) and sodium vapor lamps (soft yellow light). They require 2-5 minutes to light when cold and longer periods to relight when hot.

21. A light source for perimeter fence lighting should be located sufficiently within the protected area and above the fence so the light pattern will cover a ground area.

1. Barriers

2. Employee and visitor control

3. Facility planning

4. Guard patrols, weapons

5. Materials control

6. Mechanical, electrical and electronic devices and equipment

7. Parking, traffic control, communications and security transportation

8. Perimeter boundaries, gates, lobbies

9. Protective lighting

10. Security surveys

11. Alarms

CPP Study Guide

Formulate a detailed study plan which will cover the following key concepts:

1. Barriers, fences, and walls

2. Gates, windows, and doors

3. Security lighting

4. Burglary-resistant glass

5. Locks and keys

6. Traffic control

7. Access control

8. Alarms and alarm systems

9. Security survey

10. Closed circuit surveillance

11. Intrusion detection systems

12. Vulnerability assessment

13. Executive protection

14. Employee and visitor control

15. Parking

ASIS International. (2008). *Protection of Assets Manual*. Alexandria, VA: ASIS International. The following chapters are pertinent:

– Introduction to Assets Protection

– Vulnerability

– Barrier/Hardware

– Locking

– Alarm Sensors

– Sensor Integration

– Communications

– Identification

– Parking and Traffic Control

– Physical Security Planning

– Security Awareness

Fennelly, Lawrence J. (2004). *Handbook of Loss Prevention and Crime Prevention*, (4th ed.), Elsevier/Butterworth/Heinemann, Burlington, MA.

Fischer, Robert J., Halibozek, Edward, and Green, Gion, (2008). *Introduction to Security*, (8th ed.), Elsevier/Butterworth-Heinemann, Burlington, MA.

> THE TERMS "SECRET" AND "CONFIDENTIAL" IN THIS DOCUMENT **DO NOT** INDICATE CLASSIFICATION AS DEFINED IN ANY GOVERNMENTAL PROGRAM

I. Proprietary Information:

A. Information of value, owned by or entrusted to a company or person, which relates to the operations of the company and which has not been publicly disclosed. It is normally protected against general disclosure.

B. All proprietary information is confidential; not all confidential information is proprietary.

C. The most important distinction is between trade secret data and other types of proprietary or confidential information.

II. Trade Secrets:

A. From the Restatement of the Law of Torts – "A trade secret may consist of any formula, pattern, device, or compilation of information which is used in one's business and which gives an opportunity to gain an advantage over competitors who do not know or use it. It may be a formula for a chemical compound, a process of manufacturing, treating or preserving materials, a pattern for a machine or other device, or a list of customers. It differs from other secret information as to single or ephemeral events . . . A trade secret is a process or device for continuous use in the operation of the business."

B. From the Uniform Trade Secrets Act—Trade secret means information including a formula, pattern, compilation, program, device, method, technique, or process, that:

　1. Derives independent economic value, actual or potential, from not being generally known to, and not being readily ascertainable by proper means, by other persons who can obtain economic value from its disclosure or use, and

　2. Is the subject of efforts that are reasonable under the circumstances to maintain its secrecy.

C. Trade secrets are entitled by law to more protection than other kinds of proprietary information. For example, a company can protect against threatened disclosure of a trade secret by injunction. If the information is not a trade secret, the remedy is for damages after disclosure and, in order to recover, it will be necessary to show that some actual damages were incurred.

CPP Study Guide

D. To protect a trade secret, it will be necessary to prove all of the following elements:

1. The information is identifiable by group or type;

2. The information is not available in public sources;

3. It may be disclosed only to persons with a duty to protect it;

4. Persons to whom the information is disclosed must know that it is secret;

5. The owner must be able to prove positive action taken to protect the information from disclosure.

E. If information is wrongfully obtained by one person and disclosed in such a fashion that others gain knowledge of it without being aware that it is, or was, the secret of someone else, the wrongful discloser is the only person against whom the original owner has recourse.

HOWEVER

If the data involved is a trade secret and the persons to whom it is disclosed are relatively few and are put on notice of the existence of the trade secret before they change their positions in the use of the data, the trade secret may be protected. Also, in addition to the recourse available against the wrongful discloser, in that, the third parties are now on notice, they too will become wrongful disclosers if they further disclose or use the information.

F. For an established trade secret, the owner may get his protection through the fiduciary status of, or through a written agreement with, the employee.

G. The most serious internal threat to trade secrets is the employee.

H. All sensitive information are not trade secrets. Examples which are not:

1. Salary information

2. Customer usage information

3. Profit margins

4. Unit costs

5. Personnel changes

III. Patents:

A. A patent for an invention is the grant of a property right to the inventor, issued by the United States Patent and Trademark Office. Generally, the term of a new patent is 20 years from the date on which the application for the patent was filed in the United States or, in special cases, from the date an earlier related application was filed, subject to the payment of maintenance fees. U.S. patent grants are effective only within the United States, U.S. territories, and U.S. possessions. Under certain circumstances, patent term extensions or adjustments may be available.

B. The primary distinctions between patents and trade secrets:

1. Requirements for obtaining a patent are specific. To qualify for a patent, the invention must be more than novel and useful. It must represent a positive contribution beyond the skill of the average person.

2. A much lower level of novelty is required of a trade secret.

3. A trade secret remains secret as long as it continues to meet trade secret tests while the exclusive right to patent protection expires after twenty (20) years.

IV. Copyright:

A. Copyright provides protection for original works by providing the creator or publisher exclusive rights to the work (e.g., books, periodicals, movies, music, software programs).

B. Material identified by a copyright symbol – ©.

C. Copyright permits "fair use" under the following conditions:

1. Purpose (commercial versus non-commercial)

2. Nature (critique versus business use)

3. Amount (1 versus 1,000)

4. Effect on potential market value

D. Digital Millennium Copyright of 1998: A refinement of the copyright laws, which essentially prohibits individuals from attempting to "break" encryption programs designed to protect digital versions of movies, music and literary works.

V. Trademark and Servicemark:

A trademark is a word, name, symbol (™), or device that is used in trade with goods to indicate the source of the goods and to distinguish them from the goods of others. A servicemark is the same as a trademark except that it identifies and distinguishes the source of a service rather than a product. The terms "trademark" and "mark" are commonly used to refer to both trademarks and servicemarks.

Trademark rights may be used to prevent others from using a confusingly similar mark, but not to prevent others from making the same goods or from selling the same goods or services under a clearly different mark. Trademarks which are used in interstate or foreign commerce may be registered with the United States Patent and Trademark Office.

VI. Legal:

Civil law is the statutory and common law in which private rights and remedies are found.

A. Two (2) concepts are recognized with regard to proprietary information:

1. Under the property concept, trade secret information has independent value.

2. Fiduciaries, who occupy special positions of trust and confidence, have a duty not to divulge proprietary information or to use proprietary information to their own advantage without the consent of the owner.

B. To protect the "property" of proprietary information, the owner has the right to:

1. Sue for damages for loss or destruction;

2. Recover profits under the equity theory of unjust enrichment;

3. Restrain another from the use of the property; and

4. Retain the exclusive use of the property.

C. The two (2) general forms of relief are:

1. Money, and

2. Injunctions.

D. Prior to instituting litigation, consider that:

1. The owner may have to expose the very secrets he is trying to protect.

2. The cost may be too high.

3. The trade secret owner may lose the case.

E. The objective is to prevent the loss of the information.

The United States has enacted a number of statutes designed to protect information and threats to communication systems (i.e., telecommunications, computers, and their network systems). The following are examples of such federal laws:

Statute	Description
Computer Fraud and Abuse Act of 1986 (amended 1994, 1996, 2001 and 2006)	Protects against threats from computer related acts and offenses
Computer Security Act of 1987	Requires all federal computer systems that contain classified information to have surety plans in place, and requires periodic security training for all individuals who operate, design, or manage such systems
The Telecommunications Deregulation and Competition Act of 1996	Regulates interstate and foreign telecommunications, which affects telephone and cable services
Digital Millennium Copyright Act of 1998	Prohibits individuals from attempting to "break" encryption programs designed to protect digital versions of movies and music
The Economic Espionage Act of 1996	Protects against persons converting a trade secret to his/her own benefit or the benefit of others
USA Patriot Act	Protects against terrorist crime, including breach of security and unauthorized use of information
Sarbanes-Oxley Act of 2002	Enforces accountability for executives of publicly traded companies - and there are requirements for information control and reporting

[Source: Whitman, Michael E. and Mattord, Herbert J. (2008). *Management of Information Security,* (2nd ed.). Boston: Thomson Course Technology, pp. 436-438.]

VII. Protecting Information:

A. Methodology:

It is clearly understood that information needs to be protected in some manner. There are varying methodologies for the design and implementation of information protection. This usually varies by organizational needs and dynamics. When designing this protection system, it is imperative that one examine the life cycle of data that will be collected and its use by employees—and any vulnerabilities. The recognized method for planning information security follows these key phases:

1. Investigation Phase:

In this first stage, the intent is to understand the scope of the potential threat facing the organization. Assessing all those vulnerabilities and then addressing economic, technical, and behavioral factors that would influence this process.

2. Analysis Phase:

Following the investigative phase, the analysis should focus on the organization's ability for implementing such a program and its capabilities in terms of system management.

3. Logical Design Phase:

The analysis phase is utilized to develop proposed system for solutions to those business problems that threaten the environment.

4. Physical Design Phase:

Under this phase, the intent is to select specific technologies that will support the protection systems.

5. Implementation Phase:

This phase focuses on software engineering and hardware installations to ensure that both data and systems are protected.

6. Maintenance Phase:

While the maintenance phase is often overlooked, it is probably the most expensive and requires long-term commitment. It requires that a constant vigilance be made to support and modify systems that are in constant motion throughout the life cycle.

B. Evaluation of Potential Threats:

In evaluation process of potential threats to information security, *Management of Information Security* identifies several categories of threats. These types (and examples of each) are as follows:

Type of Threat	Examples
Acts of human error or failure	Accidents, employee mistakes
Compromises to intellectual property	Piracy, copyright infringement
Deliberate acts of espionage or trespass	Unauthorized access and/or data collection
Deliberate acts of information extortion	Blackmail of information disclosure
Deliberate acts of sabotage or vandalism	Destruction of systems or information
Deliberate acts of theft	Illegal confiscation of equipment or information
Deliberate software attacks	Viruses, worms, macros, denial-of-service
Deviations in quality of service from service providers	Power and WAN service issues
Forces of nature	Fire, flood, earthquake, lightning
Technical hardware failures or errors	Equipment failure
Technical software failures or errors	Bugs, code problems, unknown loopholes
Technological obsolescence	Antiquated or outdated technologies

[Source: Whitman, Michael E. and Mattord, Herbert J. (2008). *Management of Information Security*, (2nd ed.). Boston: Thomson Course Technology, p. 41.]

C. Needs Assessment:

As previously mentioned, an analysis of information security needs to be conducted. There are certain stages within this analysis that include:

1. Identifying vulnerabilities (i.e., types of threats) and ranking these vulnerabilities in terms of likeliness to affect the organization.

2. Developing controls that can be placed to mitigate these types of risk.

3. Undertaking economic feasibilities to determine what the cost benefit of this protection system would be to the organization. That is, it is important to determine whether an alternative control is worth the associated cost. In some cases, the cost may outweigh the value of installing a protection system or approach.

D. Education, Training, and Awareness Programs:

Another integral part of any information security program is to have designed a security education, training, and awareness program. Each one of these three elements should be instituted within the organization.

E. Security Policy:

While it is recognized that planning (based on the evaluation of potential threats) and education coincide with one another in terms of protecting information, the program needs to have articulated structure. Most organizations refer to this articulated structure in the form of policy and procedures. As such, the policy only shapes the behavior of employees relative to information security. The organization's management must recognize this and develop proper guidelines for its employees.

Types of Information Security Policies:

1. Enterprise Information Security Program Policy:

   This policy identifies the strategic direction, scope, and purpose for the security efforts.

2. Issue-Specific Information Security Policy:

   This policy provides guidance for all members of the organization in connection with information technology.

3. System-Specific Information Security Policy:

   This policy provides a guide for management and technical specifications of a particular technology or system utilized by that organization.

F. Project Management:

When undertaking a project for information security, there is a methodology that must be followed in this process, which includes:

1. Integration: an emphasis on coordinating the various elements.

2. Scope: Understanding various tasks that need to be performed.

3. Time: Vetting schedules to perform tasks and controlling the same.

4. Cost: Articulating an economic value and completing these tasks within the budget.

5. Quality: Assuring that tasks are performed within satisfactory needs of the organization.

6. Resources: Identify the appropriate individuals who can perform the necessary task.

7. Communications: Develop an efficient and effective process for conveying information to those involved in the process.

8. Risk: Understanding those diversities that affect the organization and develop a response and control process.

9. Procurement: Acquiring those resources (both human and technology) needed for the course of the project.

VIII. Personnel and Security:

A. Employee Vulnerabilities:

Employees are our greatest vulnerability in terms of any information security program.

In order to mitigate threats to information security within an organization, all employees must be knowledgeable (i.e., through education, training, and awareness programs) as to the types of attacks that would affect an organization. Employees have to understand their role, including threats to the organization and be empowered to limit these risks in a thoughtful way. The social engineering of employees plays into this process.

B. Other Risks Involving Employees:

1. Sales presentations;

2. Seminars, trade association meetings, and conventions;

3. Discussions with suppliers;

4. Off premises statements; and

5. Press releases, publications, and public relations.

C. Theft of the Information by an Outsider:

1. False job interviews with a competitor's employees;

2. Access to premises;

3. Trash cover;

4. Romantic relationships with employees;

5. Social engineering; and

6. Electronic access (hacking).

IX. Information Security Program Focuses:

A. Identification, Classification, and Marking Sensitive Material:

1. Identify and group at least two (2) categories of information. That which:
   a. Is critical to the ongoing viability of the enterprise;
   b. Should not be released to the public.

2. The smallest possible bodies of information are desired.

3. Designate employees authorized to classify information.

4. Mark the information or data.

B. Control of Information:

1. Origination.

2. Transmission (Local Area Network, courier, postal service, delivery service).
   a. Encrypted voice, data, facsimile transmission technology.

3. Reproduction (copy machines, print shops).

4. Storage (desk, file cabinet, data terminal or PC access).

5. Use (clean desk, work station, conference room).

6. Destruction (shredder, disintegrator, data deletion).

C. Human Resource Management:

1. Preemployment screening.

2. Non-disclosure and non-compete agreements.

3. Information in new employee/temp employee orientation.

4. Information in the employee handbook.

5. Security training and awareness program. (Signed forms)
   a. Existence and need for the program.
   b. Recognition of sensitive information.
   c. Proper use and disposition of sensitive information.
   d. Report attempts to solicit information.

6. Employee identification and badging.

7. Unsolicited telephone query procedures.

8. Employee exposure documentation.

9. Security related questions during exit interviews.

D. Vendors and Visitors:

1. Visitor Controls.

2. Vendor/contractor/visitor non-disclosure agreements.

3. Due diligence inquiries.

4. Information in contractor orientation.

E. Administrative Controls:

1. Pre-publication review.

2. Trade show/off-site meeting procedures.

3. Media/public affairs procedures.

4. Internal and independent security audits.

5. Notice to new employers of former employee access and responsibility.

6. Informed monitoring of routine activities.

7. Set records retention periods and destroy on schedule.

F. Physical Security Measures:

1. Access control.

2. Identification of all personnel in sensitive areas. (Color code)

3. Escort visitors and challenge strangers.

4. Standards for storage containers. (Remove key numbers)

5. Key and combination control.

6. Warning screens on access to sensitive databases.

7. Examine electronic access (hackers).

8. Use of technical services countermeasures.

9. Monitor trash.

G. Electronic Data Processing Centers:

Should have the same physical security protection as any other business or industrial establishments.

H. Personal Computer Systems:

Should have access limited to authorized users only.

1. Protect the computer.

2. Protect the storage media (e.g., hard drives, tapes, disks).

X.Threats to Information System:

A. Eavesdropping: Unauthorized listening.

Black's Law Dictionary defines eavesdropping as "knowingly and without lawful authority: (a) entering into a private place with intent to listen surreptitiously to private conversations or to observe the conduct of any other person or persons therein; or (b) installing or using outside a private place any device for hearing, recording, amplifying, or broadcasting sounds originating in such place, which sounds would not ordinarily be audible or comprehensible outside, without the consent of the person or persons entitled to privacy therein; or (c) installing or using any device or equipment for the interception of any telephone, telegraph, or other wire communication without the consent of the person in possession or control of the facilities for such wire communication . . . "

B. Wiretapping - interception of a communication circuit.

C. Bugging - interception of a communication using an electronic device.

D. Recording of Conversations:

Under federal law, one (1) party consent is necessary to electronically monitor the conversation between two (2) parties. HOWEVER, some states prohibit electronic monitoring of a conversation without two (2) party consent (e.g., Maryland, Pennsylvania, and California).

1. Wired Microphones:
   a. Carbon microphone - commonly used in a standard telephone set.
   b. Crystal microphone - generates a small electric current when the crystal is vibrated by sound waves.
   c. Contact microphone - usually a crystal mike is installed on a common wall with the target area.

    d. Spike microphone - A type of contact microphone which is installed in a hole in a common wall with the target area (not fully through to the other side of the wall).

        (1) Disadvantages of using a contact microphone or a spike microphone:

           —Signals are generally too weak to travel very far over wire.

           —Other sounds (doors slamming, water running and other building sounds) may mask sounds in the target area.

           —The microphone is affected by variations in temperature and humidity.

    e. Dynamic microphone - movement of a small wire near a permanent magnet converts sound into electrical energy. Requires no power source and is usually very small. Good eavesdropping device which is available with a built-in amplifier.

    f. Pneumatic cavity device - has a specially designed small cavity which picks up surface vibrations. (Glass tumbler effect)

    g. Condenser microphone - high fidelity use. Fragile and sensitive.

    h. Electret microphone - used primarily in public address systems and for audio recording. Extremely small.

    i. Omnidirectional microphone - used in conference rooms - picks up sound from many directions around the room.

    j. Cardioid microphone - picks up sounds from directly in front of the microphone.

    k. Parabolic microphone - resembles a TV dish antenna. Concentrates audio energy gathered over an area equal to the diameter of the parabolic reflector (typically between 12 and 4 feet) and directs it to a conventional microphone in the center of the reflector.

  l. Shotgun microphone - a bulky arrangement of tubes gathers the sound and sends it to a microphone connected to the tubes.

2. Wireless Microphone - A radio frequency ("RF") device consisting of a microphone, transmitter, power supply, antenna, and receiver.

For example, the U.S. Department of State found a wireless electronic eavesdropping device known as a "store and burst" inside a strip of wall molding in a conference room of the Oceans and Environmental Bureau. This recent technology is a solid state tape recorder that can compress voice data and be interrogated remotely.

    a. The steel structure of a building or foil backed insulation in a home can seriously attenuate the radio signal. A transmitter or receiver functions poorly when inside an automobile and a transmitter inside a metal container is completely ineffective.

C. Light Amplification by Stimulated Emission of Radiation ("LASER")

Laser eavesdropping is done without any equipment in the area under surveillance. A laser beam is aimed at a window which vibrates with the sound waves of the conversation in the room. The vibrations are transferred to the laser's reflected beam and an amplifier is used to change the light beam variations into electrical current.

Under controlled conditions this is an excellent technique which produces very high quality audio. Surveillance conditions are rarely ideal. This is an infrequently used surveillance tool.

V-13

1. Infrared Light Wave Transmission uses a microphone within the room to convert sound waves to electronic pulses. The pulses are used to modulate infrared light waves. The infrared transmissions of certain speaker phones can also be targeted for interception.

2. Light wave devices must be in line-of-sight of the intended receiver.

3. Light wave eavesdropping can be countered by drawing the window blinds or holding sensitive conversations in an interior room without windows. Laser beams can also be countered by placing an operating radio, or a white noise generator, against the window glass to induce noise into the glass.

F. Electromagnetic Radiation:

Detected electromagnetic energy is generated by electronic information processing devices. Detection is possible for several hundred feet. The Faraday cage or Tempest shielding is used for very sensitive equipment.

G. Telephone Eavesdropping:

1. The telephone company voltage on the lines can be utilized to power eavesdropping devices. The existing wires in the system may be used to carry audio signals and the telephone instrument handset transmitter may be utilized as a microphone.

2. Telephone system vulnerabilities include:
   a. Direct interceptions;
   b. Radio transmitters;
   c. Pen registers;
   d. Voice mail intercepts; and
   e. Manipulation of system software.

3. Interception from the lines. Information acquired includes voice, facsimile, teletype, or data. Two common methods are used:
   a. Direct physical connection anywhere on the line between the target area and the telephone central office. The power in the telephone system can be used to drive the interception device and batteries do not have to be provided. The wire system is highly reliable and its range is virtually unlimited.
   b. Inductive coupling which does not require a physical connection.

4. Use of existing wire. After renovations and after replacement of a telephone system, original, but now unused, wiring frequently remains in place. Unused pairs of wires can be used to transmit data that has been intercepted through electronic eavesdropping. The extra pairs are accessed at various points in a building or neighborhood. If a room telephone is not being tapped, conversation within a room can be picked up by a hidden microphone and sent to a remote listening post over telephone wiring.

5. Use of telephone equipment in the target area. Requires physical entry into the target area.
   a. Wiring alteration of the telephone set - requires technical knowledge.

b. Drop-in radio transmitter.

c. Infinity transmitter (harmonica bug) - can be accessed using any other telephone. Not used in electronic telephone switch systems.

6. Digital Systems - originally thought to be secure.

a. Digital signal can be recorded and converted to analog and speech.

7. Remote Maintenance Access Terminal ("RMAT") - Telephone system control software of a Private Board Exchange ("PBX") can be accessed via an onsite terminal or by calling the telephone system's remote maintenance port telephone number. An intruder accessing the control software can:

a. Create a bridge tap to allow silent monitoring from other extensions.

b. Activate the hands-free intercom feature to monitor a room from any other phone.

c. Activate executive override privileges to allow forced access to busy extensions.

d. Activate or modify direct inward system access ("DISA") to allow free access to WATS and outside lines.

e. Completely de-program the system.

f. Perform surveillance of station message detail recording ("SMDR") to determine who calls whom.

8. Dialed number recorder [commonly referred to as a pen register]- records and prints detailed information of telephone calls initiated, time and frequency. Generally will require a physical search to detect.

9. Cellular and cordless, analog and digital, transmit radio frequency ("RF") signals which can be intercepted. Digital signals, thought to be secure, can be recorded and converted back to analog signals for use by the interloper.

Cordless Telephones - Intercepted with a receiver tuned to the proper frequency.

a. Range normally 700 to 1000 feet.

b. Illegal to intercept.

10. Cellular Telephones - Intercepted with a receiver tuned to the proper frequency.

a. Illegal to intercept.

b. Variable Path Encryption ("VPE") is particularly useful to secure cellular signals. A call is made to the toll free number of the VPE provider. A unit attached to the cellular set and a unit attached to the VPE provider alter the communication between them. The signal is sent in the clear from the VPE provider to the intended designation of the call.

H. Computer Technology Risks:

As technology advances, with our Internet access and network systems, so do the methods for attacking information systems. These attacks can vary from monitoring transactions to stealing or destroying information. The following are recognized methods for affecting computer systems.

1. Virus:

A virus is any hidden computer code that copies itself onto other programs. The attacks on the data within the computer system may vary, depending on the type of virus design. There are programs available to mitigate certain types of virus attacks.

2. Trojan Horse:

A Trojan horse program is designed to appear innocent allowing the unsuspecting party to download the information onto their individual system. Once inside the system, the Trojan horse program can then affect the data.

3. Bomb:

A bomb is a computer code inserted by a programmer into legitimate software. It is similar to the Trojan horse program. There are two (2) basic types of bombs. One is sensitive to a time schedule which is triggered by a date or time. The other is a logic bomb which is triggered by an event (i.e., the copying of a file).

4. Data Manipulation:

This is a rather common form in which anyone having access to the computer system can create, monitor, convert, transform, and affect data transactions.

5. Trapdoors and Back Doors:

The programmer designs a means to access the program. There are two (2) forms of this design. Trapdoors are intentionally created and inserted during program development. These trapdoors are supposed to be removed once the software is completed. However, a back door is an unintentional access to the software code.

6. Cookie Monster:

This is an improper modified log-on (access control for remote resource-sharing computer) program. The log-on program allows the party to extort unauthorized service from a user seeking access. For example, e-commerce companies maintain certain data from the customer user (as a result of prior transactions) in order to make sales transactions easier for the user. This data that is collected (i.e., credit card information, address, name) by the host server can be accessed by the unauthorized party using the improper modified log-on program.

The best way to protect any type of data is to encrypt it. Encryption scrambles the information so that it is not usable unless there is knowledge of the code to translate the data.

7. Theft of Hardware:

The unlawful taking of the computer, whether it is a laptop or PC, is probably the greatest risk to the individual as well as the company, particularly if it has capabilities of gaining access to the company's network system and/or has sensitive data (on its hard drive, disks, or CDs).

I. Other Technology Risks:

1. Facsimile Machines:
   a. Many plain paper fax machines use a disposable film. The used film retains a perfect negative image of all the information printed.
   b. Some fax machines have a memory which stores received messages. If the machine is equipped with a modem, the intruder can access the memory to download the received messages.
   c. Facsimile machine security devices and techniques include:

      Fax encryption to render intercepted transmissions unintelligible to the eavesdropper. Compatible encryption devices are required at the transmitting machine and at the receiving machine.

      Fax vaults to store received transmissions in memory. A password is required to print out the transmission.

2. Computer Modems and Facsimile Boards - Many computers are equipped with modems and facsimile boards. Telephone lines connected to the rear panel indicate the probable presence of a modem or facsimile board. Laptop docking stations be similarly equipped.

3. Speaker Phones - are excellent hiding places for eavesdropping devices. Some conference room models are actually wireless microphones which transmit via radio waves or infrared light waves.

4. Video Teleconferencing Equipment - Many systems cannot communicate directly with one another. Video teleconferences between incompatible systems are conducted through network translator nodes and are monitored by third party telecommunications technicians.

J. Technical Countermeasure Sweeps:

1. Physical Search - detailed, time consuming expensive task conducted in specific areas only. Required for a complete countermeasures survey.
   a. All furniture is moved and examined.
   b. Baseboards are examined for signs of modification.
   c. Walls are examined in detail for holes, mismatched paint, new plaster.
   d. All wiring, including optical fiber, traced and accounted for. Any wire not in use is removed.
   e. Light switches and fixtures are pulled out and examined.
   f. Ventilation duct covers are removed and ducts examined.
   g. Space above a dropped ceiling (plenum) is examined.

2. Telephone Search - done by a technician familiar with the specific equipment.
   a. Handsets are examined for drop-in transmitters or wiring alteration.
   b. All cables are inspected for unusual attachments or bulges.
   c. Junction boxes and wiring closets are examined and all connections verified.
   d. Telephone distribution room wiring is verified.

3. Electronic Search - *NO REMOTE DEVICE OR TECHNIQUES CAN GUARANTEE TO FIND A WELL INSTALLED DEVICE INSTALLED BY AN EXPERIENCED TECHNICIAN.*
    a. Time domain reflectometry - an electronic picture of a telecommunications line at a given time which is compared to the same line at a future time.
    b. Telephone analyzer - Electronic analysis of the telephone set and of the telephone line for wiring modification or an installed radio transmitter.
    c. Field strength meter - measures the relative radio frequency energy present at a given point. Not as good as the countermeasures receiver.
    d. Countermeasures radio receiver - searches a large part of the radio spectrum to isolate and identify a signal.
    e. Spectrum analyzer - displays a large part of the RF spectrum and the corresponding side bands. Used in conjunction with the countermeasures receiver to find all signals and give a visual analysis of the signal.
    f. Metal detector - not very reliable.
    g. Non-linear junction detector - Transmits a microwave signal. A semiconductor re-radiates the beam at a multiple (harmonic) of the original frequency. Will find a semiconductor device which is dead. Now considered very reliable.

1. All proprietary information is sensitive while not all sensitive information is proprietary. An example of information which is not proprietary even though the organization would treat it as sensitive is:
   a. The customer database of the organization
   b. Confidential personnel data in employee files
   c. Strategic marketing plans in which the use of outside marketing firms is contemplated
   d. Specifications for product components which are produced by a subcontractor

2. Trade Secrets are generally afforded greater legal protection than other proprietary information. Which of the following in not an element of the test for a trade secret?
   a. Be identifiable
   b. Not already be available in public sources
   c. Be disclosed only to persons with a duty to protect it
   d. Be technical or product related

3. The major reason for the loss of sensitive information is?
   a. Espionage
   b. Intentional disclosure by an insider
   c. Inadvertent disclosure
   d. Disclosure through legal proceedings

4. Competitive intelligence gathering is a legitimate activity which is engaged in by many firms throughout the world. The most important function of competitive intelligence is to:
   a. Alert senior management to marketplace changes in order to prevent surprise
   b. Alert senior management as to the personal habits of competitive senior management
   c. Alert government intelligence agencies to marketplace changes
   d. Alert senior management to changes in protocol in foreign countries

5. A microphone with a large disk-like attachment used for listening to audio from great distances is known as:
   a. Contact microphone
   b. Spike microphone
   c. Parabolic microphone
   d. Moving coil microphone

6. Sound waves too high in frequency to be heard by the human ear, generally above 20 KHZ are known as:
   a. Microwaves
   b. Ultrasonic
   c. High-frequency
   d. Short-wave

V-19

7. Two methods of protection against telephone line eavesdropping are apparently reliable. The first method is "don't discuss sensitive information" and the other is:
   a. To use wire tap detector
   b. To use radio jammer
   c. To use audio jammer
   d. To use encryption equipment

8. The unauthorized acquisition of sensitive information is known as:
   a. Industrial espionage
   b. Embezzlement
   c. Larceny
   d. False pretenses

9. Proprietary information is:
   a. Information which must be so classified under government order
   b. Private information of highly sensitive character
   c. Defense data which must be classified according to federal regulations
   d. Anything that an enterprise considers relevant to its status or operations and does not want to disclose publicly.

10. A Trade secret is:
    a. Any formula, pattern, device or compilation of information which is used in one's business and which gives that business an opportunity to gain an advantage over competition who do not know or use it
    b. All information about a company which the company desires to protect
    c. Information of a company which is registered as such with the U.S. Patent Office
    d. Information so designed by the government

11. The control software of a Private Board Exchange (PBX) can be accessed and compromised by calling the telephone number of a device on the PBX from a computer and modem. What is this access device called:
    a. Time Domain Reflectometer
    b. Remote Maintenance Access Terminal
    c. Current Carrier Signaling Port
    d. Internal and Remote Signal Port

12. Which of the following is generally not true with regard to proprietary information?
    a. Secret information does not have to be specifically identifiable
    b. Secret information must be such that it can be effectively protected
    c. The more narrowly a business defines what it regards as secret, the easier it is to protect that body of information
    d. It is difficult to protect as a trade secret that which can be found in publicly-accessible sources

Copyright © 2008 by ASIS International

13. With respect to trade secrets it may be decided that its disclosure by another was innocent rather than wrongful even in the case where the person making the disclosure really was guilty of malice or wrong intent. This situation may occur when:

    a. There is absence of evidence that an owner has taken reasonable precautions to protect confidential information

    b. Trade secret was not registered

    c. The trade secret did not involve national defense information

    d. The trade secret was not in current use

14. The class of person under a duty to safeguard a proprietary secret is known as:

    a. Agents

    b. Principals

    c. Fiduciaries

    d. Business Associates

15. Which of the following is **not** a correct statement, or a general rule, involving the protection of proprietary information:

    a. By operation of common law employees are presumed to be fiduciaries to extent they may not disclose secrets of their employers without authorization

    b. As a class, employees are the largest group of persons bound to secrecy because of their status or relationship

    c. Other than employees, any other persons to be bound to secrecy must agree to be bound

    d. Any agreements to bound must always be in writing and are not implied from acts

16. The term "eavesdropping" refers to:

    a. Wiretapping only

    b. "Bugging" only

    c. Both wiretapping and "bugging"

    d. Mail covers

17. A microphone which has the characteristics of requiring no power source to operate it is quite small, relatively difficult to detect, and is offered by equipment suppliers in such items as cuff links and hearing aids is known as:

    a. Carbon microphone

    b. Dynamic microphone

    c. Contact microphone

    d. Parabolic microphone

18. A microphone which is normally installed on a common wall adjoining a target area when it is impractical or impossible to enter the area to make a microphone installation is:

    a. Carbon microphone

    b. Dynamic microphone

    c. Contact microphone

    d. Parabolic microphone

19. Which of the following is **not** true with regard to electronic eavesdropping?
    a. A listening device installed in a wire will cause a crackling sound, click, or other noise that can be heard on the line
    b. An effective countermeasures survey to detect evidence of electronic eavesdropping in telephone equipment must be conducted by a person technically familiar with such equipment
    c. All wiring should be traced out and accounted for in a countermeasures survey
    d. In a countermeasures survey to detect electronic eavesdropping a physical search should be utilized as well as an electronic search

20. In designing a proprietary information protection program, the area of greatest vulnerability is:
    a. Personnel files
    b. Marketing data
    c. Employees
    d. Computers

21. A nonlinear junction detector is used to locate eavesdropping devices by:
    a. Detecting the semi-conductor components which comprise their circuits
    b. Recording changes in the voltage on a telephone line
    c. Measuring the distance from a known point to the indicated location of a telephone line attachment
    d. Detecting infrared emissions

22. Which of the following statements is incorrect with regard to an information security program?
    a. A good information security program will provide absolute protection against an enemy spy
    b. The information security program is an attempt to make theft of sensitive information difficult, not necessarily eliminate it
    c. A trust relationship must be established and maintained with employees
    d. The good will and compliance of employees is crucial for success

23. A specially-constructed microphone attached directly to an object or surface to be protected and which responds only when the protected object or surface is disturbed is known as:
    a. Parabolic microphone
    b. Special audio device
    c. Contact microphone
    d. Surreptitious microphone

24. "Social engineering" is:
    a. The conversation involved in the beginning of a romantic relationship
    b. A function of the personnel department in which like persons are teamed together in workshops or seminars for maximum productivity
    c. The subtle elicitation of information without revealing the true purpose of the call
    d. The specific design of a business structure to facilitate the interaction of the inhabitants

25. A former employee, who had access to your trade secret information, is now employed by a competitor and is apparently using the trade secret information to gain market share. There are several serious factors you should consider before you institute litigation in the matter. Which of the following is **not** a serious factor to be considered?
    a. You may have to expose the very secrets you are attempting to protect
    b. The cost of the litigation may exceed the value of the secret information
    c. You may lose a law case
    d. Other employees may leave the company and attempt to use trade secret information in the business of a new employer

26. Electromagnetic radiation is detectable electromagnetic energy generated by electronic information processing devices. Which of the following is used to protect very sensitive equipment?
    a. A current carrier device
    b. Pneumatic cavity shielding
    c. Tempest shielding
    d. Pen register shielding

27. Piracy refers to the illegal duplication and distribution of recordings. Which form is **not** considered piracy?
    a. Pirating
    b. Downloading
    c. Bootlegging
    d. Counterfeiting

28. To prevent cybercrime, it is **not** a good strategy to:
    a. Install a fire protection system
    b. Assign passwords or codes
    c. Disable unused computer services
    d. Update software for improving security

29. Which federal statute does **not** protect information and communication systems?
    a. U.S.A. Patriot Act
    b. Economic Espionage Act
    c. Civil Rights Act
    d. Sarbanes-Oxley Act

1. b. Confidential personnel data in employee files
   Source: *Protection of Assets Manual*

2. d. Be technical or product related
   Source: *Protection of Assets Manual*

3. c. Inadvertent disclosure
   Source: *Protection of Assets Manual*

4. a. Alert senior management to marketplace changes in order to prevent surprise
   Source: *Protection of Assets Manual*

5. c. Parabolic microphone
   Source: *Protection of Assets Manual*

6. b. Ultrasonic
   Source: *Protection of Assets Manual*

7. d. To use encryption equipment
   Source: *Protection of Assets Manual*

8. a. Industrial espionage
   Source: *Protection of Assets Manual*

9. d. Anything that an enterprise considers relevant to its status or operation and does not want to disclose publicly.
   Source: *Protection of Assets Manual*

10. a. Any formula, pattern, device, or compilation of information which is used in one's business and which gives that business an opportunity to gain an advantage over competition that do not know or use it
    Source: *Protection of Assets Manual*

11. b. Remote Maintenance Access Terminal
    Source: *Protection of Assets Manual*

12. a. Secret information does not have to be specifically identifiable
    Source: *Protection of Assets Manual*

13. a. There is absence of evidence that an owner has taken reasonable precautions to protect confidential information
    Source: *Protection of Assets Manual*

14. c. Fiduciaries
    Source: *Protection of Assets Manual*

15. d. Any agreements to bound must always be in writing and are not implied from acts
    Source: *Protection of Assets Manual*

16. c. Both wiretapping and "bugging"
    Source: *Protection of Assets Manual*

17. b. Dynamic microphone
    Source: *Protection of Assets Manual*

18. c. Contact microphone
    Source: *Protection of Assets Manual*

19. a. Listening device installed in a wire will cause a crackling sound, click, or other noise that can be heard on the line
    Source: *Protection of Assets Manual*

20. c, Employee
    Source: *Protection of Assets Manual*

21. a. Detecting the semi-conductor components which comprise their circuits
    Source: *Protection of Assets Manual*

22. a. A good information security program will provide absolute protection against an enemy spy
    Source: *Protection of Assets Manual*

23. c. Contact microphone
    Source: *Protection of Assets Manual*

24. c. The subtle elicitation of information without revealing the true purpose of the call
    Source: *Protection of Assets Manual*

25. d. Other employees may leave the company and attempt to use trade secret information in the business of a new employer
    Source: *Protection of Assets Manual*

26. c. Tempest shielding
    Source: *Protection of Assets Manual*

27. b. Downloading
    Source: *Introduction to Security,* p. 471

28. a. Install a fire protection system
    Source: *Security Loss and Prevention,* pp. 392-394

29. c. Civil Rights Act
    Source: *Management of Information Security,* pp. 436-438

ASIS International. (2008). *Protection of Assets Manual.* Alexandria, VA: ASIS International.

Fennelly, Lawrence J. (2004). *Handbook of Loss Prevention and Crime Prevention,* (4th ed.), Elsevier/Butterworth/Heinemann, Burlington, MA.

Fischer, Robert J., Halibozek, Edward, and Green, Gion (2008). *Introduction to Security,* (8th ed.), Elsevier/Butterworth-Heinemann. Burlington, MA.

Whitman, Michael E. and Mattord, Herbert J. (2008). *Management of Information Security,* (2nd ed.), Boston: Thomson Course Technology.

I. Security Management

A. Security's Role in the Organization

1. Security provides protective services for the organization. The protective service of prevention is a primary service provided.

2. Special services provided include:
   a. Executive protection and home security surveys
   b. Investigative services
   c. Emergency services such as fire fighting, emergency medical, and disaster management

3. Educational Programs provided include:
   a. General security
   b. Supervisory training
   c. Employee self protection
   d. Security awareness

4. Downsizing has forced the security department which primarily performed protective services to generally evolve into an assets protection department with additional functions.

5. The assets protection department might include:
   a. Fire protection
   b. Safety
   c. Risk and Insurance Management
   d. Internal Audit

6. From an effective organizational standpoint, a security director should report to a member of senior management, preferably vice-president or higher.

7. Key resources for an effective security operation:
   a. Human resources - Identification of staffing needs and selection, training, leading, and retaining of effective personnel
   b. Financial resources - Identification and justification of funds
   c. Administrative resources - Equipment and supplies to operate effectively
   d. Operational resources - basic and technology based equipment to complete mission

B. Security Training

1. The controlling element in a training program is the competency of the instructors. The competency can be judged in two areas:
   a. Knowledge of the subject
   b. The ability to communicate the knowledge

2. An instructor training course includes:
   a. Learning theory
   b. Instructional strategies and methods
   c. Learning aids
   d. Lesson plan writing
   e. Development of practical exercises

3. Training must be ongoing and continuous.

4. Since documentation is a strong defense to a charge on negligent training, records must be kept of each aspect of every employee's training.

5. The employees must know:
   a. WHAT they are to do (POLICY)
   b. WHY they are to do it (OBJECTIVES)
   c. HOW they are to do it (PROCEDURES)

C. Risk Assessment

1. The possibility and probability of a risk resulting in loss depends on the risk itself and the preventative measures taken.

2. Close interaction is required between security and senior management in handling risk decisions.

3. Defining the problem
   a. Loss event profile
   b. Loss event probability
   c. Loss event criticality

4. Methods for handling a risk
   a. Accept
   b. Eliminate
   c. Reduce
   d. Transfer (insurance)

D. Risk Management

1. Risk is exposure to possible loss; crime, fire, product obsolescence, shrinkage, and work stoppage all are examples.

2. Loss prevention practitioners are primarily interested in crime, shrinkage, fire, and accidents. Risk Managers generally have more interest in fire and safety issues.

3. The concept of risk management is derived from business, the two types of risk are:
   a. **Pure risk** - a risk in which there is no potential of benefits to be derived
   b. **Dynamic risk** - A risk that can produce gain or profit

4. Crime and incident analysis is one of the first tools to be applied to the assessment of risks in order to determine vulnerability.

5. When assessing vulnerability and the response to risks, **PML** factors must be considered.

6. **PML** stands for:
   a. **Possible maximum loss** - maximum loss sustained if a given target is **totally destroyed** or removed
   b. **Probable maximum loss** - amount of loss a target is **likely to sustain**

7. The abbreviation ALE stands for Annual Loss Expectancy which is part of the Risk Analysis Assessment.

8. Once PML is assessed, the five principal crime risk management methods can be considered, which are critical to the crime prevention manager.
   a. **Risk Avoidance** - removal of target altogether
   b. **Risk Reduction** - minimizing potential loss to extent possible
   c. **Risk Spreading** - spreading target over as large an area as possible
   d. **Risk Transfer** - transfer risk to someone else
   e. **Risk Acceptance** - risk is simply accepted

9. Risk Management and Insurance
   a. Insurance defined: The transfer of risk from one party to another in which the insurer is obligated to indemnify the insured for an economic loss caused by an unexpected event during a period of time covered by such insurance

10. Insurance rates are dependent upon two primary variables:
    a. Frequency of claims
    b. Cost of each claim

11. There are many types of insurance available, i.e., crime insurance and bonds, fire insurance and liability insurance.

12. Two basic types of protection against crime are:
    a. Fidelity and Surety Bonds
    b. Burglary, robbery, and theft insurance

13. Fidelity bonds require that an employee be investigated by the bonding company to limit the risk of dishonesty; if the employee violates the trust, the insurance company indemnifies the employer for the amount of the policy. There are two types of fidelity bonds:
    a. Those in which the employee is specifically bonded by name or position
    b. Blanket bonds which cover a whole category of employees

14. Surety bonds compensate if there is a failure to perform specified acts within a certain period of time. An example is a contract bond which guarantees that construction will be completed by a given date.
    a. Fiduciary bonds - ensures that persons appointed by the court to supervise property will be trustworthy
    b. Litigation bonds - ensure specific conduct by defendants and plaintiffs
    c. License and permit bonds guarantee the payment of taxes and fees

15. Burglary, robbery and theft insurance can be limited, provide very specific coverage or be very comprehensive.

E. Guard Forces

1. Advantages of contract forces
   a. Monetary savings
   b. Scheduling flexibility
   c. Contract company is responsible for personnel issues
   d. Expertise of the contract company
   e. Experience of the force

2. Advantages of a proprietary force
   a. Tighter control and supervision
   b. Better training
   c. Employee loyalty
   d. Company interests are better served

F. Ethics

1. A code of ethics is a set of rules by which members of a profession regulate their conduct.

2. The code of ethics established for all members of ASIS International is:
   a. A member shall perform professional duties in accordance with the law and the highest moral principles
   b. A member shall observe the precepts of truthfulness, honesty and integrity
   c. A member shall be faithful and diligent in discharging professional responsibilities
   d. A member shall be competent in discharging professional responsibilities
   e. A member shall safeguard confidential information and exercise due care to prevent its improper disclosure
   f. A member shall not maliciously injure the professional reputation or practice of colleagues

II. Loss Prevention

A. History/Principles of Crime Prevention and Security

1. Definition of loss prevention: any method used to increase the likelihood of preventing and controlling loss.

2. Historical overview
   a. First codification of law occurred around 1800 BC with Hammurabi's Code
   b. Modern policing has its roots in England where Sir Robert Peel, in 1829, marked the beginning of a police role in crime prevention

3. In 1980, the International Association of Chiefs of Police adopted a resolution that all police agencies should consider crime prevention as a standard police function and form specialized crime prevention units.

4. Crime Prevention/Loss Prevention are allied fields:
   a. Crime Prevention Officer (CPO) - a public servant with police powers
   b. Loss Prevention Officer (LPO) - private sector individual deriving authority from an employer

B. Environmental Design

1. Environmental design, or physical planning, is an approach to preventing crime and to improve security in residential and commercial areas by coordinating efforts of architects, loss prevention practitioners, and police.

2. Crime prevention through environmental design (CPTED) advocates that the proper design and effective use of the building environment leads to a reduction in crime and in the fear of crime.

3. Oscar Newman's book entitled, *Defensible Space,* presented ideas and applied strategies from a New York housing project. The essence of the concept is that better residential security can be brought about through environmental and architectural design and other planning coordinated with crime prevention methods.

4. Environmental Security (E/S) is an urban planning and design process which integrates crime prevention with neighborhood design and urban development.

5. The basic premise of E/S is that deterioration in the quality of urban life can be prevented (or minimized) by design and redesign of urban environments so that crime opportunities are reduced. It has little or no effect on white collar crime, embezzlement, and fraud.

6. Reduction of crime through E/S maximizes opportunities for apprehension in four ways:
   a. **Increased perpetration time** - more difficult to commit crime
   b. **Increased detection time** - enhanced by lighting, landscaping, etc.
   c. **Decreased reporting time** - better overall observation by more people
   d. **Decreased police response time** - better planning of streets, clearly marked exits and pathways

7. Defensible Space concept by Newman is divided into four categories:
   a. **Territoriality** - attitude of maintaining perceived boundaries. Outsider quietly recognized, observed
   b. **Natural Surveillance** - ability of inhabitants of particular territory to casually and continually observe public areas
   c. **Image and milieu** - involve the ability of design to counteract the perception that the area is isolated and vulnerable to crime
   d. **Safe area** - locales that allow for high degree of observation by police

8. Barriers and physical security measures play a large role in support of the concept.

C. Security Surveys

1. A security survey is a critical, on-site examination and analysis to ascertain the security status, identify deficiencies or excesses, determine protection needed, and make recommendations for overall security.

2. The cost of protection is measured in:
   a. Protection in depth
   b. Delay time

3. A security surveyor requires good investigative skills with an understanding of criminal methods and operations as well as the knowledge of limitations of security devices.

4. Compilation of well-thought out checklist is **essential** in conducting a security survey. No checklist exists which can be used as a master checklist for all premises. They must be tailored to the premises being surveyed.

D. Prevention of Internal and External Threats

1. Internal theft is the greatest ongoing threat to business.

2. It is difficult to obtain accurate statistics as to the shrinkage attributable to employee theft .

3. Internal losses occur by several methods:
   a. **Pilferage** - stealing in small quantities over a long period
   b. **Embezzlement** - taking money/property entrusted to their care
   c. **Shrinkage** - loss of inventory through any means

4. Two major causes of employee theft are personal problems and environment (inadequate socialization).

5. The theft triangle consists of three elements: motivation + opportunity + rationalization. Loss prevention techniques are designed to eliminate the opportunity.

6. Danger signs that are readily visible are:
   a. **Conspicuous consumers** who are visibly extravagant
   b. Those showing a **pattern of financial irresponsibility**
   c. Those who are **financially squeezed**

7. Research shows that dissatisfied employees are most frequently involved in internal theft.

8. Effective pre-employment screening also deters theft in the workplace.

9. Security tools used by the crime prevention manager are the four D's of crime prevention:
   a. **Deter** criminal attack
   b. **Detect** attacks that occur
   c. **Delay** attack to allow time for response by authorities
   d. **Deny** access to selected targets

E. Crime Analysis and Crime Prevention

1. Crime analysis, a systematic approach to studying crime problems, collects, categorizes, and disseminates accurate, timely and useful information to line personnel.

2. The specific steps that comprise the crime analysis procedure are:
    a. **Data collection**
    b. **Analysis**
    c. **Dissemination**
    d. **Feedback**

3. The usefulness of crime analysis products is a basic measure of success, and accuracy is important to its credibility.

F. Safety and Loss Prevention

1. Unsafe acts cause 85 percent of all accidents, unsafe conditions cause the remaining 15 percent.

2. A loss prevention program must assess the concept of loss in its broadest sense. Any unwanted or undesired event which degrades the efficiency of the business operation is considered an incident.
    a. An **incident** is anything from serious injury to a breakdown in quality control
    b. An **accident** is an undesired event resulting in physical harm to a person or damage to property

3. Some acceptable ways to remedy untimely accidents:
    a. Constant inspections
    b. Job safety analysis
    c. Early discovery of unsafe conditions
    d. Identification and control of hazards
    e. Investigation of all accidents and near misses as soon as possible

4. Hazardous material program (HAZMAT):
    a. Identify hazards that are present
    b. Know how to respond to an incident
    c. Set up necessary safeguards
    d. Employee training

III. Liaison

A. In our context, defined as: "A linking up or connecting of the parts of a whole in order to bring about proper coordination of activities."

B. The major research questions addressed by Hallcrest studies were:

1. Roles, functions, and contributions of private security and public law enforcement to crime prevention and control.

2. The mutual expectations/perceptions of private security and law enforcement.

3. Communication/cooperation between private security and law enforcement.

4. Competition and conflict between private security and law enforcement.

5. Characteristics and standards of the labor and technological resources of both.

6. Identification of emerging issues.

C. Perceptions:

1. Contract security managers, police, and proprietary security managers rated private security firms "poor" in quality of personnel, preemployment background checks, training, supervision, and familiarity with legal powers. The proprietary security managers rated their own personnel higher.

2. Law enforcement gave private security a fair-to-poor rating in most areas, with the highest ratings in reporting criminal incidents, responding to alarms, reasonable use of force, and proper use of weapons. A significant minority of law enforcement had infrequent contact with private security.

3. Proprietary security managers rated their own operations as "good" but gave contract security personnel lower ratings in most performance categories.

4. Contract security managers generally gave "poor" ratings to the performance of security firms in their geographical area with the exception of alarm response.

5. Both law enforcement and private security managers felt that private security was relatively effective in reducing the dollar loss of crime, and relatively ineffective in apprehending criminals.

D. Interaction Between Law Enforcement and Private Security:

1. Law enforcement officers regarded themselves as professional and saw private security personnel as non-professional.

2. Private security managers felt that police cooperated with their investigations, and were satisfied with the speed of police response and the degree to which police supported the decisions they had made.

3. Only 20 percent of law enforcement at field-study sites were satisfied with the way security personnel handled incidents in which they were involved. Among detectives, about half were satisfied with their private security interaction.

4. Private security occasionally assists law enforcement investigations. Typically, the assistance consists of providing investigators, undercover operatives, investigative accountants, photographic, CCTV, or surveillance equipment; money for rewards, "buys," overtime pay and, information which is the most frequently exchanged item.

E. Both public and private police suggested improving private security quality by:

1. Improving training.

2. Improving personnel selection methods.

3. Paying higher wages.

4. Establishing and improving licensing and regulations.

F. How to Improve Public and Private Sector Relations?

1. Closer cooperation.

2. Management meetings.

3. Understand respective roles.

4. Information exchanges.

5. Improving communication.

G. Private security and law enforcement growth contrasts:

1. The increasing growth of private security and the limited growth of public law enforcement are due to four main factors:
   a. Increasing workplace crime
   b. Increasing fear of crime
   c. Decrease in government spending
   d. Increasing awareness and use of private security products and services as cost-effective protective measures

2. The use of locks, security lighting, burglar alarms, citizen patrols, etc., suggests that the public's fear of crimes is growing while the rate of most property crimes is steady or decreasing.

3. Public law enforcement at an average annual growth rate of 4 percent and will reach only $44 billion by the turn of the century.

4. Employment in private security is projected to grow at 2.3 percent annually until 2000 while law enforcement is expected to grow 1 percent annually.

H. Relationship Between Private Security and the Police:

1. Law enforcement administrators are interested in transferring responsibility to the private sector for responding to burglar alarms and completing incident reports when the victim declines prosecution or files for insurance purposes.

2. Police moonlighting in private security:
    a. 81% of departments permit moonlighting with 150,000 law enforcement officers regularly engaged in off-duty private security jobs
    b. Law enforcement executives often oppose it because of conflict of interest situations, liability issues and preparedness for duty problems with officers working long hours off duty
    c. Common methods to hire off-duty officers are 1) direct hire, 2) department contracts with the firm, and 3) through unions or associations
    d. Contract agencies feel that it is unfair competition

3. Police response to false alarms
    a. 10 percent to 30 percent of all calls for police service were for alarms
    b. 95 percent to 99 percent are false

I. Economic Crime - financially motivated crime with a direct impact on the economy.

1. Much economic crime is resolved privately. Private sector reservations about public adjudication include:
    a. Administrative delays in prosecution
    b. Prosecutorial policy objectives
    c. Differing "output goals" of business and criminal justice
    d. Policies on governmental release of information and rules of discovery
    e. Unsympathetic attitude of the courts to business losses

2. Indirect costs of economic crime include:
    a. Effects on business
    b. Effects on government
    c. Effects on the public

3. Liability is the largest indirect cost of economic crime for the past 20 years.

4. Obstacles to the development of an ongoing reporting system:
    a. No accepted definition of economic crime
    b. No data base to build on
    c. Businesses lack collection and reporting methods
    d. The reluctance to release loss information

J. Forecasts and recommendations:

1. The percentage of residents with alarm systems will double to 28 percent before 2000.

2. Private security personnel are becoming younger and better educated.

3. The number of armed private personnel will decrease to 5 percent or less by 2000.

4. There is a need for economic crime research, for studies of the cost effective benefits of security measures, and for a national study of false alarms.

5. Personnel screening should be upgraded.

6. By the year 2000, the ratio of private security personnel to public police will be three to one respectively.

IV. Substance Abuse

A. GENERAL

1. "Psychological Dependence" is the condition in which the repeated use of a drug results in increasing tolerance which requires progressively larger doses to attain the desired effect.

2. "Physical Dependence" refers to an alteration of the normal functions of the body which necessitates the continued presence of a drug to prevent the withdrawal syndrome which is characteristic of addictive drugs.

B. NARCOTICS

1. General Information:
   a. The term "narcotic" in its medical meaning refers to opium and opium derivatives or synthetic substitutes
   b. Under medical supervision, narcotics are administered orally or by intramuscular injection. As drugs of abuse, they may be:
      1) Sniffed
      2) Smoked
      3) Subcutaneously injected (skin-popping)
      4) Intravenously injected (mainlining)
   c. Possible effects of use of narcotics are:
      1) Pinpoint pupils
      2) Drowsiness
      3) Euphoria
      4) Reduced vision
      5) Respiratory depression
      6) Nausea

d. Generally, there is no loss of motor coordination or slurred speech

e. Withdrawal symptoms involving narcotics are:

 1) Watery eyes

 2) Runny nose

 3) Yawning

 4) Loss of appetite

 5) Irritability

 6) Tremors

 7) Panic

 8) Chills and sweating

 9) Cramps

 10) Nausea

f. Effects of overdose of narcotics are:

 1) Slow and shallow breathing

 2) Clammy skin

 3) Convulsions

 4) Possible death

C. NARCOTICS OF NATURAL ORIGIN – The poppy, cultivated in many countries around the world, is the main source of nonsynthetic narcotics.

1. **Opium**

 a. The 25 alkaloids extracted from opium fall into two general categories:

  1) The phenanthrene alkaloids represented by morphine and codeine which are used as analgesics and cough suppressants

  2) The isoquinoline alkaloids represented by papaverine (an intestinal relaxant) and noscapine (a cough suppressant)

 b. Both physical and psychological dependence are rated high with the use of opium

 c. Opium is usually administered orally or smoked

2. **Morphine**

 a. Morphine is one of the most effective drugs known for the relief of pain

 b. Its legal use is restricted primarily to hospitals

 c. It is odorless, tastes bitter, and darkens with age

 d. Addicts usually administer it intravenously but, it is also taken orally or smoked

 e. Physical and psychological dependence are rated high with the use of morphine

3. **Codeine**

 a. Most codeine is produced from morphine

 b. Compared with morphine, codeine produces less analgesia, sedation, and respiratory depression

 c. It is widely distributed in tablets, alone or combined with other products such as aspirin, or in liquid cough preparations

 d. It is by far the most widely used "naturally occurring narcotic"

4. **Thebaine**
   a. It is the principal alkaloid in a species of poppy which has been grown experimentally in the U.S.
   b. It is converted into a variety of medical compounds including codeine

5. **Heroin**
   a. Pure heroin is a white powder with a bitter taste
   b. Pure heroin is rarely sold on the street, but is diluted with sugar, starch, powdered milk, and quinine
   c. Street heroin varies from white to dark brown with a purity of 1 percent to 98 percent
   d. "Black Tar" heroin, primarily from Mexico, is 20 percent to 80 percent pure heroin
   e. Heroin is usually:
      1) Injected
      2) Sniffed
      3) Smoked
   f. Both physical and psychological dependence are rated high with the use of heroin

6. **Hydromorphone**
   a. Highly marketable with a potency is two to eight times as great as morphine
   b. Both physical dependence and psychological dependence are rated as high

7. **Oxycodone**
   a. Synthesized from Thebaine, it is similar to codeine but more powerful and has a higher dependence potential

8. **Etorphine and Diprenorphine**
   a. Both of these substances are made from Thebaine
   b. Etorphine is more than a thousand times as potent as morphine in its analgesic, sedative, and respiratory depressant effect
   c. There is a great danger of overdose in the use of this drug
   d. Diprenorphine is used to counteract the effects of Etorphine

D. Synthetic Narcotics (produced entirely within the laboratory)

1. **Meperidine (Pethidine)**
   a. Probably the most widely used drug for the relief of moderate to severe pain
   b. Administered either orally or by injection
   c. Both physical and psychological dependence is rated high

2. **Methadone and Related Drugs**
   a. Methadone was synthesized during World War II by German scientists because of a shortage of morphine
   b. Methadone is almost as effective when administered orally as it is by injection
   c. Designed to control narcotic addiction, it has been a major cause of overdose death
   d. Both physical and psychological dependence of this drug are rated as high

E. Narcotic Antagonists

1. A class of compounds developed to block and reverse the effects of narcotics.

F. DEPRESSANTS

1. **General Information**
   a. Used in excessive amounts, depressants induce a state of intoxication similar to that of alcohol
   b. Depressants have a high potential for physical and psychological dependence
   c. As prescribed by a physician, they may be beneficial for the relief of anxiety, irritability, and tension
   d. In contrast to the effects of narcotics, intoxicating doses of depressants result in:
      1) Impaired judgment
      2) Slurred speech
      3) Loss of motor coordination
      4) Disorientation
      5) Drunken behavior without the odor of alcohol
   e. The effects of overdose are:
      1) Shallow respiration
      2) Cold and clammy skin
      3) Dilated pupils
      4) Weak and rapid pulse
      5) Coma
      6) Possible death
   f. The withdrawal syndrome regarding depressants includes:
      1) Anxiety
      2) Insomnia
      3) Tremors
      4) Delirium
      5) Convulsions
      6) Possible death

2. **Chloral Hydrate**
   a. The oldest of sleep inducing drugs, known as hypnotic drugs
   b. Its popularity declined after introduction of barbiturates but is still widely used by older adults
   c. It is a liquid with a slightly acrid odor and a bitter, caustic taste
   d. Withdrawal symptoms resemble delirium tremens
   e. Both physical and psychological dependence are rated as moderate

3. **Barbiturates**
   a. Widely prescribed to induce sleep and sedation, barbiturates are classified as:
      1) Ultrashort
      2) Short
      3) Intermediate
      4) Long-acting
   b. All barbiturates result in a build-up of tolerance and dependence on them is widespread
   c. Physical and psychological dependence are classified as "high moderate"

4. **Methaqualone**
   a. A synthetic sedative, it has been widely abused because it was once mistakenly thought to be non-addictive and effective as an aphrodisiac
   b. Both the physical and psychological dependence of this drug are rated as high

5. **Meprobamate**
   a. A muscle relaxant prescribed primarily for the relief of anxiety, tension, and muscle spasms
   b. Excessive use can result in psychological dependence

6. **Benzodiazepines**
   a. Depressants which relieve anxiety, tension, and muscle spasms as well as producing sedation and preventing convulsions
   b. The margin of safety of these drugs is greater than that of other depressants
   c. Physical and psychological dependence drug are rated as low but prolonged use of excessive doses may result in physical and psychological dependence

G. STIMULANTS

1. **General Information**
   a. Of all abused drugs, stimulants are the most powerfully reinforcing
   b. They can lead to increasingly compulsive behavior
   c. The two most prevalent stimulants are nicotine in tobacco and caffeine, which is an active ingredient in coffee, tea, and some bottled beverages
   d. In moderation, nicotine, and caffeine tend to relieve fatigue and increase alertness
   e. The consumption of stimulants may result in temporary exhilaration, hyperactivity, super-abundant energy, extended wakefulness, and a loss of appetite
   f. They may also induce irritability, anxiety, and apprehension
   g. The protracted use of stimulants is followed by a period of depression known as "crashing"
   h. The possible effects generally associated with the use of stimulants are:
      1) Increased alertness
      2) Excitation
      3) Euphoria
      4) Increased pulse rate and blood pressure
      5) Insomnia
      6) Loss of appetite

    i. The effects of overdose of stimulants are:
1) Agitation
2) Increase in body temperature
3) Hallucinations
4) Convulsions
5) Possible death

    j. Withdrawal syndrome characteristics are:
1) Apathy
2) Long periods of sleep
3) Irritability
4) Depression
5) Disorientation

2. **Cocaine**
   a. The most potent stimulant of natural origin, it is extracted from the leaves of the coca plant
   b. Illicit cocaine is distributed as a white, crystalline powder, often diluted by sugars and local anesthetics
   c. It is most commonly administered by "snorting" through the nasal passages
   d. It has the potential for extraordinary psychic dependency
   e. Excessive doses of cocaine may cause seizures and death from respiratory failure
   f. While a stimulant, it has been designated as a narcotic in the U.S. Controlled Substance Act
   g. "Crack", the chunk or "rock" form of cocaine, is a ready to use freebase
      1) Smoking crack delivers large quantities of cocaine to the lungs with an immediate effect comparable to intravenous injection
      2) The effects are very intense and quickly over

3. **Amphetamines**
   a. First used clinically to treat narcolepsy, the medical use of amphetamines is now limited to narcolepsy, hyperkinetic behavioral disorders in children, and some cases of obesity
   b. The illicit use of these drugs closely parallels that of cocaine in both short-term and long-term effects
   c. The physical dependence potential is rated as possible whereas the psychological dependence potential is rated as high
   d. Crystalline methamphetamine hydrochloride, or "**Ice**" is smoked

4. **Methcathinone**
   a. A structural analogue of methamphetamine known as "**Cat**"
   b. Most commonly snorted, but can be used orally or injected
   c. Toxic levels may produce convulsions, paranoia and hallucinations

5. **Khat**
   a. The fresh young leaves of the "Catha Edulis" shrub which are chewed
   b. Used in a social context similar to coffee primarily in East Africa and the Arabian peninsula
   c. Chewed in moderation, khat alleviates fatigue and reduces appetite

    d. Compulsive use may result in manic behavior with grandiose delusions or in a paranoid type of illness, sometimes accompanied by hallucinations

    e. As the leaves mature or dry, the stimulatory properties are reduced

6. **Phenmetrazine and Methylphenidate**

    a. Phenmetrazine is used medically as an appetite suppressant

    b. Methylphenidate is mainly used medically for treatment of hyperkenetic behavioral disorder in children

H. HALLUCINOGENS

1. **General Information**

    a. Generally, both natural and synthetic substances which distort the perception of reality; the senses of direction, distance, and time become disoriented

    b. They excite the central nervous system with a change of mood, usually euphoric; the mood may also become severely depressive; depression sometimes becomes so severe that suicide results

    c. In large doses, the drug produces delusions and visual hallucinations

    d. The most common danger is the impairment of judgment which often leads to rash decisions and accidents

    e. Long after hallucinogens are eliminated from the body, users may experience "flashbacks," fragmentary recurrences of psychedelic effects

    f. Recurrent use produces tolerance which tends to encourage resorting to

2. **Peyote and Mescaline**

    a. The primary active ingredient of the peyote cactus is mescaline which comes from the fleshy parts or bottoms of the cactus plant, but can also be produced synthetically

3. **Psilocybin and Psilocyn**

    a. These drugs are obtained from the psilocybe mushrooms, but can now be made synthetically

4. **LSD**

    a. LSD is an abbreviation of the German expression for lysergic acid diethylamide

    b. It is produced from lysergic acid, which in turn is derived from the ergot fungus which grows on rye

    c. Commonly known as acid and microdot, it is usually sold in the form of tablets, thin squares or gelatin or impregnated paper

    d. Tolerance develops rapidly

5. **Phencyclidine (PCP)**

    a. Commonly known as PCP, Angel Dust and HOG, most phencyclidine is produced in clandestine laboratories

    b. It is unique among popular drugs of abuse in that it is able to produce psychoses indistinguishable from schizophrenia

I. CANNABIS

1. **General Information**
   a. The source of cannabis is the hemp plant which grows wild throughout most of the tropic and temperate regions of the world
   b. Cannabis is usually smoked in the form of loosely rolled cigarettes called "joints"
   c. The possible effects of the use of cannabis products are:
      1) Euphoria
      2) Relaxed inhibitions
      3) Increased appetite
      4) Disoriented behavior
   d. The possible effects of overdose are:
      1) Fatigue
      2) Paranoia
      3) Possible psychosis

2. **Marihuana**

   a. Marihuana is also known by the following names:
      1) Pot
      2) Acapulco Gold
      3) Grass
      4) Reefer
      5) Sinsemilla
      6) Thai Sticks

3. **Hashish**
   a. Consists of secretions of the cannabis plant which are collected, dried, and then compressed into forms such as balls, cakes, or cookie-like sheets

J. INHALANTS

1. Inhalants are psychoactive substances in solvents commonly found in adhesives, lighter fluids, cleaning fluids, and paint products.

2. Between 5 percent and 15 percent of young people in the United States have tried inhalants, although the vast majority of these youngsters do not become chronic abusers.

3. Inhalants may be sniffed directly from an open container or "huffed" from a rag soaked in the substance and held to the face.

4. Blood levels peak rapidly with effects resembling alcohol inebriation. Stimulation and loss of inhibition are followed by depression at high doses. Other effects are distortion in perceptions of time and space, headache, nausea or vomiting, slurred speech, loss of motor coordination, and wheezing.

5. Memory impairment, attention deficits, and diminished non-verbal intelligence have been associated with the abuse of inhalants. Deaths resulting from heart failure, asphyxiation, or aspiration have occurred.

K. ALCOHOL

1. It is our most used and most abused recreational drug. Physical dependence can occur if alcohol is taken regularly in large quantities.

L. SUBSTANCE ABUSE PROGRAMS

1. Rationale:
   a. The problem is widespread and growing
   b. Control and rehabilitation is more humane and cost effective than termination of abusing employees

2. Substance Abuse Policy:
   a. The substance abuse policy of the organization includes:
      1) The attitude of the organization on drug abuse
      2) The criteria to be applied
      3) The actions that will be taken
   b. Having the policy does not imply that production or safety problems will be ignored
   c. With the decision made on an individual case basis, using the whole man rule, termination of employment or disqualification of an applicant can be sustained

3. Drug Screening:
   a. Enzyme Multiplied Immunoassay Technique (EMIT) screens
      1) Easy to administer and relatively inexpensive
      2) Can be used for a combination of substances
   b. Gas Chromatography/Mass Spectrometry, highly reliable, are used for confirming tests
   c. Initial positives are confirmed before any personnel action is taken
   d. Confirming tests should be done on the same specimen

4. Legal Issues:
   a. To avoid liability in the screening process:
      1) Notify all to be tested of the screening program
      2) Get consent from persons tested
      3) Provide prior notice to incumbents that testing is a condition of continued employment
      4) Define the circumstances under which testing is done
      5) Insure a positive identification and chain of custody for specimen collection, identification, and handling
      6) Limit dissemination of test results
      7) Maintain an Employee Assistance Program
      8) Regularly verify results from test facilities

5. Critical Job Situations:
   a. An abuser using judgment or skills where improper performance would result in harm to people or damage to assets may not assume the duties until a fitness check is conducted
   b. The direct supervisor conducts the check prior to assumption of duty on each tour
   c. An abuser who will not participate in daily fitness checks or in rehabilitation efforts may not continue in the critical assignment
   d. Failure of the employer to take proper care, resulting in damage or injury, is the basis for tort liability

1. From an organizational standpoint, the head of security should report to:
    a. Superintendent of buildings
    b. Manager of buildings and grounds
    c. Head housekeeper
    d. A vice-president or higher

2. The most conspicuous role of the security department in any organization is that of:
    a. Educational services
    b. Management services
    c. Special services
    d. Protective services

3. Training sessions consisting of a security awareness program for new employees should be conducted by:
    a. Special training officers
    b. Security personnel
    c. Consultants skilled in training
    d. Member of management

4. There are necessary and legitimate exceptions to the principle of unity of command. One condition which sometimes allows for shifting in supervision is:
    a. When order is given by the rank of captain or above
    b. When order is given by the head of a department
    c. When the order is given by the head of internal affairs
    d. During emergencies

5. Perhaps the most common shortcoming in the security industry is:
    a. Lack of support by top management
    b. Failure to properly prepare and equip new supervisors with tools to discharge their important responsibilities (supervisory training)
    c. Lack of planning
    d. Lack of monetary resources

6. Which of the following is **not** recommended policy with regard to security manuals?
    a. It must be updated on regular basis
    b. Employee should not be allowed to have possession of it
    c. The manual should be put in the hands of all regular security personnel
    d. It should include procedural instructions for specific incidents

7. Which of the following is not an advantage of using in-house (career) personnel?
    a. Career personnel develop a loyalty to the department
    b. Career personnel tend to be more ambitious
    c. There is more stability among career personnel
    d. Career personnel constitute a fixed, limited cadre or pool of manpower resources

8. Which of the following is known to be one of the disadvantages of contract security services?
   a. Turnover
   b. Cost
   c. Manpower resource
   d. Skills

9. Ideally, the person who should conduct the inspection of a security department is:
   a. An outside consultant
   b. The second ranking person
   c. The security director or security manager
   d. The ranking sergeant

10. The process of determining the probability and cost of potential loss is known as:
    a. Probability analysis
    b. Risk assessment
    c. Potential loss analysis
    d. Physical survey

11. The ultimate responsibility for the internal security in a department should rest with:
    a. The president
    b. Chairman of the board
    c. Security director
    d. The line supervisor

12. The issuance of weapons to guards is usually **not** justified:
    a. In a situation where deterrence is needed in handling control of large amounts of cash
    b. In situations in which terrorism is a real threat
    c. In a situation where there would be greater danger to life safety without weapons than with them
    d. In a situation where there is no danger to life safety

13. In issuing policy statements regarding the handling of disturbed persons, the primary consideration is:
    a. Legal liability to the disturbed
    b. Reducing the disturbed person to a form of benevolent custody and eliminating the immediate danger
    c. Legal liability to employees and third persons if restraint not achieved
    d. Employee-community public relations

14. Spotting the individual loss events that might take place is the primary step in dealing with security vulnerability. This process is called:
    a. Loss event probability
    b. Threat assessment process
    c. Loss event profile
    d. Actual threat analysis

15. The likelihood or probability of risks affecting the assets becoming actual loss events is known as:
    a. Loss event probability
    b. Loss event profile
    c. Treat analysis control
    d. Threat target control

16. The impact or effect on the enterprise if the loss occurs is known as:
    a. Loss event profile
    b. Loss event probability
    c. Loss event criticality
    d. Security survey analysis

17. Which of the following is considered to be one of the three basic functions of risk management?
    a. Lock control
    b. Barrier control
    c. Disaster management
    d. Loss control

18. Oscar Neuman published a classic in which he presented ideas and applied strategies from the New York public housing project to aid in reducing the risk of being victimized and reducing fear of crime when on the streets. What is the name of this book?
    a. Crime Prevention
    b. Crime Reduction
    c. Defensible Space
    d. Crime in Architectural Planning

19. From a security perspective, what is the first factor to be considered in facility construction:
    a. The identity of experienced consultants
    b. An effective security plan
    c. An architect with knowledge of physical security
    d. The building site itself

20. A critical on-site examination and analysis of an industrial plant business, home or public or private institution to ascertain the present security status, to identify deficiencies or excesses to determine the protection needed and to make recommendations to improve the overall security is the definition of:
    a. Security survey
    b. Risk analysis
    c. Full-field inspection
    d. Crime prevention assessment

21. There are two generally accepted definitions of risk. These are most commonly known to risk managers and security officers as:
    a. Potential risk and dynamic risk
    b. Profit risk and dynamic risk
    c. Potential risk and pure risk
    d. Pure risk and dynamic risk

22. The most effective deterrent to shoplifting is:
    a. Highly competent and educated security officers
    b. Widespread use of sensor devices
    c. Well positioned CCTV's
    d. Well trained personnel

23. A simplified answer to the question of why employees steal is:
    a. Sickness in family
    b. To feed drug habit
    c. To live on a higher level
    d. The theft triangle

24. Many experts agree that the most important deterrent to internal theft is:
    a. Threat of dismissal
    b. Fear of discovery
    c. Threat of prosecution
    d. Conscience pangs

25. Crime analysis is a key element in focusing the use of police and security resources to address crime problems. Data collection and analysis are two specific steps. The other two are:
    a. Inspection and discovery of facts
    b. Response and feedback
    c. Feedback and corrective action
    d. Dissemination and feedback

26. It is generally accepted that insurance rates are dependent upon two primary variables. These are:
    a. Cost of claims and competitors rates
    b. Competition among insurance companies and frequency of claims
    c. Cost of claims and frequency of claims
    d. Cost of claims and government regulations

27. The basic types of protection which security personnel realize as best can be described by the following:
    a. Fidelity Bonds
    b. Surety Bonds
    c. Burglary/Robbery/Theft Insurance
    d. All of the above

28. Bonds which require that an employee be investigated by the bonding company to limit the risk of dishonesty, and if that trust is violated, the insurance company must indemnify the employer, are called:
    a. Surety Bonds
    b. Fidelity Bonds
    c. Insurance Bonds
    d. Blanket Bonds

29. Protection for a corporation, if there is a failure to perform specified acts within a certain period of time, is known as a:
    a. Contract Bond
    b. Blanket Bond
    c. Surety Bond
    d. Fiduciary Bond

30. The urban planning and design process which integrates crime prevention techniques with neighborhood design is known as:
    a. Urban Development Planning
    b. Conceptual Modeling in Architecture
    c. Environmental Design
    d. Environmental Security (E/S)

31. The ability of design to counteract the perception that the area is isolated and criminally vulnerable is known as:
    a. Natural Surveillance Techniques
    b. Image and Milieu
    c. Soft Area Protection
    d. Territoriality Cleansing

32. The greatest ongoing threat to any business is:
    a. Shoplifting
    b. Shrinkage
    c. Internal Theft
    d. Pilferage

33. Pilferage is defined as stealing in small quantities over a long period of time. The taking of property entrusted to someone's care is called:
    a. Mistake of fact
    b. Misprison of a felony
    c. Uttering
    d. Embezzlement

34. The theft triangle consists of the following components:
    a. Desire, skill, and training
    b. Motivation, skill, and opportunity
    c. Opportunity, desire, and skill
    d. Motivation, opportunity, and rationalization

35. A key element in focusing the use of police and security resources to address crime problems is commonly called:
    a. Data collection and analysis
    b. Systematic evaluation of data available
    c. Crime analysis
    d. Analysis and feedback

36. The practice of preventing unauthorized persons from gaining information by analyzing electromagnetic emanations from electronic equipment is often termed:
    a. Tempest
    b. Veiling
    c. Bugging
    d. Hardening

37. Which of the following is not a correct statement with regard to narcotics?
    a. The term "narcotic" in its medical meaning refers to opium and opium derivatives of synthetic substitutes
    b. They are the most effective agents known for the relief of intense pain
    c. They have been used for a long period of time as a remedy for diarrhea
    d. They tend to intensify vision and increase alertness

38. Which of the following characteristics does not pertain to morphine?
    a. It is the principal constituent of opium
    b. Its legal use is restricted primarily to hospitals
    c. It tastes sweet and is marketed in the form of yellow crystals
    d. Tolerance and dependence develop rapidly

39. Most of this substance is produced from morphine; but it is often combined with other products such as aspirin or Tylenol. It is often used for relief of coughs; and it is by far the most widely used naturally occurring narcotic in medical treatment. It is:
    a. Barbiturates
    b. Mescaline
    c. Chloral Hydrate
    d. Codeine

40. German scientists synthesized methadone during World War II because of a shortage of morphine. Which of the following is **not** characteristic of methadone and its usage?
    a. Although chemically unlike morphine and heroin, it produces many of the same effects
    b. It was distributed under such names as amidone, dolophine and methadone
    c. It was widely used in the 1960's in the treatment of narcotic addicts
    d. It is only effective when administered by injection

41. Which of the following characteristics do not pertain to the use or effects of depressants generally?
    a. The usual methods of administration are oral or injected
    b. Excessive use results in drunken behavior similar to that of alcohol
    c. There is no danger of tolerance developing
    d. Taken as prescribed, they may be beneficial for the relief of anxiety and tension

42. Another widely abused depressant is methaqualone. All of the following are factually descriptive of methaqualone except one. Identify this exception.
    a. It is chemically unrelated to the barbiturates
    b. It was once mistakenly thought to be effective as an aphrodisiac
    c. It is administered orally
    d. It is one of the depressants that does not lead to tolerance and dependence

43. All of the following are controlled substances grouped as stimulants except one. Identify the exception.
    a. Cocaine
    b. Amphetamines
    c. Phenmetrazine
    d. Mescaline

44. All of the following are factual statements descriptive of illicit cocaine except one, which is:
    a. It is distributed on the street as a white to dark brown powder
    b. It is often adulterated to about half its volume by a variety of other ingredients
    c. This substance is only used through the process of injection
    d. It is popularly accepted as a recreational drug

45. Which of the following is another name for cocaine?
    a. Adipex
    b. Bacarate
    c. Piegine
    d. Snow

46. Which of the following statements does not pertain to cocaine?
    a. It has a medical use as a sedative
    b. There is a possibility that sustained use could result in physical dependence
    c. There is a high possibility that sustained use could result in psychological dependence
    d. Tolerance is a distinct possibility

47. The effects of illusions and hallucinations with poor perception of time and distance possibly indicates the use of which of the following substances?
    a. Cannabis
    b. Hallucinogen
    c. Stimulants
    d. Depressants

48. All of the following are hallucinogens except:
    a. LSD
    b. Marihuana
    c. Mescaline
    d. Phencyclidine

49. The source of marihuana is the:
    a. Peyote cactus
    b. Mushrooms
    c. Coca plant
    d. Cannabis plant

50. Cannabis products are usually taken:
    a. Through sniffing
    b. Injection
    c. Smoking
    d. By rubbing into the skin

51. The condition whereby a user develops an attachment to the use of a substance due to its ability to satisfy some emotional or personality need of the person is known as:
    a. Tolerance
    b. Physical dependence
    c. Addiction
    d. Psychological Dependence

52. The state of periodic or chronic intoxication produced by the repeated consumption of a substance is known as:
    a. Tolerance
    b. Addiction
    c. Habituation
    d. Drug dependence

1. d. A vice-president or higher
    Source: *Effective Security Management*

2. d. Protective services
    Source: *Effective Security Management*

3. b. Security personnel
    Source: *Effective Security Management*

4. d. During emergencies
    Source: *Effective Security Management*

5. b. Failure to properly prepare and equip new supervisors with tools to discharge their important responsibilities (Supervisory training)
    Source: *Effective Security Management*

6. b. Employee should not be allowed to have possession of it
    Source: *Effective Security Management*

7. d. Career personnel constitute a fixed, limited cadre or pool of manpower resources
    Source: *Effective Security Management*

8. a. Turnover
    Source: *Effective Security Management*

9. c. The security director or security manager
    Source: *Effective Security Management*

10. b. Risk assessment
    Source: *Protection of Assets Manual*

11. d. The line supervisor
    Source: *Protection of Assets Manual*

12. d. In a situation where there seems to be no danger to life safety
    Source: *Protection of Assets Manual*

13. b. Reducing the disturbed person to a form of benevolent custody and eliminating the immediate danger
    Source: *Protection of Assets Manual*

14. c. Loss event profile
    Source: *Protection of Assets Manual*

15. a. Loss event probability
    Source: *Protection of Assets Manual*

16. c. Loss event criticality
    Source: *Protection of Assets Manual*

17. d. Loss control
    Source: *Protection of Assets Manual*

18. c. Defensible Space
    Source: *Handbook of Loss Prevention and Crime Prevention*

19. d. The building site itself
    Source: *Handbook of Loss Prevention and Crime Prevention*

20. a. Security survey
    Source: *Handbook of Loss Prevention and Crime Prevention*

21. d. Pure Risk and Dynamic Risk
    Source: *Handbook of Loss Prevention and Crime Prevention*

22. d. Well trained personnel
    Source: *Security and Loss Prevention*

23. d. The theft triangle
    Source: *Handbook of Loss Prevention and Crime Prevention*

24. b. Fear of discovery
    Source: *Handbook of Loss Prevention and Crime Prevention*

25. d. Dissemination and feedback
    Source: *Handbook of Loss Prevention and Crime Prevention*

26. c. Cost of claims and frequency of claims
    Source: *Security and Loss Prevention*

27. d. All the above
    Source: *Security and Loss Prevention*

28. b. Fidelity Bond
    Source: *Security and Loss Prevention*

29. c. Surety Bond
    Source: *Security and Loss Prevention*

30. d. Environmental Security (E/S)
    Source: *Handbook of Loss Prevention and Crime Prevention*

31. b. Image and Milieu
    Source: *Handbook of Loss Prevention and Crime Prevention*

32. c. Internal Theft
    Source: *Security and Loss Prevention*

33. d. Embezzlement
    Source: *Security and Loss Prevention*

34. d. Motivation, opportunity and rationalization
    Source: *Handbook of Loss Prevention and Crime Prevention*

35. c. Crime Analysis
     Source: *Handbook of Loss Prevention and Crime Prevention*

36. a. Tempest
     Source: *Protection of Assets Manual*

37. d. They tend to intensify vision and increase alertness.
     Source: *Protection of Assets Manual*

38. c. It tastes sweet and is marketed in the form of yellow crystals.
     Source: *Protection of Assets Manual*

39. d. Codeine
     Source: *Protection of Assets Manual*

40. d. It is only effective when administered by injection.
     Source: *Protection of Assets Manual*

41. c. There is no danger of tolerance developing.
     Source: *Protection of Assets Manual*

42. d. It is one of the depressants that does not lead to tolerance and dependence.
     Source: *Protection of Assets Manual*

43. d. Mescaline
     Source: *Protection of Assets Manual*

44. c. This substance is only used through the process of injection.
     Source: *Protection of Assets Manual*

45. d. Snow
     Source: *Protection of Assets Manual*

46. a. It has a medical use as a sedative.
     Source: *Protection of Assets Manual*

47. b. Hallucinogen
     Source: *Protection of Assets Manual*

48. b. Marihuana
     Source: *Protection of Assets Manual*

49. d. Cannabis plant
     Source: *Protection of Assets Manual*

50. c. Smoking
     Source: *Protection of Assets Manual*

51. d. Psychological Dependence
     Source: *Protection of Assets Manual*

52. b. Addiction
     Source: *Protection of Assets Manual*

1. The number of security personnel required to cover a single post around the clock on three eight-hour shifts is 4-1/2 to 5 persons — **not** 3.

2. Well-trained, well-supervised security personnel may be the best possible protection available to a company.

3. The accounting department of a company is the most vulnerable to major loss due to crime.

4. The security manager should have the necessary authority to carry out responsibilities. To accomplish this, the security manager should occupy a position where the manager reports directly to a vice president or higher.

5. "Risk analysis" is a management method used to minimize risks through application of security measures commensurate with the threat.

6. The major resource required for a risk analysis is manpower.

7. The primary objective in implementing a protection program within an organization should be to motivate every employee to become part of the protection team.

8. Both private security and public law enforcement have, as their primary mission, the prevention of crime and protection of persons and property.

9. "Economic crime" is defined as the illicit behavior having as its object the unjust enrichment of the perpetrator at the expense of the economic system as a whole.

10. Private security relies upon both commercial security services and government agencies for intelligence gathering and crisis management planning.

11. Private security frequently avoids or bypasses police with regard to white collar or economic crime.

12. Business crime is most effectively attacked through sound management controls. The emphasis on loss prevention rather than the "offender" involved in the incident is a distinguishing characteristic of private security.

13. About 95 percent to 99 percent of activated alarms are "false."

14. The main deterrent value of a burglar alarm system is that the alarm signal enunciated locally or transmitted to a central station brings a police response.

15. Employee theft was the most frequently investigated crime by private security.

16. As a general rule, local law enforcement has very little effect on many crimes against business. Exceptions are burglaries, robberies and arson.

17. Frequently cited measures for improving private security are:
    a. More or better training
    b. Mandated training
    c. Improved selection processes

    d. Higher wages

    e. Establishment or improvement of licensing and regulation

18. The two problems in police and security relationships which seem to have the greatest intensity of feelings are:

    a. Secondary employment or moonlighting by police officers in private security

    b. Police response to activated alarms which are largely false

19. The two major components of economic crime are white collar and ordinary crime.

20. 80 percent of computer security incidents result from insider attacks by dishonest and disgruntled employees.

21. Only one percent of computer security incidents annually are attributed to "hackers."

22. The practice of preventing unauthorized persons from gaining intelligence information by analyzing electromagnetic emanations from electronic equipment such as computers, is often termed "tempest."

23. The term "narcotic" in its medical meaning refers to opium and opium derivatives or synthetic substitutes.

24. "Drug dependence" is a condition resulting from repeated use whereby the user must administer progressively larger doses to attain the desired effect, thereby reinforcing compulsive behavior.

25. "Physical dependence" refers to an alteration of the normal functions of the body that necessitates the continued presence of a drug in order to prevent the withdrawal or abstinence syndrome.

26. The poppy (papaver somnifferum) is the main source of the non-synthetic narcotics.

27. Examples of synthetic narcotics, which are produced entirely within the laboratory, are meperidine and methadone.

28. Depressants have a potential for both physical and psychological dependence. Some examples of "depressants" are:

    a. Chloral Hydrate

    b. Barbiturates

    c. Benzodiazepines

29. When "depressant" drugs are used to obtain a "high" they are usually taken in conjunction with another drug, such as alcohol.

30. "Stimulants" are drugs which may produce a temporary sense of exhilaration, superabundant energy and hyperactivity including extended wakefulness. Examples are cocaine and amphetamines.

31. The two most prevalent stimulants are nicotine and caffeine, both accepted in our culture.

32. The most potent stimulant of natural origin is cocaine which is extracted from the leaves of the coca plant.

33. Excessive doses of cocaine may cause seizures and death. There is no "safe" dose of cocaine.

34. "Marijuana" refers to cannabis plant parts and extracts that produce somatic or psychic changes in humans.

35. The hemp plant grows wild throughout most of the tropic and temperate regions of the world.

36. "Hallucinogenic" drugs distort the perception of objective reality. Examples are:
    a. LSD
    b. Mescaline and peyote
    c. Phencyclidine (such as PCP)
    d. Amphetamine Variants (such as DOM and DOB)

37. Long after hallucinogens are eliminated from the body, users may experience "flashbacks."

38. DOM, DOB, JDA, MDMA, DET and MDA are hallucinogens which are synthesized in the laboratory.

39. Another source of hallucinogens (psilocybin and psilocyn) is psilocybe mushrooms.

40. "Designer" drugs are analogues of controlled substances with slight variations in their chemical structure so as not to be specifically listed as controlled substance.

41. A "drug" is a substance which, because of its chemical make-up, alters the mood, perception or consciousness of the user. All drugs are not illegal.

42. The most abused "drug" is alcohol and the most used drug is also alcohol.

43. "Tolerance" is a body condition wherein ever-increasing amounts of a drug are needed to gain the desired effect.

44. The street name of PCP is "angel dust."

45. The person most likely to become an alcoholic is a white male over 40 who is living alone.

46. The following behavioral characteristics are associated with substance abuse:
    a. Abrupt changes in attendance, quality of work grades and work output
    b. Attitude changes
    c. Withdrawal from responsibility
    d. Breakdown in personal appearance
    e. Wearing sunglasses at inappropriate times (hide dilated or constricted pupils)
    f. Wears long-sleeved garments to hide needle marks
    g. Association with known substance abusers
    h. Excessive borrowing of money
    i. Stealing small items from home, work or school
    j. Secretive habits

A. The application of accepted doctrines and techniques of general management to the security task resources.

1. Countermeasures selection

2. Vulnerability assessment

3. Risk Assessment

4. Countermeasures

5. Policies

6. External relations: Federal, State and Local

7. Disposition of abusers

8. Identification of abusers

9. Prevention programs

10. Types of substances

Review the general concepts set out in the "classification scheme" prepared by the Professional Certification Board.

Secondly, formulate a detailed study plan which will enable you to become knowledgeable concerning the following specified key concepts as a minimum.

1. Security director / manager's role

2. Inspections - formal and informal

3. Risk assessment and management

4. Security vulnerability assessment

5. Systems approach to security

6. Threat analysis

7. Loss reporting techniques

8. Characteristics of private security personnel

9. Problems associated with rapid growth of private security

10. Police role in crime prevention and control

11. Transfer of law enforcement activities to private security

12. Interaction and cooperation between police and private security

13. Exchange of resources and information between police and private security

14. False alarms - effect on relationship between police and private security

15. Heroin and other opiates

16. Cocaine and other synthetic stimulants

17. Hallucinogens - natural and synthetic

18. Depressants - barbiturates

19. Marijuana - and other cannabis preparations

20. Dependence - physical and psychological

21. Narcotics - definition

22. Recognition of drug abusers

23. Alcohol - alcoholism

24. Effects of overdose

25. Withdrawal syndrome

26. Prevention program

ASIS International. *Protection of Assets Manual.* (2008). Alexandria, VA: ASIS International. The following chapters are pertinent:

- Vulnerability

- Guard Operation

- Theft and Fraud

- Insurance

- Security and Labor Relations

- Ethics

- Alcohol and Drug Abuse Control

- Security Aspects of OSHA

- Training

- Security Awareness

Fennelly, Lawrence J. (2004). *Handbook of Loss Prevention and Crime Prevention,* (4th ed.), Elsevier/Butterworth-Heinemann, Burlington, MA.

Purpura, Philip P., CPP (2008). *Security and Loss Prevention: An Introduction,* (5th ed.), Elsevier/Butterworth-Heinemann, Burlington, MA.

Sennewald, Charles A., CPP (2003). *Effective Security Management,* (4th ed.), Elsevier/Butterworth-Heinemann, Burlington, MA.

I. GENERAL MANAGEMENT

A. Basic Principles, Definitions, and Concepts

1. **Line executives** are those who are delegated chain of command authority to accomplish specific objectives in the organization.

2. **Staff functions** are those functions which are advisory or service oriented to the line executive.

3. As a general rule, the security manager serves in a staff capacity.

4. The security manager, in exercising authority delegated by the senior executive to whom the security manager reports, is exercising **functional authority**.

5. The security manager exercises full line authority over his own department.

6. From an organizational standpoint security cuts across department lines and relates to the activity of the company.

7. **Chain of Command** is the path along which authority flows.

8. Security personnel should be directly supervised only by security management.

9. There are six basic principles of organization:
   a. A logical division of work as to:
      1. Purpose
      2. Process or method
      3. Clientele
      4. Time
      5. Geography
   b. Clear lines of authority as set forth in the organizational chart
   c. **Limited Span of Control** – the number of personnel which one individual can effectively supervise:
      1. Ideal ration is 1 supervisor to 3 employees.
      2. Good ratio is 1 supervisor to 6 employees.
      3. Acceptable ratio is 1 supervisor to 12 employees.
   d. Unity of command – an employee should be under the direct control of only one immediate supervisor
   e. Proper delegation of responsibility and authority – the most common management weakness is the failure to properly delegate responsibility and the authority to carry out the responsibility
   f. Coordination of efforts through training and communication

10. The two key points to remember about an organizational chart are:
    a. The horizontal plane indicates the division of areas of responsibility
    b. The vertical plane defines the levels of authority

11. Organizational structure should be flexible to be most effective.

12. Authority – refers to the rights inherent in a managerial position to give orders and expect the orders to be obeyed.

13. Organizational structure – defines how job tasks are formally divided, grouped, and coordinated.

14. Work specialization – division of labor and the degree to which tasks in the organization are subdivided into separate jobs.

15. Work team – group whose individual efforts result in a performance that is greater than the sum of those individual inputs.

16. Departmentalization – the basis on which jobs are grouped together.

17. Centralization – the degree to which decision making is concentrated at a single point in the organization.

18. Decentralization – the degree to which lower level personnel provide input or are actually given the discretion to make decisions.

19. Formalization – the degree to which jobs within the organization are standardized.

20. Organization – a systematic arrangement of two or more people who fulfill formal roles and share a common purpose.

21. Organizing – management function encompassing:
    a. The determination of what tasks are to be done
    b. Who is to do them
    c. How the tasks are to be grouped
    d. Who reports to whom
    e. Where in the organization decisions are to be made

22. Simple Structure – characterized by:
    a. Low degree of departmentalization
    b. Wide spans of control
    c. Authority centralized in a single person
    d. Little formalization
    e. Widely practiced in small businesses

23. Bureaucracy – characterized by:
    a. Highly standardized operating tasks that are specialized
    b. Formalized rules and regulations
    c. Tasks grouped in functional departments
    d. Centralized authority
    e. Narrow spans of control
    f. Decision making follows the chain of command

24. Environment – institutions and forces that are outside the organization and can affect the organization's performance.

B. Behavioral Theories

1. Dr. Abraham Maslow developed a five-step process which describes man's behavior in terms of the needs he experiences. These needs are:
   a. Food and shelter (basic needs)
   b. Safety, such as security, protection, and avoidance of harm and risk
   c. To belong, such as membership and acceptance by a group and its members
   d. Ego status, such as achieving some special recognition
   e. Self-actualization, such as being given assignments which are challenging and meaningful

2. Frederick Herzberg's "Motivational-Hygiene Theory" – defined two independent categories of needs – hygiene factors and motivators.
   a. The hygiene factors in Herzberg's theory consist of:
      1. Salary
      2. Fringe benefits
      3. Security (Civil Service)
      4. Rules and regulations
      5. Supervision
   b. The motivators in Herzberg's theory consist of:
      1. Challenging assignments
      2. Increased responsibility
      3. Recognition for work
      4. Individual growth
   c. Herzberg believed that hygiene factors do not produce growth in the individual or increase work output but they do prevent losses in performance
   d. Herzberg felt that motivators had some positive effect upon the employee, resulting in increased job satisfaction and increased total output capacity
   e. There is a close relationship between Herzberg's theory of Motivation and Maslow's theory
   f. Herzberg's theory is also known as the "Work Motivation Theory" in that genuine motivation for work comes from work itself and not from so-called "hygiene factors".

3. "Theory X" developed by Douglas McGregor holds that traditional managers have the following basic assumptions:
   a. It is management's rule to organize resources in a structure which requires close supervision of all employees and brings about maximum control.
   b. It is management's responsibility to direct the efforts of the personnel of the agency, to keep them motivated, to control all their actions, and to modify their behavior to fit the needs of the organization.
   c. If management does not take an active part in controlling the behavior of the employees, they will be passive to the needs of the organization.

    d. The average employee is by nature, lazy and will work as little as possible.

    e. The average employee lacks ambition, dislikes responsibility and authority, and prefers taking orders to being independent.

    f. The employee is basically self-centered, has no feeling for organizational needs, and must be closely controlled.

    g. By nature, the average employee resists change.

    h. The average employee does not have the ability to solve problems creatively

4. "Theory Y" developed by McGregor holds that Theory Y managers assume:

    a. It is management's role to organize resources to reach organizational goals.

    b. Work can be an enjoyable part of one's life if the conditions are favorable.

    c. People are not by nature lazy, passive, or resistant to the needs of the organization but have become so as a result of their experience working within the organization.

    d. Management does not place the potential for development within the employee. It is management's responsibility to recognize the potential which is present within each individual and allow the individual the freedom to develop his abilities.

    e. People possess creativity and can solve organizational problems if encouraged by management.

    f. The essential task of management is to develop organizational conditions and operational procedures so the individual can attain his goals by directing his efforts towards organizational goals and objectives.

5. Immaturity/Maturity Theory of Chris Argyris – seven personality changes that should occur if the employee is to develop into a mature person and an asset to the organization:

    a. From passive to active

    b. From dependence to independence

    c. From restricted behavior patterns to diversified behavior

    d. From erratic shallow interests to short time perspective

    e. From short time perspective to long time perspective

    f. From subordinate position to an equal or superior position

    g. From lack of self-awareness to awareness and control over self

6. The Autocratic Theory – dates back to the Industrial Revolution of the 1750s.

    a. The manager's position is one of formal and official authority

    b. Management has complete control over the employee

    c. This theory gets results up to a point but does nothing to develop the potential of the employee

7. The Custodial Theory – key points are:

    a. This theory's aim is to make the employee happy and contented through the wealth of the company, which provides economic benefits to the employee

    b. This theory does not adequately motivate the employee

    c. Employees look in areas other than the job to secure fulfillment or challenge

8. The Supportive Theory – key points are:
   a. The prime element of this theory is leadership which thinks in terms of "we" rather than "they".
   b. Little supervision is required as employees will take on added responsibility with the knowledge that support is available from the supervisory level of management.

9. Manifest Needs Theory – proposes:
   a. Needs have two components – direction and intensity
   b. Identifies more than twenty needs
   c. Argues that most needs are learned and activated by environmental cues
   d. States that multiple needs motivate behavior simultaneously.

10. Learned Needs Theory – three needs acquired from culture of a society that are important sources of motivation:
    a. Need for achievement (NACH) – drive to excel and succeed
    b. Need for affiliation (NAFF) – desire for interpersonal relationships
    c. Need for power (NPOW) – need to make others behave in a way they would not have behaved otherwise

11. Expectancy Theory – proposes:
    a. Employees will be motivated to exert high levels of effort when they believe the effort will lead to good performance appraisal.
    b. That a good appraisal will lead to organization rewards
    c. Rewards will satisfy personal goals

C. Basics of Human Behavior – Personality Traits

1. Of the many different personality traits, a small number have been found to be valuable in providing insights into employee behavior.
   a. Locus of Control – the degree to which people believe they are masters of their own fate
      1. Internals – control their own destinies
      2. Externals – see their lives as being controlled by outside forces
   b. Machiavellianism – the degree to which an individual is pragmatic, maintains emotional distance, and believes that ends can justify means
   c. Self-esteem – the degree to which an individual likes or dislikes themselves
   d. Self-monitoring – a personality trait that measures an individual's ability to adjust his or her behavior to external, situational factors
   e. Risk taking – a propensity to assume or avoid risk has been shown to have an impact on decision making and information gathering within certain time frames
   f. Type-A Personality – aggressive involvement in a chronic, incessant struggle to achieve more and more in less and less time and, if necessary, against the opposing efforts of other things or people
   g. Type-B Personality – rarely harried by the desire to obtain a wildly increasing number of things or participate in an endless growing series of events in an ever decreasing amount of time

2. Personality-Job Fit Model – identifies six personality types and proposes that the fit between personality type and occupational environment determines satisfaction and turnover.
   a. Realistic – prefers physical activities requiring skill
   b. Investigative – prefers activities involving thinking and organizing
   c. Social – prefers activities that help and develop others
   d. Conventional – prefers rules and orderly activities
   e. Enterprising – prefers opportunities to influence and gain power
   f. Artistic – prefers activities that allow creative expression

3. Attribution Theory – when individuals observe behavior, they attempt to determine whether it is internally or externally caused. Determination depends on three factors:
   a. Distinctiveness – everyone reacts differently
   b. Consensus – everyone reacts the same way
   c. Consistency – person responds the same way over time

4. Job Satisfaction – an individual's general attitude toward his or her job.

5. Job Involvement – the degree to which a person identifies psychologically with his or her job and considers his or her perceived performance level to be important to self-worth.

6. Organization Commitment – the degree to which an employee identifies with a particular organization and its goals and wishes to maintain membership in the organization.

7. Operant Conditioning – a type of conditioning in which desired voluntary behavior leads to a reward or prevents a punishment.

8. Four Methods of Shaping Behavior
   a. Positive Reinforcement – following a response with something pleasant
   b. Negative Reinforcement – following a response by terminating or withdrawing something unpleasant
   c. Punishment – causing an unpleasant condition in an attempt to eliminate an undesirable behavior
   d. Extinction – eliminating any reinforcement that is maintaining a behavior

9. Schedules of Reinforcement
   a. Continuous Reinforcement – a desired behavior is reinforced each and every time it is demonstrated
   b. Intermittent Reinforcement – a desired behavior is reinforced often enough to make the behavior worth repeating, but not every time it is demonstrated

10. Learning Styles – a recurring process that cycles through the following four stages:
    a. Concrete Experience – learn by new experiences
    b. Reflective Observation – passively observe and then reflect
    c. Abstract Conceptualization – develop workable theories
    d. Active Experience – learn by doing

11. Performance Appraisal – criteria includes:
    a. Individual task outcomes – quantity of work
    b. Behaviors – outcomes directly attributable to employee's actions
    c. Traits – weakest set of criteria because they are furthest removed from actual performance of the job

12. Methods of Performance Appraisal
    a. Written Essays – simplest method describing employee strengths, weaknesses, past performance, potential, and suggestions for improvement
    b. Critical Incidents – focus on behaviors that concentrate on effectiveness or ineffectiveness in doing the job
    c. Graphic Rating Scale – rates specific factors on a numeric scale
    d. Multi-Person Comparison – evaluates one person's performance against the performance of one or more others

13. Job Analysis – defines the jobs within the organization and the behaviors that are necessary to perform those jobs.

14. Job Characteristics Model (JCM) – identifies five core job dimensions and their relationship to personal and work outcomes
    a. Skill Variety – jobs vary and require different skills and talents
    b. Task Identity – degree to which the job requires competition of a whole and identifiable piece of work
    c. Task significance – degree to which a job has substantial impact on the work of others
    d. Autonomy – job provides freedom to determine procedures to be used in carrying it out
    e. Feedback – work activities result in information about the effectiveness of performance

15. Job Description – written statement of what a job holder does, how it is done, and why it is done.

16. Job Specification – states the minimum acceptable qualifications an incumbent must possess to perform a given job successfully.

D. Finances

1. A budget, a plan in financial terms, is an essential element of management planning and control. Three purposes of budgeting include:
   a. Estimate the costs and expected revenues of planned activities
   b. Provide a warning mechanism when variances occur in actual numbers
   c. Exercise uniformity in fiscal control

2. If the contribution of an operating function cannot be quantified or cannot be shown to result in greater net revenue, it is an axiom of sound management that the function be reduced or eliminated.

3. **Zero based budgeting** requires that the benefits from an activity be weighed against the benefits to be lost if the planned activity is carried out at a lesser level or not done at all.

4. Incremental budget – each period's budget begins by using the last period as a reference point.

5. Top-down vs. Bottom-up budgeting – budgets initiated, controlled, and directed by top management.

6. Activity-based budgeting – allocates costs for producing a good or service on the basis of the activities performed and services employed.

7. Revenue budget – projects future sales.

8. Expense budget – lists primary activities undertaken by a unit and allocates a value to each.

9. Cash budget – forecasts how much cash is on hand and how much is needed to meet expenses.

10. Financial ratios
    a. Data from financial statements that compare two significant figures and express them as a percentage or ratio
    b. Managers use ratios as internal control devices for monitoring how efficiently the organization uses its assets, debt, inventories, etc.

11. Audits – a formal verification of an organization's accounts, records, operating activities, or performance.

E. Budget for Loss Prevention

1. Management is viewed in terms of the functions a manager performs, i.e. planning, decision making, organizing, directing, and controlling.

2. The budget is simply a plan stated in financial terms.

3. It is a realistic estimate of the resources needed to achieve planned objectives.

4. A budget is also an instrument which records work programs in terms of appropriations needed to put them to work.

5. It is also a management tool which is devised to ensure that work programs are carried out as planned.

6. Any budget identification must include plans and programs.

7. A budget requires a manager to operate his plan in three dimensions:
   a. The operation/project **must unfold as planned**
   b. The operation/project **must take place when planned**
   c. It will **not exceed the planned costs**

8. Budgets are normally prepared annually or biannually.

9. Loss prevention budgets must be based upon intelligently anticipated and predictable conditions, which means planning must use good judgment and good decision making estimates about the future.

10. Budgeting approaches can be bottom-up and top-down or top-down and bottom-up.

11. Top-down and bottom-up is preferred by some because senior management initiates the process by establishing acceptable expenditure limits and guidelines prior to detailed planning by middle or operating management.

12. Budgeting processes follow a logical sequence or pattern to bring about interaction between senior and middle management. This sequence involves planning, budget building/development, evaluation and review, establishment of the final budget, and allocation of funds.

13. There are three types of budgets to be familiar with in respect to Loss Prevention Planning:
    a. **Line item budgets** – each item is listed by separate line
    b. **Program budgets** – funds are allocated by specific activity
    c. **Capital budgets** – used for infrequently purchased high dollar items

14. Budget costs are classified under one of three categories; salary expenses, sundry expenses, and capital expenses.

15. Capital expenditures are for physical improvements, physical additions, or major expenditures for hardware, generally considered one-time expenses.

16. All ongoing non-salary expenses are considered sundry expenses.

F. Planning, Management, and Evaluation

1. Plans must be based on sound judgment and good decision making estimates of the future.

2. Plans must be in alignment with the overall strategy of the company, considering:
    a. The approach to business
    b. The organizational approach , i.e. Management By Objectives (MBO), etc.

3. Planning is an activity concerned with proposals for the future, an evaluation of those proposals, and methods for achieving the proposals.

4. Management is the activity which plans, organizes, and controls activities in an organization.

5. Matrix management uses assets over a wide spectrum of activity by forming ad hoc teams to work on shorter term projects.

6. MBO is a systematic way of achieving agreed to goals set ahead of time.

7. In MBO the supervisor and the subordinates establish agreed upon goals, review them, and periodically evaluate progress.

8. Continuous evaluation is important in a management arena, since its purpose is to evaluate operational effectiveness.

9. There is a planning and evaluation cycle that is continuous. It involves planning which requires management and implementation, and continuous evaluation so more planning can be done.

10. This sort of approach enables the organization to clarify purpose, organize information that is relevant, create necessary alternatives, gives the whole program direction and purpose, and ultimately results in proactive and less crisis oriented efforts.

11. The planning/evaluation cycle relies heavily on data and an accurate analysis of the data. The successful security manager will know where to find the data, how to collect and organize it, and how to turn it into meaningful information to employ successfully.

12. It is also necessary to be able to measure program effectiveness and its impact. This needs to relate to what is ultimately achieved as defined by the program goals, objectives, and strategies.

13. Steps for successful planning:
    a. Identify the problem
    b. Collect the facts
    c. Review available information
    d. Identify alternative plans
    e. Select most appropriate plan
    f. Consult/involve others
    g. Implement the plan
    h. Evaluate

G. Communications

1. Management should strive for an open climate of communication.

2. Open communication depends on the willingness to listen and respond; all employees should be free to communicate with the security director.

3. The art of effective communication is the most important skill for successful management.

4. For better understanding, communications should be in writing whenever possible.

5. When a job is done poorly, it is usually because the manager failed to communicate clearly.

H. Personnel Management

1. Discipline
    a. Discipline should be as positive as possible
    b. Constructive discipline (positive) is the training which develops disciplined conduct and corrects, molds, and strengthens an employee

    c. Any punishment connected with discipline should be a means to an end; organizational, not personal

    d. All employees require constructive discipline

    e. Rules of the disciplinary process:

        1. Put rules in writing

        2. Discipline in private

        3. Be objective and consistent

        4. Educate, do not humiliate

        5. Keep a file on all employee interactions

        6. Exercise discipline promptly

2. Promotions

    a. Objective is to identify and select the best qualified candidates

    b. Primary qualification factors are:

        1. The employee's performance record in present job

        2. Anticipated/expected performance in new job

    c. Educational achievement, ability to articulate, etc. should be considered later

    d. Disqualifiers are valid for one time only

1. One supervisor can effectively control only a limited number of people and that limit should not be exceeded. This principle is called:
   a. Unity of command
   b. Supervisory limits
   c. Span of control
   d. Line discipline

2. An important principle of organization is that an employee should be under the direct control of one and only one immediate superior. This principle is:
   a. Unity of command
   b. Supervisory limits
   c. Span of control
   d. Line discipline

3. As a rule, which department of the company administers the recruiting activity?
   a. Security department
   b. Administrative department
   c. Personnel department
   d. Internal affairs

4. In non-entry level recruiting, the recommended technique is:
   a. "Blind ad"
   b. Open advertisement in newspaper
   c. Advertisement in trade journal
   d. Word of mouth on selective basis

5. Every applicant's first interview should be with:
   a. The security manager or director
   b. The security supervisor
   c. A security line employee
   d. A personnel interviewer

6. The heart of personnel selection is:
   a. Polygraph test
   b. Review of application
   c. Interview
   d. Background investigation

7. Discipline is primarily the responsibility of:
   a. The supervisor
   b. The employee
   c. The security manager or director
   d. The inspection division

8. Among classical theories of human behavior in the work environment, one emphasizes negative aspects of employee behavior, which is known as:

   a. The autocratic theory

   b. The custodial theory

   c. The supportive theory

   d. McGregor's "Theory X"

9. Among classical theories of human behavior in the work environment is one which suggests that employees do not inherently dislike work and will actually seek responsibility and better performance if encouraged to do so. It is known as:

   a. McGregor's "Theory Y"

   b. McGregor's "Theory X"

   c. The supportive theory

   d. The motivational theory

10. Dr. Frederick Herzberg developed a position that motivation comes from work itself, not from those factors such as salary and job security. This theory is known as:

    a. The supportive theory

    b. The work motivation theory

    c. The custodial theory

    d. McGregor's "Theory X"

11. In conducting background investigations, it is good policy to:

    a. Not let prospective employees know an investigation is being conducted

    b. Restrict the investigation to "confidential" record checks

    c. Restrict the investigation to employment checks

    d. Advise the applicant of forthcoming investigation and secure his permission

12. The behavioral scientist whose key concept is that every executive relates to his subordinates on the basis of a set of assumptions termed theory X and theory Y was formulated by:

    a. Abraham Maslow

    b. Douglas McGregor

    c. Warren Bennis

    d. B.F. Skinner

13. The term "knowledge worker" is used to describe those workers:

    a. Whose primary task is to use information to produce value

    b. Who have a detailed knowledge of the physical tasks that they perform

    c. With a Ph.D.

    d. Whose education has progressed to at least a Masters Degree

14. Motivational theory that argues that the strength of a tendency to act in a certain way depends on the strength of an expectation that the act will be followed by a given outcome and on the attractiveness of that outcome to the individual is known as:
    a. Goal-setting theory
    b. Manifest needs theory
    c. Learned needs theory
    d. Expectancy theory

15. A line item budget is the traditional and most frequently used method of budgeting. Two other commonly used budgeting techniques include:
    a. Management and program budgets
    b. Capital and program budgets
    c. Program and exception item budgets
    d. Fund allocation and capital budgets

16. A management tool wherein there is a systematic method of achieving agreed upon goals set in advance is known as:
    a. Matrix management
    b. Proactive management
    c. Scheduling management
    d. Management By Objective (MBO)

17. The activity concerned with proposals for the future, an analysis of those proposals, and methods for achieving them is known as:
    a. Effective management
    b. Evaluation techniques
    c. Planning
    d. Budgeting

18. Stewardship means:
    a. The function of serving passengers on a cruise ship
    b. Serving as the head of the wine cellar in a quality restaurant
    c. To hold something in trust for another
    d. To serve on the board of directors in an enterprise

19. Administrative management does not:
    a. Expressly state the objectives of the security organization
    b. Indicate organizational relationships, responsibilities and authority
    c. Identify the regular and extraordinary methods of communication
    d. Provide required financial resources

20. When an assets protection program is planned or implemented input should be sought from:
    a. Experienced security personnel only
    b. Anyone with whom the protection organization has a relationship
    c. Local law enforcement personnel only
    d. Anyone within the enterprise being protected

21. In a protection program, a prime objective should be to motivate which of the following to become a part of the protection team:
    a. All management personnel
    b. Senior management
    c. Local law enforcement personnel
    d. All employees

22. Any plan that no longer serves a useful purpose should be:
    a. Revised
    b. Abandoned
    c. Reviewed
    d. Filed for historical reference

23. Which of the following techniques would not contribute directly to cost effective management?
    a. Doing things in the least expensive way
    b. Maintaining the lowest costs consistent with required results
    c. Maintaining a high level of personnel training
    d. Assuring that amounts spent generate high returns

1. c. Span of control
   Source: *Effective Security Management*

2. a. Unity of command
   Source: *Effective Security Management*

3. c. Personnel department
   Source: *Effective Security Management*

4. a. "Blind ad"
   Source: *Effective Security Management*

5. d. A personnel interviewer
   Source: *Effective Security Management*

6. c. Interview
   Source: *Effective Security Management*

7. a. The supervisor
   Source: *Effective Security Management*

8. d. McGregor's "Theory X"
   Source: *Protection of Assets Manual*

9. a. McGregor's "Theory Y"
   Source: *Protection of Assets Manual*

10. b. The work motivation theory
    Source: *Protection of Assets Manual*

11. d. Advise the applicant of forthcoming investigation and secure his permission
    Source: *Effective Security Management*

12. b. Douglas McGregor
    Source: *Protection of Assets Manual*

13. a. Whose primary task is to use information to produce value.
    Source: *Protection of Assets Manual*

14. d. Expectancy Theory
    Source: *Protection of Assets Manual*

15. b. Capital and program budgets
    Source: *Security and Loss Prevention*

16. d. Management By Objective (MBO)
    Source: *Security and Loss Prevention*

17. c. Planning
    Source: *Security and Loss Prevention*

18. c. To hold something in trust for another
     Source: *Protection of Assets Manual*

19. d. Provide required financial resources
     Source: *Protection of Assets Manual*

20. b. Anyone with whom the protection organization has a relationship
     Source: *Protection of Assets Manual*

21. d. All employees
     Source: *Protection of Assets Manual*

22. b. Abandoned
     Source: *Protection of Assets Manual*

23. c. Maintaining a high level of personnel training
     Source: *Protection of Assets Manual*

1. In the organizational structure of proprietary firms, security may provide both line and staff functions.
   a. When advising senior executives, the security manager performs "staff" duties
   b. In security operations, the security manager carries out "line" duties

   As a general rule, "line" duties are considered to be operational in nature and "staff" duties are of a support nature.

2. When security managers exercise authority delegated by a senior executive to whom they report, such authority is known as "functional" authority.

3. Security functions cut across departmental lines and consist of involvement into every activity of the company but should not involve significant interference.

4. Probably the most common security management failure is the inability to delegate responsibility and the authority necessary to carry it out.

5. "Span of Control" is a management term which refers to the number of personnel over which one can effectively supervise.

6. The largest single item of expense in the security operation is the cost of security personnel.

7. "Chain of command" is a management term which refers to the path along which authority flows.

8. "Unity of command" is a management concept which means that an employee should have only one immediate superior to whom the employee should report.

9. The "Theory X" management theory holds that the average employee has little ambition, dislikes work, and must be coerced, controlled, and directed to achieve organizational objectives.

10. The "Theory Y" management theory holds that the average employee does not dislike work, is self-directed, is creative and imaginative, accepts responsibility, and is committed to achieving organizational needs and objectives.

11. Theory X and Theory Y were developed by Douglas McGregor.

12. Those in management who believe the behavioral assumption of "Theory X" take an autocratic approach to get work done, whereas "Theory Y" encourages managers to support and encourage employees in efforts to higher achievement.

13. The three main theories of organizational behavior are:
    a. Autocratic theory
    b. Custodial theory
    c. Supportive theory

14. The "autocratic theory" holds that management is all-powerful and employees are obligated to follow orders without question.

15. The "custodial theory" holds that the aim of the company is to make the employee happy and contented through economic benefits and thus they will be positively adjusted to their work. This theory does not motivate employees to produce to their full capacity.

16. The "supportive theory" holds that through good leadership, management will provide a climate where employees will take on added responsibilities and thus make greater contributions to the growth of the company.

17. "Herzberg's theory" is a management theory which holds that motivation comes from work achievement satisfaction and not from such things as salary and job security.

18. "Theory Z" is a recent management style used effectively by the Japanese. This theory emphasizes humanized working conditions along with attention by management to enhance trust and close personal relationships.

19. Management by Objective (MBO) was introduced by Peter Drucker. In this approach, both subordinate and superior agree on measurable goals to be achieved primarily by the subordinate over a stated period of time.

20. A "budget" is a plan stated in financial terms. It sets forth in dollars the necessary allocation of funds to achieve the plan.

21. The most important management skill is the ability to communicate effectively.

22. Written communication is the best means to communicate.

A. The application of accepted doctrines and techniques of general management to the security task resources.

1. Financial management

2. Management systems

3. Personnel management

4. Planning, organization, leading, and communications management

5. Policies and procedures

6. Methods of communications

7. Measuring organization's productivity

8. Interviewing techniques

9. Job analysis

10. Performance evaluation

11. Training

Review the general concepts set out in the "classification scheme" prepared by the Professional Certification Board.

Secondly, formulate a detailed study plan which will enable you to become knowledgeable concerning the following specified key concepts as a minimum.

1. Organizational principles including lines of authority, span of control, unity of command, and logical division of work

2. Functional authority

3. The horizontal and vertical planes of an organizational chart

4. Basic rules of disciplinary process

5. McGregor's Theory X and Theory Y

6. Autocratic, custodial, and supportive theories of organizational behavior

7. Herzberg's work motivation theory

8. Budget management

9. Personnel management

10. Key management rules

ASIS International. (2008). *Protection of Assets Manual*. Alexandria, VA: ASIS International. The following chapters are pertinent:

- Strikes and Labor Disturbances

- Proprietary Data

- Insurance

- Security and Labor Relations

- Organization and Management

- Human Relationships

- Security Awareness

- Accounting and Financial Controls

- Workplace Violence

Fennelly, Lawrence J. (2004). *Handbook of Loss Prevention and Crime Prevention*, (4th ed.), Elsevier/Butterworth-Heinemann, Burlington, MA.

Purpura, Philip P., CPP (2008). *Security and Loss Prevention: An Introduction*, (5th ed.), Elsevier/Butterworth-Heinemann, Burlington, MA.

Sennewald, Charles A., CPP (2003). *Effective Security Management*, (4th ed.), Elsevier/Butterworth-Heinemann, Burlington, MA.

OVERVIEW

When one defines the law, this is a process which recognizes legislation, judicial precedents, and the accepted legal principles for social control. Law is designed to protect persons, in their rights and relations, to safeguard their property interests, enforce their contractual rights, hold them accountable for wrongful conduct, punish them for criminal behavior, by means of remedies administered by government.

In the United States, law is derived from four (4) sources. These sources are:

The United States and State Constitutions;

Legislation or Statutory law;

Judicial decisions or case law; and

Administrative law or the rules and regulations of governmental agencies.

It is important to understand that regardless of the various sources of law, the Constitution (either federal and state) prevail over statutes, and, as a general rule, statutes prevail over common-law principles established in court decisions.

There are specific areas of law that govern societal and individual activities. For the purpose of this *CPP Study Guide*, the emphasis will be on the following specific areas:

Civil Law;

Criminal Law; and

Administrative Law.

CIVIL LAW

I. Basic Concepts:

A. Civil law is the statutory and common law in which private rights and remedies are found. Under certain legal matters, the government may be a party. However, the principle cause of action may stem from statutory and criminal law that addresses the rights among private parties such as individuals and business entities.

Federal Statute is codified in the 50 titles of the United States Code ("USC"). Generally, Title 18 defines crimes and offenses. The balance of the other titles are primarily civil and relate to various federal activities such as General Provisions, the President, and the Congress (i.e., Titles 1, 2 and 3) through Commerce and Trade, Conservation and Copyrights (i.e., Titles 15, 16 and 17) to Transportation and War and National Defense (i.e., Titles 49 and 50).

B. Contract Liability:

1. The basic elements of a contract are:
   a. An agreement;
   b. Between two or more parties;
   c. To do or not to do a particular thing;
   d. A valid consideration (obligation) flowing to each party;
   e. The parties must be competent and have a legal capacity to contract; and
   f. The subject matter of the contract must be legal.

2. Contractual agreements are enforced by court action requiring a party to perform its obligation or assessment of money damages to compensate an injured party for failure of performance of the other party.

3. Contractual liability is pertinent to private security in that:
   a. The company providing contract security forces may be liable for breach of contract.
   b. The private company which hires its own security employees does so by employment contracts with its employees.

4. An **Express Contract** is an actual agreement of the parties, the terms of which are openly uttered or declared (usually in writing) at the time the contract is made.

5. An **Implied Contract** is one not created or evidenced by the explicit agreement of the parties, but is inferred by law.

6. **Price** is the dollar value stated in the contract.

7. **Reasonable value** is the dollar value of goods and/or services determined by a court or arbitrator.

8. Unless a written agreement specifically states that it is the complete agreement between the parties, oral agreements which are not inconsistent with the written terms may well be considered binding.

9. Recovery of damages under a contract may be estopped[1] by a **"time bar"** clause.

C. Warranties:

1. A warranty is a statement that the goods or services provided are actually as they are described or said to be.

2. A person or entity that relied on the warranty in using the services or product may generally collect monetary damages, to the extent of any "injury," if the service or product warranted was not as represented.

3. A "limitation of warranty" is normally included in a warranty contract by security product and services providers.

---

[1]Estoppel, in this instance, is a legal bar against filing a claim for breach of contract.

D. Torts (Civil Wrongs):

1. A tort is a willful or negligent wrong done by one person to another. **No agreement between the parties is required.**

2. The concept of tort liability operates to:
   a. Compensate a victim for his loss;
   b. Act a deterrent for future conduct of the same kind; and
   c. Serve as evidence of society's disapproval of the wrong.

3. The basic elements of intentional tort liability are:
   a. An act or omission,
   b. Which brought about the intended result.

4. Examples of intentional torts:
   a. Battery
   b. Assault
   c. False Arrest and False Imprisonment
   d. Trespass to Land
   e. Trespass to Chattels (Conversion)
   f. Fraud/Misrepresentation
   g. Defamation
   h. Invasion of Privacy
   i. Malicious Prosecution

5. A basic concept in tort liability, **Negligence,** is the failure to exercise a reasonable or ordinary amount of care in a situation that causes harm to someone or something. The standard used to ascertain whether conduct constitutes negligence is that of a "reasonable person." The standard is higher when "professionals" are involved; those who operate as specialists in the field of security are obliged to be aware of the standards of the industry.

   "Negligence" consists of four elements:
   a. A standard of care,
   b. A breach of this standard,
   c. Proximate cause, and
   d. Harm or injury produced.

6. Generally, the injured party must prove that:
   a. The tort feasor[2] acted negligently, and
   b. The negligent act was the cause of the loss or injury.

7. **Gross negligence or reckless conduct** shows a greater lack of concern for the rights of others than ordinary negligence. Where gross negligence is shown, punitive damages are available.

---

[2]Tort feasor is a wrong-doer; one who has committed the wrongful act.

E. Agency Relationship - Established when one person acts for another. The agent can be acting on his own, but in behalf of another. Agency can be:

   a. An express appointment,

   b. Ratification of actions taken,

   c. Permitting one with apparent authority to act.

1. The doctrine of **Respondeat Superior** (let the master respond) is well established in common law. The employer (master) is responsible for the actions of his employee (servant) while the employee is acting in the employer's behalf. In litigation, the Plaintiff must prove that the employee's actions were within the scope of his/her employment, thus implying that liability was contingent on whether the employer *knew or should have known* about the alleged actions.

2. The right of control and not necessarily the exercise of that right is the test of the relation of the employer to the employee. It is the distinction between a person who is subject to orders as to how he does his work and one who agrees only to do the work in his own way.

3. Generally, proprietary security officers are employees. Contract security personnel are employees of the supplying agency and therefore may not be considered employees of the employing organization. The key to liability under contract law is whether the security officer is acting within the scope of his employment and commits a wrongful act. Factors which determine if the security officer was acting within the scope of employment include:

   a. Was the act one of the kind which the offender was employed to perform?

   b. Did it occur substantially within the authorized time and space limits of the employment?

   c. Was the offender motivated, at least in part, by a desire to serve his employer?

4. The hiring organization may take a totally hands off position with regard to contract personnel to avoid liability for their wrongful acts; however, the legal concept of **"non-delegable duty"** provides that there are certain duties and responsibilities which cannot be delegated to others including an independent contractor. Courts may find negligence on the part of the hiring organization which has neglected to exercise any control over the selection and training of contract personnel.

5. **Vicarious liability** means that the employer is *automatically liable* for the illegal actions of its employee. Negligence of the agent is imputed by law to the principal, provided the employee was acting within the scope of his employment when the injury occurred.

6. Liability for the acts of another may be avoided if the hiring contract has established the relationship of the tort feasor as an **"independent contractor."** However, the employer may be held liable for the acts of an independent contractor when one of the following exist:

   a. The work contracted for is wrongful per se, or

   b. The work contracted for is a public nuisance, or

   c. The work contracted for is inherently dangerous, or

   d. The act of the independent contractor violates a duty imposed on the employer by contract, or

   e. The wrongful act by the independent contractor violates a statutory duty.

7. **Strict Liability** is a liability that is not dependent upon actual negligence or intent to harm, but is based on the breach of an absolute duty to make something safe. This concept of strict liability most often applies to either ultra-hazardous activities or in products-liability cases. The term is also referred to as *absolute liability* or *liability without fault.*

F. Premises Liability for Negligent Security - When a party, who is in control of a property or premises, fails to provide reasonable security to those who depend upon such protection. A claim of this nature results when an *invitee* (e.g., customer, client, visitor) is injured by a criminal act (e.g., murdered, raped, assaulted) by a third party and that the act occurred on the premises of a business.

While premises security liability law varies from state jurisdiction to state jurisdiction, the analysis remains the same. The legal concepts to apply in examining this tort claim include:

1. *Duty* - The key element in determining whether or not a duty may exist depends on the relationship of the parties. In that, a duty may exist which may require the property owner to protect against certain dangers, make the premises reasonably safe, and/or warn against certain dangers.

2. *Foreseeability* - Under certain circumstances, a property owner may not have a duty to exercise any care until that property owner knows or has reason to know that such acts are occurring or likely to occur at the premises. If the property owner, however, knows or has reason to know, based on past experience, that there is a likelihood of certain conduct, then the legal obligation changes. As a result, the question of potential liability depends on certain factors—in particular, whether the criminal act was *foreseeable.*[3] There are two standards for determining whether the criminal act in question was foreseeable:
   a. *"Prior Similar Incidents"* - A duty may exist when the owner or party in control of the premises **knew or should have known** about similar incidents committed on the premises.
   b. *"Totality of the Circumstances"* - A broader standard in terms of the potential liability to the owner or party in control of the premises. This standard includes prior similar incidents as well as other factors, such as the nature of the business, its community environment (i.e., its neighbors), security training and whether customary or recognized industry standards were being exercised at the time of the criminal attack.

3. *Breach of Duty* - If an event was foreseeable and the property owner had a duty, then the next element would be to determine whether or not the duty was breached.

4. *Causation* - An essential factor for a cause of action for negligence is whether there was a reasonable connection between the act or omission of the property owner for which the plaintiff suffered the harm (e.g., death or injury) in connection with a criminal act.

G. Remedies - Under tort law, the means of enforcing rights and redressing wrongs are as follows:

1. An injunction[4] to prohibit continuance of the wrongful conduct.

---

[3]Foreseeable is an element of proximate cause in tort law.
[4]Injunction is a court's order to a party to do or to refrain from doing a particular act.

2. "Special damages" which are ascertainable as to amount (medical bills, property loss).

3. "General damages" not ascertainable (pain and suffering).

4. "Punitive damages" to compensate for outrageous behavior.

5. "Statutory damages" are created, defined, or required by a statute.

CRIMINAL LAW

I. Basic Concepts:

A. The basis for the definition of certain conduct as a "crime" is the concept that the prohibited conduct is a threat to the public welfare. A "crime" can be an act or omission.

B. Whether a wrong will be considered a "crime" or a civil wrong (**TORT**) is determined by the legislature. The *main body* of Federal Criminal Law is found in Title 18 of the United States Code.

C. The Law of Precedence, **"Stare Decisis"** holds that when a court has decided a case by applying a legal principle to a set of facts, the court should hold to that principle and apply it to all later cases with similar facts, unless there is a good strong reason to the contrary.

D. Crimes Classifications:

1. **Felony -** Federal statutes provide for five classes of felonies ranging in punishment from imprisonment for a term exceeding one year to death or life imprisonment.

2. **Misdemeanor -** Federal statutes provide three classes of misdemeanors as follows:

    Class A Misdemeanor - One year or less but more than 6 months.

    Class B Misdemeanor - Six months or less, but more than 30 days.

    Class C Misdemeanor - Thirty days or less, but more than 5 days.

3. **Infraction -** Federal statutes provide for one class of infraction for which the penalty ranges from five days or less imprisonment to no authorized penalty.

E. **"Jurisdiction"** is the geographical area within which a court or public official has the right and power to operate, or the power of the court to handle a case.

F. **"Venue"** is the place at which the crime was committed.

G. **"Color of Law"** is the pretense of law which grants one the authority to act.

H. "Due Process" is that a person should always have notice and a chance to present his/her side in a legal dispute without law or government obstruction.

II. The Basic Elements of a Crime:

A simple definition of a crime is that: *"A crime is an offense against the government punishable by a fine and/or imprisonment by the government."*

A. Every crime contains several elements:

1. A law defining the crime, which is to say a law commanding or prohibiting the act;

2. A material element called the ***actus reus*** [means the act of wrongful conduct];

3. A mental element called the ***mens rea*** [means the state of mind of the actor or intent];

4. An injury or result;

5. A causal relationship between the act or conduct and the injury or result; and

6. A prescribed penalty.

[**Note:** The *actus reus,* the *mens rea,* the nature of the required injury, and to some extent the degree of causal connection between the act and injury, vary from crime to crime.]

B. The **"Corpus Delicti"** (the body of the crime) is the combination of the elements which provide proof of the crime. The corpus delicti of every true crime consists of:

1. Mens Rea (criminal intent)

2. Actus Reus (the forbidden act)

3. Coming together of the criminal intent and the criminal act.

C. The law [The Law of Causation] says that before criminal sanctions can be imposed, the offenders conduct must constitute the **"proximate cause"** of the injury or result. This means that the conduct of the offender, operating in a natural and continuous sequence, must produce the injury or result. There must also be a showing that *without* the offenders conduct, the harm or injury would not have occurred.

D. Motive is ***not*** an essential part of a crime; it is not part of the *corpus delicti.*

E. Crimes are classified into two (2) basic categories - *mala in se* or *mala prohibita.*

1. **Mala in se** - is a crime which is inherently wrong or wrong of itself (i.e, murder and rape).

2. **Mala Prohibita** - is defined as a crime or "wrong" by statute, though not inherently wrong (i.e., failure to pay taxes). Generally, no proof of criminal intent is required. The mere accomplishment of the act is sufficient for criminal liability.

F. **"Recklessness"** - a wrongful state of mind of a lesser degree than intent, implies that one has acted in complete disregard for the rights and safety of others, resulting in harm.

G. **"Criminal negligence"** is often called **gross negligence** or **culpable negligence.** If conduct is grossly negligent, the same conduct can render one both civilly and criminally liable.

H. The test in ascertaining whether the standard of care was met is that of the **"reasonable person."** The test is whether the accused exercised the same amount of care that a reasonable, prudent person exercising ordinary caution would have used under the same circumstances.

I. **"Negligence"** differs from recklessness. In recklessness, conduct is governed by the actual state of mind of the accused.

J. **"Transferred Intent"** is the term applied to a situation in which an individual intends one criminal wrong but accomplishes another. The necessary criminal intent is present by means of "transfer" from the original act to the second act.

III. Defenses:

Information offered by a defendant as a reason in law or fact why he is not guilty.

A. The **"alibi"** defense is one of physical impossibility. The testimony of an alibi witness must cover the entire time of the crime.

B. The **"mistake of fact"** defense is used when one commits a violation of the law in good faith with a reasonable belief that certain facts existed, which would make the act innocent if indeed they did exist.

C. **"Entrapment"** is an act of a government official or agent inducing a person to commit a crime that the person would not have committed without the inducement.

IV. Law of Arrest:

A. The Fourth Amendment to the United States Constitution reads as follows:

> "The right of the people to be secure in their persons, houses, papers, and effects, against unreasonable searches and seizures, shall not be violated, and no warrants shall issue, but upon probable cause, supported by oath or affirmation, and particularly describing the place to be searched, and the persons or things to be seized."

Since an arrest is a seizure of the person, a person is given the same protection against an illegal arrest as he is against an unreasonable search and seizure of his house, papers, and effects.

B. The basic elements which constitute an arrest are:

1. A purpose or intention to affect the arrest.

2. An actual or constructive seizure or detention of the person to be arrested.

3. A communication by the arresting officer to the arrestee of his intention to place him under arrest.

4. An understanding by the person to be arrested that he is being arrested.

C. The mere words "you are under arrest" will not satisfy the seizure or detention element of arrest. Moreover, no formal words are necessary to constitute an arrest, and no touching is required. If an officer, with the intention to arrest says, "Come with me," and the individual, *knowing he is not free to leave the presence of the officer,* quietly submits himself to the officer's custody and control, there has been an arrest.

D. Arrest Authority Under a Warrant:

1. Arrest with a warrant places the determination of probable cause in the hands of impartial judicial authority. **"Probable Cause"** exists when the facts and circumstances within a persons knowledge and of which he has reasonable trustworthy information are sufficient to warrant a person of reasonable caution and prudence to believe that an offense has been committed or is being committed by a specific person.

2. If the warrant is proper on its face and the officer acted within the scope of his authority, the officer is protected against civil liability for false arrest.

3. A *warrant* is an order by a court for the arrest of a person. A *summons* directs the defendant to appear before a court at a stated time and place.

E. When a private citizen acts in aid of a known law enforcement officer, the citizen has the same rights and privileges as the officer and is protected from liability even if the officer was acting illegally.

F. Arrest Authority Without a Warrant:

1. Generally, law enforcement officers may make an arrest for any offense which they have "probable cause" to believe was committed by the person arrested. A law enforcement officer needs only to have "probable cause." If the officer was right or wrong in making the arrest, it is still a legal arrest.

2. Generally, private citizens may arrest any person who has committed an offense in their presence or for a felony not committed in their presence. **BUT,** the arrest can be justified only by further showing that the felony was actually committed by the person arrested.

V. Use of Force:

A. Reasonably necessary force is the least amount of force needed to accomplish the lawful purpose for which it is used. Reasonably necessary force is allowable:

1. In self defense, defense of others, defense of property or premises;

2. In restraining a person about to do himself serious bodily harm;

3. By a parent correcting a minor child;

4. By a law enforcement officer, or a person directed to assist the officer, in arresting a criminal or preventing escape; and

5. By a private citizen in arresting a criminal or preventing escape.

B. The use of force must cease when resistance stops.

C. Deadly Force may **only** be used when deadly force has been threatened or is reasonably believed to be imminent.

D. Defense of Premises:

1. To prevent or stop what is "reasonably believed" to be a criminal trespass, the person in responsible charge of the premises may use the amount of force reasonably necessary (but not fatal force).

VI. Search and Seizure With a Warrant:

A. A search warrant is an order in writing by a judge (Magistrate) in the name of the people, commanding a law enforcement officer to search for certain personal property and bring it before the judicial authority named in the warrant.

B. For a search warrant to be valid:

1. The proper official must issue the warrant.

2. A warrant may be issued only for authorized objects. Examples:
   a. Fruits of a crime,
   b. Instrumentalities of a crime,
   c. Contraband,
   d. Property that might constitute evidence of a crime.

3. The warrant must be issued on probable cause supported by oath or affirmation.

4. The place to be searched and things to be seized must be particularly described.

C. A search under a search warrant may extend to all parts of the premises described in the warrant, provided it is reasonable to assume items could be concealed therein.

D. The **"Exclusionary Rule"** excludes evidence, otherwise admissible, obtained by methods which violate Constitutional guarantees of the Fourth Amendment.

E. The **"Fruit of the Poisoned Tree"** doctrine states that any evidence obtained as a result of an unreasonable search cannot be used against the accused. Other evidence obtained as a result of the original unlawful invasion is dubbed the "fruit of the poisoned tree" and may not be used against the person whose privacy was violated.

VII. Search and Seizure Without a Warrant:

A. The Fourth Amendment does not specifically authorize a search without a warrant. We have legal searches without a warrant because of court decisions.

B. A search incidental to a lawful arrest is permitted:

1. To protect the arresting officer.

2. To avoid destruction of evidence by an arrested person.

C. In a search incidental to arrest, the area of search is limited:

1. Generally, a full search of the person of the arrestee may be made and evidence may be seized even though it had no direct connection with the arrest.

2. A search inside a building where an arrest is made is limited to the area where the arrestee *might reach* for a weapon or conceal or destroy evidence.

3. If an arrest is made outside the residence, the search is limited to the person of the arrestee and the surrounding area into which he *might reach.*

D. The burden of showing that the accused consented to a search is on the prosecution.

1. Consent must be voluntary.

2. The extent of the search is limited by the exact words of the one giving consent.

3. Consent may be withdrawn.

4. The person giving consent must have the capacity to do so.

E. The **"Plain View Doctrine"** holds that if a law enforcement officer is legally in an area and sees contraband, instrumentalities of crime or other evidence which he has the right to seize, he may legally seize that which is in "plain view." (Where no search is necessary, there is no need for constitutional protection against an illegal search.)

VIII. Confessions and Admissions:

A. A **confession** is a statement in which a person acknowledges guilt of a crime.

B. An **admission** is a statement in which a person admits a fact or facts which would tend to prove him guilty of a crime, but which does not constitute a full acknowledgment of guilt of a crime.

C. Right to legal counsel is guaranteed in the Sixth Amendment to the United States Constitution. Under *Miranda v. Arizona,* 384 U.S. 436 (1966), when a person has officially been taken into custody (detained by law enforcement), **but before any interrogation takes place,** police must inform this person of their right to remain silent and to have an attorney present during questioning.[5] The accused must be informed clearly and unequivocally that:

1. He has the right to remain silent and that anything said can and will be used against the individual in court.

---

[5]A person is considered to be "in custody" any time this person is placed in an environment in which he/she does not believe he/she is free to leave. Police can question witnesses at a crime scene without advising them of their Miranda Rights. In the event that a party implicates himself/herself in the crime during such questioning, his/her statements could be used against him/her in a court of law.

2. He has the right to consult with a lawyer and have the lawyer with him during the interrogation.

3. If he is indigent and cannot afford a lawyer, one will be appointed to represent him.

D. Key points regarding the *Miranda* Ruling:

1. Give the warnings if there is any doubt whether or not they apply.

2. Courts generally hold that questioning a suspect in his home or place of business (assumes that the party believes that they are free to leave) without arrest is not custodial interrogation.

3. Admissions made by a suspect in response to interrogation by private citizens will be admissible in court despite lack of warnings.

E. The fundamental test regarding the use of confessions and admissions is the **"free and voluntary"** test.

IX. Special Legal Aspects of Private Security:

A. Constitutional safeguards protect the citizen against governmental action, not against other private citizens; but, constitutional limitations can apply to the conduct of private security personnel when they act in concert with public police or as their agents.

B. A security officer's authority may be:

1. The same authority as a private citizen.

2. Obtained through deputization or commission by a public agency.

3. A mixture of civilian and special power added by statute or regulation.

C. Arrest and Detention Powers of Private Security:

1. Private security officers do not usually have broad authority to detain or arrest. Primary sources for the arrest authority of private security personnel:
   a. Statutes, such as deputization, which grant qualified private security personnel arrest powers similar to public police.
   b. Statutes which grant shop owners and agents authority to arrest and detain.

2. Most states authorize a merchant or employee to arrest or detain, upon probable cause, a person believed to have stolen goods.

D. Interrogation:

1. A person who has been legally detained may be interrogated as a general rule of law. Any confession obtained will be scrutinized by the courts to ensure that it was voluntarily given.

2. A private security officer, not operating under special authority of the state, is not required to advise the suspect of his rights, as is the public officer.

E. Searches:

1. A private security officer has only the search authority of a private citizen. The Fourth Amendment does not apply to searches by private persons.

2. Evidence discovered by private search is admissible in a criminal trial and not subject to the Exclusionary Rule.

3. The search of employee lockers, packages, or automobiles on the employers' premises is usually dictated by company policy and the employment contract. These searches are usually made with the consent of the searched, validating the search unless the element of "unreasonableness" enters the picture.

X. Selected Criminal Violations Significant to the Security Function:

A. Larceny, or theft crimes, include petit and grand larceny; embezzlement; fraud; extortion; and false pretenses. These crimes consist of:

1. The wrongful taking, obtaining, or withholding

2. Property of another

3. With intent to deprive the owner of the use and benefit thereof, or appropriate the property to the taker or to a third party.

B. Embezzlement involves:

1. Conversion of personal property

2. By a person

3. To whom property was entrusted.

C. False Pretenses consist of:

1. Obtaining personal property

2. Of another

3. With intent to deprive the owner of the use and benefit thereof

4. By use of false pretenses in misrepresenting a past or present fact.

D. Receiving Stolen Property consists of:

1. Receiving or concealing

2. Stolen property

3. Knowing the property to be stolen

4. With intent to obtain a monetary gain, or

5. To prevent the rightful owner from the enjoyment of his property.

E. Robbery, a specific intent crime, has the following elements:

1. Felonious taking

2. Of personal property

3. In the possession of another

4. From that person's person or presence

5. By means of force or fear.

F. Essential elements of **burglary** are:

1. Unlawful entry or *remaining within a building*

2. With the intent to commit some crime therein.

3. The degree, or severity, of the offense will be altered if:
   a. Physical injury is done or threatened;
   b. A dangerous weapon is possessed or used;
   c. The unlawful entry is at night, or;
   d. The building is a dwelling.

4. **It will be necessary to show that the area involved was defined and that actual or constructive notice to that effect was given.**

G. The basic elements of the crime of **Forgery** are:

1. Falsely making or altering

2. A writing of legal significance

3. With intent to defraud.

H. Uttering, a separate offense from Forgery, occurs when a person draws a check on an account with insufficient funds to cover the check. The basic elements of the crime are:

1. Giving or attempting to give

2. Another person

3. An instrument

4. Knowing it to be forged.

I. False Imprisonment may be committed by private citizens as well as police officers. The basic elements of the crime are:

1. Unlawful restraint

2. By one person

3. Of another.

J. The basic elements of the crime of **Perjury** are:

1. Deliberately and knowingly

2. Testifying falsely under oath

3. To a material matter

4. In a court proceeding.

K. Trespass of Real Property is a tort as well as a crime. Generally, one who enters the land of another and does nothing else is not subject to criminal liability. Most jurisdictions require that trespass notices be posted before there can be a violation. The key elements of trespass:

1. Unlawful

2. Violation of the person or property

3. Of another.

XI. Key Points of Criminal Procedure:

A. An arrestee must be brought before a Magistrate "without unnecessary delay."

B. The purpose of a preliminary hearing is to determine probable cause. The defendant may waive preliminary hearing and the case would then go directly to the Grand Jury.[6]

C. The accusatory documents used to bring the charge are an indictment or information. The indictment is issued by the Grand Jury whereas the information is signed and issued by the prosecuting attorney.

D. Bail may be refused if it can be established that the defendant will be a danger to the community. Bail may also be refused on the grounds that no amount will ensure that the defendant will appear for later proceedings.

E. The defendant may plead:

  1. Not guilty

  2. Guilty

  3. Nolo Contendre (no contest)

F. The right to trial by jury may be waived by the defendant and the trial may be held before a judge only.

G. Guilt must be proven **"beyond a reasonable doubt"** to find the defendant guilty in a criminal trial. Proof in a civil action need only be that of a **"preponderance of the evidence."**

H. Probation is the release of a convicted person, under certain conditions, for a specified period of time. **Parole** is the release from confinement, under certain conditions, after the person has served a period of confinement.

---

[6]Grand Jury is a body of citizens empowered and authorized to hear criminal matters and can return indictments. Whereas, Petit Jury is an ordinary jury of twelve citizens who are fact finders in criminal trials.

XII. Eavesdropping: Unauthorized listening.

A. Black's Law Dictionary defines eavesdropping as "knowingly and without lawful authority: (a) entering into a private place with intent to listen surreptitiously to private conversations or to observe the conduct of any other person or persons therein; or (b) installing or using outside a private place any device for hearing, recording, amplifying, or broadcasting sounds originating in such place, which sounds would not ordinarily be audible or comprehensible outside, without the consent of the person or persons entitled to privacy therein; or (c) installing or using any device or equipment for the interception of any telephone, telegraph, or other wire communication without the consent of the person in possession or control of the facilities for such wire communication . . . "

B. Wiretapping is the interception of a communication circuit.

C. Bugging is the interception of a communication using an electronic device.

XIII. Interception of Communications (18 U.S.C. '2500 et seq):

A. Federal law prohibits the intentional:

1. Interception or attempt to intercept any wire, oral or electronic communication;

2. Use or attempt to use any electronic, mechanical, or other wire or radio device to intercept oral communications;

3. Disclosure or attempt to disclose the contents or any wire, oral, or electronic communication, knowing the information to have been obtained in violation of the act; or

4. Use of or attempt to use the contents of any illegally intercepted wire, oral, or electronic communication.

B. Federal law does not prohibit interceptions:

1. By a communications company in the normal course of business;

2. By a party to, or with the consent of a party to, the communication unless the interception will further a crime or tortuous act under federal or state law;

3. On order from the Foreign Intelligence Surveillance Court;

4. Of electronic communications which are readily available to the public;

5. By law enforcement after judicial review and order.

C. Federal law prohibits the manufacture, distribution, possession and advertising of devices primarily designed for surreptitious interception.

[***Note:*** Under the Uniting and Strengthening America Act by Providing Appropriate Tools Required to Intercept and Obstruct Terrorism ("USA Patriot") Act of 2001, the Federal Government enhanced the authority for intercepting wire, oral and electronic communications relating to terrorism.]

XIV. Key Federal Agencies in Investigations:

A. The Department of Homeland Security:

Under this Department, the following are the major components:

◆ *Directorate for National Protection and Programs* – works to advance the Department's risk-reduction mission using an approach that encompasses both physical and virtual threats and their associated human elements.

◆ *Directorate for Science and Technology* – the primary research and development arm of the Department which provides federal, state and local officials with the technology and capabilities to protect the homeland.

◆ *Directorate for Management* – responsible for Department budgets and appropriations, expenditure of funds, accounting and finance, procurement; human resources, information technology systems, facilities and equipment, and the identification and tracking of performance measurements.

◆ *Office of Policy* – the primary policy formulation and coordination component for the Department of Homeland Security.

◆ *Office of Health* – coordinates all medical activities of the Department to ensure appropriate preparation for and response to incidents having medical significance.

◆ *Office of Intelligence and Analysis* – responsible for using information and intelligence from multiple sources to identify and assess current and future threats to the United States.

◆ *Office of Operations Coordination* – responsible for monitoring the security of the United States on a daily basis and coordinating activities with the Department and with governors, Homeland Security Advisors, law enforcement partners, and critical infrastructure operators in all 50 states and more than 50 major urban areas.

◆ *Federal Law Enforcement Training Center* – provides career-long training to law enforcement professionals to help them fulfill their responsibilities safely and proficiently.

◆ *Domestic Nuclear Detection Office* – works to enhance the nuclear detection efforts of federal, state, territorial, tribal, and local governments, and the private sector, and to ensure a coordinated response to such threats.

◆ *Transportation Security Administration (TSA)* – protects the nation's transportation systems to ensure freedom of movement for people and commerce.

◆ *United States Customs and Border Protection (CBP)* – responsible for protecting our nation's borders in order to prevent terrorists and terrorist weapons from entering the United States.

◆ *United States Citizenship and Immigration Services* – responsible for the administration of immigration and naturalization adjudication functions and establishing immigration services policies and priorities.

◆ *United States Immigration and Customs Enforcement (ICE)* – largest investigative arm of the Department; responsible for identifying and shutting down vulnerabilities in the nation's border, economic, transportation and infrastructure security.

◆ *United States Coast Guard* – protects the public, the environment and U.S. economic interest in the nation's ports and waterways, along the coast and on international waters.

◆ *Federal Emergency Management (FEMA)* – prepares the nation for hazards, managed Federal response and recovery efforts following any national incident and administers the National Flood Insurance Program.

◆ *United States Secret Service* – protects the President and other high-level officials and investigates counterfeiting and other financial crimes, including financial institution fraud, identity theft, computer fraud, and computer-based attacks on our nation's financial, banking and telecommunications infrastructure.

B. The Department of Justice:

This Department is headed by the Attorney General of the United States who is responsible for overseeing over 40 separate component organizations. The key component law enforcement agencies are:

1. Federal Bureau of Investigation:
   a. Investigative jurisdiction over Federal criminal violations and concurrent jurisdiction with the DEA on Narcotics and Dangerous Drugs. The priorities include:
      (1) Protect the United States from terrorist attack
      (2) Protect the United States against foreign intelligence operations and espionage
      (3) Protect the United States against cyber-based attacks and high-technology crimes
      (4) Combat public corruption at all levels
      (5) Protect civil rights
      (6) Combat transnational/national criminal organizations and enterprises
      (7) Combat major white-collar crime
      (8) Combat significant violent crime
      (9) Support federal, state, local and international partners
   b. Additional functional areas under the FBI's jurisdiction include:
      (1) National Depository of Fingerprints
      (2) National Crime Information Center (NCIC)
      (3) National Center for the Analysis of Violent Crime

(4) Violent Criminal Apprehension Program

(5) Forensic Science Training and Research Center

(6) National Bomb Data Center

2. U.S. Marshals Service:
    a. Operational priorities include:
        (1) Physical security for Federal courts
        (2) Custodian of Federal evidence
        (3) Service of Federal criminal and civil process
        (4) Witness-protection program
        (5) Federal Assets Forfeiture and Seizure Program
        (6) Transportation of Federal prisoners
        (7) Conduct of fugitive investigations

3. Bureau of Alcohol, Tobacco, Firearms and Explosives (ATF):
    a. Administration and enforcement of U.S. gun and explosives laws
    b. Training and investigative assistance in arson and bomb investigations
    c. Trace of weapons for law enforcement agencies
    d. Investigations into illegal trafficking of alcohol and tobacco products

4. Drug Enforcement Administration (DEA):
    a. Administration and enforcement of U.S. narcotics laws

C. Federal Highway Administration (FHA) (Department of Transportation):

1. Regulatory jurisdiction over safety and performance of commercial motor carriers in interstate commerce. Authorized to investigate violations of:
    a. Highway Safety Act
    b. Interstate Commerce Act
    c. Explosive and Dangerous Articles Act

D. Flood control planning should be coordinated with the U.S. Army Corp of Engineers.

E. Progressive situation reports of floods are available from the National Oceanic and Atmospheric Administration (NOAA).

F. The National Weather Service issues severe weather advisories.

ADMINISTRATIVE LAW

I. Basic Concepts:

A. Administrative law is the law concerning the powers and procedures of administrative agencies, including especially the law governing judicial review of administrative action.

B. Administrative agencies affect private rights through rulemaking, licensing, investigation, prosecution, and other informal actions. When made under the appropriate statute and within the scope of the agency, the rules and regulations have the force of law.

C. Enabling statutes, which authorize agencies, describe only the structure and powers of the agency. Generally, agencies have quasi-legislative and quasi-judicial power in that they:

1. Make rules and regulations,

    [NOTE: The Administrative agency initially publishes proposed or final regulations in the *Federal Register*. On or after the effective date, the regulations are codified in the Code of Federal Regulations ("CFR").]

2. Issue citations for violations of the rules and regulations,

3. Hold hearings and/or adjudicates the alleged violations, and

4. Assess penalties for the violations.

D. The Fair Credit Reporting Act (15 U.S.C. '1681 et seq):

1. Regulates mercantile credit, insurance, and employment investigation agencies.

2. Consumer reporting agency: provides information to third persons about the background, character, reputation, lifestyle, or habits of an individual.

3. Investigative Consumer Report: Made by a consumer reporting agency. Contains information developed through personal interviews with others with personal knowledge of the subject.

4. Any organization that procures or intends to procure an investigative consumer report on a person **who has applied** for employment, retention, or reassignment must give the applicant written notice of that intention. The notice must be on a separate sheet of paper.

5. On applicant request, the organization must describe the nature and scope of the information to be sought.

6. An internal security staff report is not an investigative consumer report.

7. A routine investigation of an incumbent without a request for personnel action, even if provided by a consumer reporting agency, does not require prior notice to the subject.

8. When adverse action is based on information in a consumer report, the employee is given a copy of the consumer rights under the FCRA, the identity of the consumer reporting agency, and is notified that the adverse action is based upon information in the report.

9. Release of any data that did not come from direct experience with the employee could constitute the employer a Consumer Reporting Agency and he may have to open his investigative files to the affected individual.

E. Fair and Accurate Credit Transactions Act of 2003 ("FACT"):

This statute amends the Fair Credit Reporting Act relative to regulation of criminal background and reference checks, as interpreted under a 1999 Federal Trade Commission ("FTC") opinion letter, known as the *Vail* letter. Under the *Vail* letter, there was a requirement that the accused in a workplace investigation be given advance consent to the investigation if conducted by third parties, such as private investigators. Title VI of the FACT nullified the *Vail* letter requirement. However, if an employer takes any adverse action based on the workplace investigation (conducted by a third party), a disclosure must be made to the affected employee.

II. Statutory Civil Rights:

A. The Civil Rights Act (42 U.S.C. 2000e): prohibits *employers with 15 or more employees* from discrimination, failure or refusal to hire, discharge, limitation, segregation, or classification in any way adverse to an employee or employment applicant on the basis of race, color, religion, sex, or national origin.

The U.S. District Court has jurisdiction in all matters that arise from claims under Title VII of the Act. A claim may be filed with the Equal Employment Opportunity Commission ("EEOC") or a deferral agency. The Federal courts become involved in such situations as:

1. The EEOC fails in an attempt at reconciliation and a suit is filed;

2. Government agencies or their employees are involved;

3. Private individuals bring suit because the EEOC has declined to file a suit, but has issued a "right-to-sue notice," allowing the individual to bring the charges before a Federal court;

4. The EEOC requests permanent or temporary injunctive relief prior to the final disposition of the case;

5. The matter is a pattern or practice case in which the EEOC can seek class action type relief, without complying with the customary requirements for a class action suit.[7]

---

[7]42 C.F.R. 2000e-5(f) et seq.

Key Cases to Remember:

1. In *Griggs v. Duke Power Company* (1971) 401 U.S. 424 – Duke's intradepartmental transfer policy requiring a high school diploma and obtaining certain scores on two aptitude tests, violated the Civil Rights Act because it prevented a disproportionate number of African-American Employees from advancement. (An adverse impact case)

2. In *Gregory v. Litton* (472 F2d 631). Gregory was denied employment on the basis of an arrest (not a conviction), which was disallowed by the Court.

B. The Age Discrimination in Employment Act of 1967 (as amended through 1991) prohibits **employers of 20 or more employees** from discrimination against applicants or employees over 40 years of age. The EEOC enforces the act. The individual may file a civil action 60 days after filing the EEOC complaint, if the EEOC has not started such action.

C. The Equal Pay Act of 1963 requires that employees receive equal pay for equal work, requiring equal skill, effort and responsibility regardless of sex. Note that the employer may pay different rates at different establishments. The Administrator of Wage and Hour Division of the Department of Labor has primary jurisdiction over this Act.

III. Labor Relations Laws:

A. The National Labor Relations Act (Wagner Act) provides employees with the right to organize, form, join, or assist labor organizations, to bargain collectively, and to refrain from such activities except when membership is required as a condition of employment.

1. Unfair labor practices include:
   a. Interfering with, restraining, or coercing employees in the exercise of their rights.
   b. Dominating or interfering with the formation of any labor organization or contributing financial or other support to it.
   c. Encouraging or discouraging membership in any labor organization by discriminating in regard to hire, tenure, or terms or conditions of employment.
   d. Discharging or discriminating against an employee because he filed charges or gave testimony under the NLRA.
   e. Refusing to bargain collectively with representatives of a majority of employees in the bargaining unit.

2. The basic question in any grievance matter is "was the aggrieving person the employer or a representative authorized to act for the employer?"

3. Ground rules:
   a. Literature distribution would be permitted on a parking lot during break or lunch hours, but would be prohibited in a patient care area of a hospital or in the sales area of a store.
   b. No management representative attends a union meeting or union organizing meeting.

c. Undercover operations are neither conducted nor authorized where and when labor organizing efforts or labor problems are occurring.

d. No information regarding the union affiliation of employment applicants is included in security reports.

e. Actions of security personnel will be considered "employer actions."

f. Have a clear reason for any requirement which may adversely affect only persons in a bargaining unit.

4. Just cause discharge:
   a. Incidents are serious infractions or involve serious misconduct.
   b. The disciplined person was actually responsible (not goaded).
   c. The incident was known to be serious and the violation known to be misconduct.

5. To sustain a just cause discharge the rules must be:
   a. Reasonable;
   b. Within the authority of management to make;
   c. Properly publicized; and
   d. Uniformly enforced.

6. The behavior of the security personnel must be reasonable.

7. Arbitration is governed by the labor contract and the state or federal arbitration law (or the common law of contracts). Arbitration includes:
   a. A final and binding decision which is enforceable by judicial decree or judgment;
   b. Provision for compelling evidence by subpoena;
   c. Absent fraud, capricious or arbitrary conduct, or a decision beyond the power of the arbitrator, the findings of the arbitrator will not be reviewed by the courts.
   d. Labor arbitrators generally admit anything either party offers in evidence.

8. Security considerations in a discipline case:
   a. Security personnel must act "reasonably" at all times.
   b. Statements by employees must be shown to have been totally voluntary.
   c. Evidence gathered in a search where an employee had an expectation of privacy or where the company had not clearly reserved the right to make the search, may be admitted but given little weight.
   d. Surveillance must not be conducted where the employee has an expectation of privacy.
   e. **Weingarten Rule:** When an employee reasonably believes that an interview may lead to or result in disciplinary action and **requests** that a union representative be present, union representation must be allowed. Key Points are as follows:
      (1) The employee must request that a co-worker/representative be present;
      (2) The rights *only* apply to investigatory interviews – not a disciplinary meeting;
      (3) The employer *only* has to allow a co-worker/representative to be present, but does not have to allow an outsider (e.g., a lawyer) to attend the meeting.

9. The **Appropriate Bargaining Unit** is a group of workers that:
   a. Excludes supervisors and managers;
   b. Excludes craft or professional workers or is restricted to such workers under certain circumstances;
   c. Consists of at least two workers; and,
   d. Does not mix guards and non-guards when NLRB certification is sought.

10. **Past Practices** are regular and recurring ways of doing things which are not in the union contract.

11. A **"past prior benefit clause"** in a union contract ensures that any condition of employment existing at the time of the contract cannot be changed by management to conditions less beneficial to the workers.

B. **The Labor Management Relations Act (Taft-Hartley Act)** forbids unions from:

1. Restraining or coercing employees in the exercise of their rights, or employers in the selection of their own collective bargaining or grievance adjustment representatives.

2. Coercing employers to discriminate against employees.

3. Refusing to bargain.

4. Engaging in secondary boycotts, coercing employers of self-employed persons to join a labor organization, or striking for the purpose of forcing an employer to bargain with one union when another union has been certified as the bargaining agent.

5. Charging excessive or discriminatory initiation fees for union membership.

6. Coercing an employer to pay for work not performed (featherbedding).

C. **The Labor Management Reporting and Disclosure Act (Landrum-Griffin Act)** which established safeguards and restrictions on union officers and management conduct regarding their members, also prohibits either union or employer from "Hot Cargo" agreements.

IV. Occupational Safety and Health:

A. **The Williams-Steiger Occupational Safety and Health Act (29 U.S.C. 651-678)** is administered by the Occupational Safety and Health Administration (OSHA) under the Department of Labor.

B. The purpose of the act was to assure that employers engaged in a business affecting commerce will furnish places of employment free from recognized hazards that cause or are likely to cause death or serious physical harm.

C. A state with legislation at least as effective as the federal legislation may regulate occupational safety and health in the state. DOL monitors to ensure compliance.

D. A temporary variance application includes:

1. Detailed statement of reasons why the employer is unable to comply with a particularly identified standard or portion thereof.

2. Steps taken, or to be taken, (with specific dates) to protect against the hazard.

3. When the employer expects to be in compliance and steps taken, and to be taken (with specific dates) to reach compliance.

4. Certification that the employees were informed by posting notices in the plant and giving a copy of the application to an employee representative.

E. For a permanent variance, a hearing provides employees an opportunity to participate. The variance is granted if the employer demonstrates that the conditions, practices, means, methods, operations, or processes used or proposed will provide a place of employment which are as safe and healthful as if he complies with the standard.

F. Enforcement - OSHA conducts inspections and issues citations and/or assesses fines for violations of standards. The limited time period given for violation abatement is often significant. A history of safety citations becomes a bargaining issue in new contract negotiations.

1. Employers must admit compliance officers without advance notice.

2. The compliance officer may inspect the physical plant and the records.

3. Employers and employees may appeal certain OSHA actions to the Occupational Safety and Health Review Commission.

4. Criminal penalties can be invoked only in extreme cases, (e.g., willful actions which lead to the death of an employee) and only by court action.

5. When they find conditions of "imminent danger," compliance officers may **REQUEST,** not demand, shutdown. If shutdown is refused, the officer may notify all employees of the hazard and request DOL to file for court action to shut down the operation.

6. OSHA inspection priorities arc:
   a. Fatalities and multiple hospitalization incidents;
   b. Employee complaints;
   c. Selected high hazard target industries;
   d. Random selection of previously un-inspected industries.

G. Safety Citations:

1. Most citations allege violations of specific safety and health standards or of the posting and record keeping requirements.

2. Citations are not issued to employees. A citation is issued to the employer if employees fail to comply with safety and health standards.

3. Citations may be issued for any of the following types of violations:
   a. Imminent Danger - any condition or practice such that a danger exists which could reasonably be expected to cause death or serious physical harm immediately, or before the imminence of such danger can be eliminated through the enforcement procedures provided by this act.
   b. Serious Violation - a substantial probability that death or serious physical harm could result and the employer knew, or with the exercise of reasonable diligence, should have known of the hazard.
   c. Non-serious Violation - the condition is likely to cause injury, but not death or serious physical harm, or the employer did not know of the hazard. (A tripping hazard on a level surface)
   d. De Minimis Violation - No immediate or direct relationship to safety or health.
   e. Willful Violation - the employer intentionally or knowingly violated the act, or was aware of a hazard and made no attempt to correct it.
   f. Repeated Violation - a second or subsequent citation for violation of the same standard or general duty clause.

H. Penalties:

1. Penalties may be assessed although the employer takes immediate action to correct the cited condition.

2. Written notice of penalties proposed may accompany the citation or follow it.

3. For a non-serious violation, a fine of $7000 or less *may* be imposed.

4. A fine not exceeding $7000 *must* be assessed for a serious violation.

5. The minimum for a willful violation is $5000, while the maximum for willful or repeated violations is $70,000.

6. When the citation or penalty is not contested, payment must be made within 15 days after receipt of the notice.

I. Citations Appeals:

1. Employees or their representatives may contest the time allowed for the abatement of an alleged violation.

2. Employers may contest:
   a. A citation;
   b. A proposed penalty;
   c. A notice of failure to correct a violation;

 d. The time allotted for correction of a violation, or

 e. A combination of any of the foregoing.

 3. Employees or their representatives are considered parties to any contested action.

J. Record Keeping:

 1. Specified types of establishments with 11 or more employees are required to maintain three basic types of injury/illness records. A summary of the total number of job-related injuries and illnesses occurring during the previous calendar year (e.g., 2008) must be posted from February 1, 2009 to March 1, 2009.

 Exempt are small employers, the self-employed, employers of domestic help, or religious organizations. Most retail, trade, finance, insurance, real estate, and service industries are exempt, but samples of these groups may be required to do so by the secretary.

 2. The local place of work is the recording and reporting unit at which two types of records must be maintained:

 a. OSHA Form #300 – Log of Work-Related Injuries and Illnesses;

 b. OSHA Form #300A – Summary of Work-Related Injuries and Illnesses;

 c. OSHA Form # 301- Injury and Illness Incident Report

 3. An "injury" results from a single incident. A one time chemical exposure is an injury.

 4. An "illness" is an abnormal condition or disorder caused by exposure to environmental factors in employment.

 5. Recordable injuries and illness are:

 a. Fatalities

 b. Lost workday cases, other than fatalities.

 c. Any diagnosed occupational illness reported to the employer, not classified as fatalities or lost workday cases, and requiring treatment other than first aid, transfer to another job, termination of employment, or involve restriction of work or motion or loss of consciousness.

 6. Special record keeping requirements involve specified environmental conditions, materials, and employee exposures. Maintenance records of specified equipment (e.g., portable fire extinguishers) are in this category.

V. Security and Employment Issues:

A. The Americans With Disabilities Act of 1990 (ADA):

 1. Regulations to implement Title I are issued by the Equal Opportunity Employment Commission (EEOC). The regulations cover all employers with 15 or more employees in industries affecting commerce.

2. Persons or organizations covered by the Act may not discriminate against a "qualified individual with a disability" in job application, hiring, advancement, discharge, compensation, training, or other terms/conditions of employment.
   a. A "qualified individual with a disability" is a person who can perform the essential functions of the job held or sought, with or without reasonable accommodation.
   b. Reasonable accommodation is making existing facilities readily accessible to and usable by individuals with disabilities, and job structuring, part-time or modified schedules, reassignments, acquisition or modification of equipment or devices, adjustment or modifications of examinations, training materials or policies, the provision of qualified readers or interpreters, and other similar accommodations.

3. Discrimination includes:
   a. Limiting, segregating or classifying a job applicant or employee, on the basis of a disability, in a way that adversely affects opportunities or status;
   b. Participating in a contract or other arrangement or relationship which subjects qualified applicants or employees to discrimination on the basis of a disability;
   c. Utilizing standards, criteria or methods of administration which discriminate on the basis of disability or perpetuate the discrimination of others subject to common administrative control;
   d. Discriminating or denying equal job benefits to a qualified person because of the known disability of one with whom that person associates;
   e. Not making reasonable accommodation to the known mental or physical limitation of an otherwise qualified person.

4. The implementing regulations provide that:
   a. Tests given to persons with impaired sensory, manual, or speaking skills must be administered so that they effectively represent the qualities or skills being tested for rather than the impaired skill, unless the test is specifically for the impaired skill.
   b. Associations with persons of known disability which may not be used as a basis for discrimination include family, business, social or other relationships.
   c. Collective bargaining agreements may not discriminate on the basis of disability.

5. Not protected under the Act are transvestites (Section 508), current illegal drug users (Section 510), homosexuals, bisexuals, persons with sexual behavior or compulsive gambling disorders, kleptomaniacs, and pyromaniacs (Section 511).

6. Employees who completed or are enrolled in a supervised drug rehabilitation program and employees erroneously thought to use drugs are protected.

7. Any medical examination or inquiry into the disability of an applicant or employee is prohibited unless the employer can show a job relationship and a consistent business necessity. Medical examinations after an offer of employment has been made must be given to all prospective employees.

8. **"Readily achievable"** means easily accomplished without much difficulty or expense. The nature and cost of the needed measure, the character and size of the facility, the size, overall financial position, and the character of the operations of the entity which operates the facility are all considered in determining if a measure is "readily achievable."

9. **"Accessibility"** means free of barriers that could prevent a person with impaired mobility from getting to a desired location in the facility, or to use lavatories, lounges, lunchrooms, public telephones, drinking fountains or other amenities.

10. The World Health Organization (WHO) definition of an **"impairment"** is a permanent or transitory psychological, physiological, or anatomical loss or abnormality of structure or function (amputated limb, paralysis after polio, diabetes, mental retardation, impaired hearing or sight).

11. The WHO definition of a **"disability"** includes restrictions on, or the prevention of, carrying out an activity because of an impairment, in the manner or within the range considered normal for a human. Under the ADA, a **"disability"** is a physical or mental impairment that substantially limits one or more of the major life activities of an individual.

12. The WHO defines a **"handicap"** as a disability which interferes with what is expected at a particular time in one's life (inability to care for oneself, communicating thoughts and concerns, developing a capacity for independent economic activity).

VI. Security and Personal Information:

A. Health Insurance Portability and Accountability Act ("HIPAA") of 1996

This Act encourages health care businesses to engage in electronic transactions and requires new safeguards to protect the security and confidentiality of transaction information for patients.

B. Gramm-Leach Bliley Act

This Act requires that financial institutions (i.e., banks, credit unions, tax services, mortgage companies and investment advisors) take steps to ensure the security and confidentiality of their customers' non-public personal information be protected from identity theft.

C. Sarbanes-Oxley Act

This Act established new or enhanced standards for all United States registered public companies and public accounting firms in connection with implementing safeguards against accounting errors and/or fraudulent management practices.

VII. The Employee Polygraph Protection Act of 1988 ("EPPA"):

The Employee Polygraph Protection Act of 1988 ("EPPA") provides for the use of polygraph examinations in the workplace in certain specific situations. It sets certain requirements for the employer and the examiner. Where those requirements are followed, polygraph examinations — both preemployment and incident-specific — may lawfully occur.

The EPPA describes the following situations in which polygraph examinations may be conducted in the workplace:

A. An employer may use polygraphs to assist in their "ongoing investigation" of certain kinds of workplace crime.

B. An employer who engages in providing certain kinds of security services may use polygraphs for pre-employment screening of certain prospective employees.

C. An employer who engages in manufacturing, distributing or dispensing certain controlled drugs may use polygraphs for some pre-employment screening of certain prospective employees and for investigation of certain incident-specific losses.

VIII. Federal Sentencing Guidelines:

A. The Organizational Sentencing Guidelines (OSG) cover antitrust, tax, money laundering, fraud, Employment Retirement Income Security Act (ERISA), securities, and environmental law violations.

B. The OSG are to encourage business to deter and detect criminal violations. They significantly increase the penalties for a business which makes no effort to detect, report, and deter crime and significantly reduce penalties for a company which does so.

C. A company found guilty of violation of a federal criminal statute will be required:

1. To make restitution to any party injured by the criminal conduct, and

2. To pay a fine which is not tax deductible.

D. The fine consists of a "base fine" which is multiplied by a "culpability score" to determine a minimum and maximum range within which the court imposes a fine.

E. The base fine is the greater of:

1. The pre-tax gain to the company from the crime, or

2. The loss to any party intentionally injured by the crime, or

3. An amount, ranging from $5000 to $72,500, determined from a "level of seriousness" table provided by the sentencing commission.

F. In determining the culpability score, every business starts with a rating of 5 and aggravating or mitigating factors move the score within the range of 0 to 10.

G. Aggravating factors include:

1. Participation, tolerance, or disregard of criminal conduct by "high level" or "substantial authority" personnel in a large organization. (Add 5 points)

2. A history of similar conduct within the last 5 years. (Add 2 points)

3. Obstruction of justice in the course of investigation, prosecution, or sentencing. (Add 3 points)

H. Mitigating factors include:

1. Self reporting, cooperation with an investigation, and accepting responsibility for the conduct of the organization. (Subtract 5 points)

2. An effective compliance program(s) to prevent and detect criminal conduct. (Subtract 3 points)

I. An effective compliance program has seven mandatory components:

1. Establishment of compliance standards which are reasonably capable of preventing criminal conduct.

2. Specific responsibility for high level management to oversee the standards.

3. Communication of standards and offering training in compliance issues to employees.

4. Tests of the compliance system with auditing, monitoring, and other tests designed to detect criminal conduct.

5. Due care to ensure that discretionary authority is not delegated to individuals with a propensity to engage in illegal conduct.

6. Enforcement using disciplinary procedures which include provisions for discipline of individuals who fail to detect or report and offense.

7. All reasonable steps, after an offense has been detected, to prevent a future similar occurrence.

J. A determination, after the fact, that an effective compliance program did not exist may result in a probation status which may require that the company:

1. Publicize its criminal acts at its own expense as directed by the court.

2. File periodic financial reports with the court.

3. Submit to periodic examination by court appointed experts.

1. A crime can be described as:
   a. A violent act
   b. A violation of one's privacy
   c. An act or omission prohibited by law for which a penalty is provided
   d. A public wrong

2. The federal definition of a felony is any offense:
   a. Which calls for punishment
   b. Punishable by death
   c. For which the minimum penalty is $500
   d. Punishable by imprisonment for a term exceeding one year

3. In federal system, the chief prosecutor is:
   a. The district attorney
   b. The state's attorney
   c. The commonwealth attorney
   d. The U.S. Attorney

4. The main purpose of a grand jury is to:
   a. Determine whether or not an individual has committed a crime
   b. Determine guilt
   c. Determine whether there is sufficient evidence that a crime has been committed and that the accused probably committed it.
   d. Determine the nature of the punishment

5. The purpose of bail is to:
   a. Confine the accused pending trial
   b. To take dangerous offenders off the streets
   c. Make certain each accused is offered his constitutional right to put up security in order to gain his release
   d. To assure the appearance of the accused in court

6. In a criminal trial, the burden of proof required to find guilt is:
   a. Preponderance of evidence
   b. Beyond a reasonable doubt
   c. Reasonableness of presentation
   d. Amount necessary to convince a majority of jurors

7. The release of a convicted person under certain conditions without having to be imprisoned is known as:
   a. Probation
   b. Parole
   c. Corpus Juris
   d. Detainer

8. The release from confinement of a person who has served part of a sentence is called:
   a. Probation
   b. Parole
   c. Reprieve
   d. Commutation

9. The process in which a court abides by a previous court decision is known as:
   a. Corpus Delicti
   b. Habeas corpus
   c. Ex-post facto
   d. Stare decisis

10. The crime of unlawful entry into or remaining within a building, with intent to commit some crime there in is:
    a. Robbery
    b. Trespass
    c. Burglary
    d. Embezzlement

11. To make proof of intent easier in proving shoplifting, many stores have a policy which requires apprehension of a suspect to be made:
    a. After the accused leaves the premises
    b. As soon as the theft occurs
    c. As soon as the material is concealed
    d. Only on issuance of a warrant

12. The private person generally may arrest without a warrant:
    a. For a felony
    b. For misdemeanors
    c. For a crime committed in his presence
    d. Where he had "reasonable cause" to believe the person arrested committed the crime.

13. The Supreme Court decision which holds that no suspect, in a custodial environment, may be asked any questions until he has first been warned that he need not make any statement and advised of other rights is the :
    a. McNabb decision
    b. Mallory decision
    c. Ennis decision
    d. Miranda decision

14. The Amendment to the U.S. Constitution which deals with searches and seizures is:
    a. 1st Amendment
    b. 4th Amendment
    c. 5th Amendment
    d. 6th Amendment

15. As a general rule, searches may be made of employee lockers and desks located on the premises of the company:
    a. If consent is given by the employee
    b. Under no circumstances
    c. If done by the local police
    d. If done by the security manager

16. When a law enforcement agent induces the commission of an offence not otherwise contemplated, the accused may use an affirmative defense known as:
    a. Hearsay
    b. Illegally induced crime
    c. Ex-post facto law
    d. Entrapment

17. The imputation of another's negligence to the employer is described as:
    a. Gross liability
    b. Vicarious liability
    c. Agency liability
    d. Net liability

18. A willful or negligent wrong done by one person to another is a:
    a. Crime
    b. Misdemeanor
    c. Felony
    d. Tort

19. The unlawful taking of property by force or threat of force constitutes the crime of:
    a. Burglary
    b. Robbery
    c. Assault and battery
    d. Larceny

20. Deadly force may be used to defend yourself if you:
    a. Reasonably believe deadly force is necessary to protect yourself or another from unlawful use of deadly force of a third party
    b. Your home is broken into
    c. You are protecting your property
    d. You are attacked by a drug addict

21. In a criminal prosecution the measure of evidence used to find the accused guilty is:
    a. Beyond a reasonable doubt
    b. Probable cause
    c. Suspicion
    d. Preponderance of evidence

22. The term "foreseeability" refers to:
    a. Illegal action
    b. Whether a harm is likely to occur
    c. Administrative law
    d. Strict liability

23. Which is **not** considered a Comprehensive Environmental Compliance Program?
    a. Discipline wrongdoers
    b. Establish an incentive program
    c. Audit and monitor all activities outside the company
    d. Evaluate the whole effort by retaining an outside expert

24. The relationship in which two parties agree that one will act as the representative of the other is known as:
    a. Contractual relationship
    b. Fiduciary relationship
    c. Partnership relationship
    d. Agency relationship

25. An agent can ordinarily act for the principal in such a way to make the principal legally responsible provided the agent:
    a. Is authorized by the principal to act that way
    b. Acts reasonable
    c. Notifies the principal within 24 hours
    d. Is eighteen years of age

26. If an employee, while acting within the scope of his/her employment, injures another party and that party dies, the employee's employer can be:
    a. Held liable in a civil suit for damages
    b. Subjected to criminal liability
    c. Held liable for both civil and criminal action
    d. Criminally liable if the act is malicious

27. The affirmative act of concealing the commission of a felony, cognizable by a court of the U.S. by someone having knowledge of the felony is a violation called:
    a. Misprison of a felony
    b. Accessory
    c. Subornation of perjury
    d. Obstruction of justice

28. Wrongful appropriation of the personal property of another to the use of the taker is a tort called:
    a. Conversion
    b. Larceny
    c. Trespass
    d. Embezzlement

29. A writ issued by a court directing the recipient to appear and testify is a:
    a. Warrant
    b. Subpoena
    c. Writ of Mandamus
    d. Writ of prohibition

30. The general rule as to the amount of force a security officer is permitted to use in order to accomplish a lawful arrest is:
    a. The amount needed to assure that the security officer is not injured
    b. Up to and including deadly force
    c. The maximum amount
    d. Only such force as is reasonably necessary

31. The federal agency in charge of disaster planning is:
    a. Federal Emergency Management Agency
    b. Office of Civil Defense
    c. Department of the Army
    d. Department of Interior

32. Question on an application left blank or field investigative inquiries dealing with union membership or affiliation should be avoided as they may lead to charges which constitute violation of:
    a. National Labor Relations Act
    b. The Civil Rights Act of 1964
    c. The Civil Rights Act of 1976
    d. The Fair Credit Reporting Act

33. Identify the act which basically prohibits discrimination, discharge, failure or refusal to hire, on any of the grounds of race, color, religion, sex, or national origin:
    a. Fair Credit Reporting Act
    b. The Civil Rights Law of 1964
    c. First Amendment
    d. Omnibus Crime Control Act

1. c. An act or omission prohibited by law for which a penalty is provided
   Source: *Protection of Assets Manual*

2. d. Any offense punishable by imprisonment for a term exceeding one year
   Source: *Protection of Assets Manual*

3. d. The U.S. Attorney
   Source: *Protection of Assets Manual*

4. c. Determine whether there is sufficient evidence that a crime has been committed and that the accused probably committed it.
   Source: *Protection of Assets Manual*

5. d. To assure that appearance of the accused in court
   Source: *Protection of Assets Manual*

6. b. Beyond a reasonable doubt
   Source: *Protection of Assets Manual*

7. a. Probation
   Source: *Protection of Assets Manual*

8. b. Parole
   Source: *Protection of Assets Manual*

9. d. Stare decisis
   Source: *Protection of Assets Manual*

10. c. Burglary
    Source: *Protection of Assets Manual*

11. a. After the accused leaves the premises
    Source: *Protection of Assets Manual*

12. c. For a crime committed in his presence
    Source: *Protection of Assets Manual*

13. d. Miranda decision
    Source: *Protection of Assets Manual*

14. b. 4th Amendment
    Source: *Protection of Assets Manual*

15. a. If consent is given by the employee
    Source: *Protection of Assets Manual*

16. d. Entrapment
    Source: *Protection of Assets Manual*

17. b. Vicarious liability
    Source: *Protection of Assets Manual*

18. d. Tort
    Source: *Protection of Assets Manual*

19. b. Robbery
    Source: *Protection of Assets Manual*

20. a. One reasonably believes deadly force is necessary to protect himself or another from unlawful use of deadly force of a third party.
    Source: *Protection of Assets Manual*

21. a. Beyond a reasonable doubt
    Source: *Protection of Assets Manual*

22. b. Whether a harm is likely to occur
    Source: *Security and Loss Prevention,* p. 76

23. c. Audit and monitor all activities outside the company
    Source: *Security and Loss Prevention,* p.80

24. d. Agency relationship
    Source: *Protection of Assets Manual*

25. a. The agent is authorized by the principal to act that way
    Source: *Protection of Assets Manual*

26. a. Held liable in a civil suit for damages
    Source: *Protection of Assets Manual*

27. a. Misprison of a felony
    Source: *Protection of Assets Manual*

28. a. Conversion
    Source: *Protection of Assets Manual*

29. b. Subpoena
    Source: *Protection of Assets Manual*

30. d. Only such force as is reasonable necessary
    Source: *Protection of Assets Manual*

31. a. Federal Emergency Management Agency
    Source: *Protection of Assets Manual*

32. a. National Labor Relations Act
    Source: *Protection of Assets Manual*

33. b. The Civil Rights Act of 1964
    Source: *Protection of Assets Manual*

ASIS International. (2008). *Protection of Assets Manual,* Alexandria, VA: ASIS International.

Fischer, Robert J., Halibozek, Edward, and Green, Gion (2008). *Introduction to Security,* (8th ed.). Elsevier/Butterworth-Heinemann, Burlington, MA.

Purpura, Philip P. (2008). *Security and Loss Prevention: An Introduction,* (5th ed.). Elsevier/Butterworth-Heinemann, Burlington, MA.

Narcotics of Natural Origin

The poppy Papaver somniferum is the source for nonsynthetic narcotics. It was grown in the Mediterranean region as early as 5000 B.C., and has since been cultivated in a number of countries throughout the world. The milky fluid that seeps from incisions in the unripe seedpod of this poppy has, since ancient times, been scraped by hand and air dried to produce what is known as opium.

A more modern method of harvesting is by the industrial poppy straw process of extracting alkaloids from the mature dried plant. The extract may be in liquid, solid or powder form, although most poppy straw concentrate available commercially is a fine brownish powder. More than 500 tons of opium or its equivalent in poppy straw concentrate are legally imported into the United States annually for legitimate medical use.

Opium

There were no legal restrictions on the importation or use of opium until the early 1900s. In the United States, the unrestricted availability of opium, the influx of opium smoking immigrants from the Orient, and the invention of the hypodermic needle contributed to the more severe variety of compulsive drug abuse seen at the turn of this century. In those days, medicines often contained opium without any warning label. Today, there are state, federal, and international laws governing the production and distribution of narcotic substances.

Although opium is used in the form of paragoric to treat diarrhea, most opium imported into the United States is broken down into its alkaloid constituents. These alkaloids are divided into two distinct chemical classes, phenanthrenes and isoquinolines. The principal phenanthrenes are morphine, codeine and thebaine, while the isoquinolines have no significant central nervous system effects and are not regulated under the CSA.

Morphine

Morphine, the principal constituent of opium, can range in concentration from 4 to 21 percent (note: commercial opium is standardized to contain 10 percent morphine). It is one of the most effective drugs known for the relief of pain, and remains the standard against which new analgesics are measured.

Morphine is marketed in a variety of forms including oral solutions (Roxanol), sustained-release tablets (MSIR and MS-Contin), suppositories and injectable preparations. It may be administered orally, subcutaneously, intramuscularly, and intravenously, the latter method being the one most frequently used by addicts. Tolerance and physical dependence develop rapidly in the user. Only a small part of the morphine obtained from opium is used directly; most of it is converted to codeine and other derivatives.

Codeine

This alkaloid is found in opium in concentrations ranging from 0.7 to 2.5 percent. Most codeine used in the United States is produced from morphine. Compared to morphine, codeine produces less analgesia, sedation and respiratory depression, and is frequently taken orally.

Codeine is medically prescribed for the relief of moderate pain. It is made into tablets either alone or in combination with aspirin or acetaminophen (Tylenol). Codeine is an effective cough suppressant and is found in a number of liquid preparations. Codeine products are also used to a lesser extent as an injectable solution for the treatment of pain. It is by far the most widely used naturally occurring narcotic in medical treatment in the world. Codeine products are encountered on the illicit market, frequently in combination with glutethimide (Doriden) or carisoprodol (Soma).

Thebaine

A minor constituent of opium, thebaine is chemically similar to both morphine and codeine, but produces stimulatory rather than depressant effects. Thebaine is not used therapeutically, but is converted into a variety of compounds including codeine, hydrocodone, oxycodone, oxymorphone, nalbuphine, naloxone, naltrexone and buprenorphine. It is controlled in Schedule II of the CSA as well as under international law.

SEMI-SYNTHETIC NARCOTICS

The following narcotics are among the more significant substances that have been derived by modification of the phenanthrene alkaloids contained in opium:

Heroin

First synthesized from morphine in 1874, heroin was not extensively used in medicine until the beginning of this century. Commercial production of the new pain remedy was first started in 1898. While it received widespread acceptance from the medical profession, physicians remained unaware of its potential for addiction for years. The first comprehensive control of heroin in the United States was established with the Harrison Narcotic Act of 1914.

Pure heroin is a white powder with a bitter taste. Most illicit heroin is a powder which may vary in color from white to dark brown because of impurities left from the manufacturing process or the presence of additives. Pure heroin is rarely sold on the street. A "bag"—slang for a single dosage unit of heroin—may contain 100 mg of powder, only a portion of which is heroin; the remainder could be sugars, starch, powdered milk, or quinine. Traditionally, the purity of heroin in a bag has ranged from 1 to 10 percent; more recently heroin purity has ranged from 1 to 98 percent, with a national average of 35 percent.

Another form of heroin known as "black tar" has also become increasingly available in the western United States. The color and consistency of black tar heroin result from the crude processing methods used to illicitly manufacture heroin in Mexico. Black tar heroin may be sticky like roofing tar or hard like coal, and its color may vary from dark brown to black. Black tar heroin is often sold on the street in its tar-like state at purities ranging from 20 to 80 percent. Black tar heroin is most frequently dissolved, diluted and injected.

The typical heroin user today consumes more heroin than a typical user did just a decade ago, which is not surprising given the higher purity currently available at the street level. Until recently, heroin in the United States almost exclusively was injected either intravenously, subcutaneously, (skin-popping), or intracuscularly. Injection is the most practical and efficient way to administer low-purity heroin. The availability of higher purity heroin has meant that users now can snort or smoke the narcotic. Evidence suggests that heroin snorting is widespread or increasing in those areas of the country where high purity heroin is available, generally in the northeastern United States. This method of administration may be more appealing to new users because it eliminates both the fear of acquiring syringe-borne diseases such as HIV/AIDS and hepatitis, and the historical stigma attached to intravenous heroin use.

Hydromorphone

Hydromorphone (Dilaudid) is marketed both in tablet and injectable forms. Its analgesic potency is from two to eight times that of morphine. Much sought after by narcotic addicts, hydrommorphone is usually obtained by the abuser through fraudulent prescriptions or theft. The tablets are dissolved and injected as a substitute for heroin.

Oxycodone

Oxycodone is synthesized from thebaine. It is similar to codeine, but is more potent and has a higher dependence potential. It is effective orally and is marketed in combination with aspirin (Percodan) or acetaminophen (Percocet) for the relief of pain. Addicts take these tablets orally or dissolve them in water, filter out the insoluble material, and "mainline" the active drug.

SYNTHETIC NARCOTICS

In contrast to the pharmaceutical products derived directly or indirectly from narcotics of natural origin, synthetic narcotics are produced entirely within the laboratory. The continuing search for products that retain the analgesic properties of morphine without the consequent dangers of tolerance and dependence has yet to yield a product that is not susceptible to abuse. A number of clandestinely-produced drugs as well as drugs that have accepted medical uses fall into this category.

Meperidine

Introduced as a potent analgesic in the 1930s, meperidine produces effects that are similar but not identical to morphine (shorter duration of action and reduced antitussive and antidiarrheal actions). Currently it is used for the relief of moderate to severe pain, particularly in obstetrics and post-operative situations. Meperidine is available in tablets, syrups and injectable forms (Demerol). Several analogues of meperidine have been clandestinely produced. One noteworthy analogue is a preparation with a neurotoxic by-product that has produced irreversible Parkinsonism.

Methadone & Related Drugs

German scientists synthesized methadone during World War II because of a shortage of morphine. Although chemically unlike morphine or heroin, methadone produces many of the same effects. Introduced into the United States in 1947 as an analgesic (Dolophine), it is primarily used today for the treatment of narcotic addiction (Methadone). The effects of methadone are longer lasting than those of morphine-based drugs. Methadone's effects can last up to 24 hours, thereby permitting administration only once a day in heroin detoxification and maintenance programs. Methadone is almost as effective when administered orally as it is by injection. Tolerance and dependence may develop, and withdrawal symptoms, though they develop more slowly and are less severe than those of morphine and heroin, are more prolonged. Ironically, methadone used to control narcotic addiction is frequently encountered on the illicit market and has been associated with a number of overdose deaths.

Fentanyl

First synthesized in Belgium in the late 1950s, fentanyl was introduced into clinical practice in the 1960s as an intravenous anesthetic under the trade name of Sublimaze. Thereafter, two other fentanyl analogues were introduced; alfentanil (Alfenta), an ultra-short (5-10 minutes) acting analgesic, and sufentanil (Sufenta), an exceptionally potent analgesic for use in heart surgery. Today, fentanyls are extensively used for anesthesia and analgesia. Illicit use of pharmaceutical fentanyls first appeared in the mid 1970s in the medical community and continues to be a problem in the United States. To date, over 12 different analogues of fentanyl have been produced clandestinely and identified in the U.S. drug traffic. The biological effects of the fentanyls are indistinguishable from those of heroin, with the exception that the fentanyls may be hundreds of times more potent. Fentanyls are most commonly used by intravenous administration, but like heroin, they may also be smoked or snorted.

Pentazocine

The effort to find an effective analgesic that is less dependence-producing led to the development of pentazocine (Talwin). Introduced as an algesic in 1967, it was frequently encountered in the illicit trade, usually in combination with tripelennamine and placed into Schedule IV in 1979. An attempt at reducing the abuse of this drug was made with the introduction of Talwin Nx. This product contains a quantity of antagonist sufficient to counteract the morphine-like effects of pentazocine if the tablets are dissolved and injected.

DEPRESSANTS

Historically, people of almost every culture have used chemical agents to induce sleep, relieve stress, and allay anxiety. While alcohol is one of the oldest and most universal agents used for these purposes, hundreds of substances have been developed that produce central nervous system (CNS) depression. These drugs have been referred to as "downers," sedatives, hypnotics, minor tranquilizers, anxiolytics, and antianxiety medications. Unlike most other classes of drugs of abuse, depressants, except for methaqualone, are rarely produced in clandestine laboratories. Generally, legitimate pharmaceutical products are diverted to the illicit market.

Although a number of depressants (i.e., chloral hydrate, glutethimide, meprobamate and methaqualone) have been important players in the milieu of depressant use and abuse, two major groups of depressants have dominated the licit and illicit market for nearly a century, first barbiturates and now benzodiazepines.

Barbiturates were very popular in the first half of this century. In moderate amounts, these drugs produce a state of intoxication that is remarkably similar to alcohol intoxication. Symptoms include slurred speech, loss of motor coordination and impaired judgment. Depending on the dose, frequency, and duration of use, one can rapidly develop tolerance, physical dependence and psychological dependence on barbiturates. With the development of tolerance, the margin of safety between the effective dose and the lethal dose becomes very narrow. That is, in order to obtain the same level of intoxication, the tolerant abuser may raise his or her dose to a level that can produce coma and death. Although many individuals have taken barbiturates therapeutically without harm, concern about the addiction potential of barbiturates and the ever-increasing numbers of fatalities associated with them led to the development of alternative medications. Today, only about 20 percent of all depressant prescriptions in the United States are for barbiturates.

Benzodiazepines were first marketed in the 1960s. Touted as much safer depressants with far less addiction potential than barbiturates, these drugs today account for about 30% of all prescriptions for controlled substances. It has only been recently that an awareness has developed that benzodiazepines share many of the undesirable side effects of the barbiturates. A number of toxic CNS effects are seen with chronic high dose benzodiazepine therapy. These include headache, irritability, confusion, memory impairment, depression, insomnia and tremor. The risk of developing over-sedation, dizziness and confusion increases substantially with higher doses of benzodiazepines. Prolonged use can lead to physical dependence even at recommended dosages. Unlike barbiturates, large doses of benzodiazepines are rarely fatal unless combined with other drugs or alcohol. Although primary abuse of benzodiazepines is well documented, abuse of these drugs usually occurs as part of a pattern of multiple drug abuse. For example, heroin or cocaine abusers will use benzodiazepines and other depressants to augment heir "high" or alter the side effects associated with over-stimulation or narcotic withdrawal.

There are marked similarities among the withdrawal symptoms seen with all drugs classified as depressants. In it mildest form, the withdrawal syndrome may produce insomnia and anxiety, usually the same symptoms that initiated the drug use. With a greater level of dependence, tremors and weakness are also present, and in its most severe form, the withdrawal syndrome can cause seizures and delirium. Unlike the withdrawal syndrome seen with most other drugs of abuse, withdrawal from depressants can be life-threatening.

Chloral Hydrate

The oldest of the hypnotic (sleep inducing) depressants, chloral hydrate was first synthesized in 1832. Marketed as syrups or soft gelatin capsules, chloral hydrate takes effect in a relatively short time (30 minutes) and will induce sleep in about an hour. A solution of chloral hydrate and alcohol constituted the infamous "knockout drops" or Mickey Finn." At therapeutic doses, chloral hydrate has little effect on respiration and blood pressure but, a toxic dose produces severe respiratory depression and very low blood pressure. Although chloral hydrate is still encountered today, its use declined with the introduction of the barbiturates.

Barbiturates

Barbiturates (derivatives of barbituric acid) were first introduced for medical use in the early 1900s. More than 2,500 barbiturates have been synthesized, and in the height of their popularity about 50 were marketed for human use. Today, only about a dozen are used. Barbiturates produce a wide spectrum of CNS depression, from mild sedation to coma, and have been used as sedatives, hypnotics, anesthetics and anticonvulsants.

The primary differences among many of these products are how fast they produce an effect and how long those effects last. Barbiturates are classified as ultrashort, short, intermediate and long-acting.

The ultrashort-acting barbiturates produce anesthesia within about one minute after intravenous administration. Those in current medical use are methohexital (Brevital), thiamylal (Surital) and thiopental (Pentothal).

Barbiturate abusers prefer the short-acting and intermediate-acting barbiturates pentobarbital (Nembutal), and secobarbital (Amytal). Other short- and intermediate-acting barbiturates are butalbital (Fiorinal, Fioricet), butabarbital (Butisol), talbutal (Lotusate) and aprobarbital (Alurate). After oral administration, the onset of action is from 15 to 40 minutes and the effects last up to 6 hours. These drugs are primarily used for sedation or to induce sleep. Veterinarians use pentobarbital for anesthesia and euthanasia.

Long-acting barbiturates include phenobarbital (Luminal) and mephobarbital (Mebaral). Effects of these drugs are realized in about one hour and last for about 12 hours, and are used primarily for daytime sedation and the treatment of seizure disorders or mild anxiety.

Glutethimide and Methaqualone

Glutethimide (Doriden) was introduced in 1954 and methaqualone (Quaalude, Sopor) in 1965 as safe barbiturate substitutes. Experience showed, however, that their addiction liability and the severity of withdrawal symptoms were similar to those of barbiturates.

By 1972, "luding out," taking methaqualone with wine, was a popular college pastime. Excessive use leads to tolerance, dependence and withdrawal symptoms similar to those of barbiturates. Overdose by glutethimide and methaqualone is more difficult to treat than barbiturate overdose, and deaths have frequently occurred. In the United States, the marketing of methaqualone pharmaceutical products stopped in 1984 and methaqualone was transferred to Schedule I of the CSA. In 1991, glutethimide was transferred into Schedule II in response to an upsurge in the prevalence of diversion, abuse and overdose deaths.

Meprobamate

Meprobamate was introduced as an antianxiety agent in 1955 and is prescribed primarily to treat anxiety, tension and associated muscle spasms. More than 50 tons are distributed annually in the United States under its generic name and brand names such as Miltown and Equanil. Its onset and duration of action are similar to the intermediate-acting barbiturates; however, therapeutic doses of meprobamate produce less sedation and toxicity than barbiturates. Excessive use can result in psychological and physical dependence.

Benzodiazepines

The benzodiazepine family of depressants are used therapeutically to produce sedation, induce sleep, relieve anxiety and muscle spasms, and to prevent seizures. In general, benzodiazepines act as hypnotics in high doses, as anxiolytics in moderate doses, and as sedatives in low doses. Of the drugs marketed in the United States that affect CNS function, benzodiazepines are among the most widely prescribed medications and, unfortunately, are frequently abused. Fifteen members of this group are presently marketed in the United States and an additional 20 are marketed in other countries.

Like the barbiturates, benzodiazepines differ from one another in how fast they take effect and how long the effects last. Shorter-acting benzodiazepines, used to manage insomnia, include estazolam (ProSom), flurazepam (Dalmane), quazepam (Doral), temazepam (Restoril) and triazolam (Halcion).

Benzodiazepines with longer durations of action include alprazolam (Xanax), chlordiazepoxide (Librium), clorazepate (Tranxene), diazepam (Valium), halazepam (Paxipam), lorazepam (Ativan), oxazepam (Serax) and prazepam (Centrax). These longer acting drugs are primarily used for the treatment of general anxiety. Midazolam (Versed) is available in the United States only in an injectable form for an adjunct to anesthesia. Clonazepam (Klonopin) is recommended for use in the treatment of seizure disorders.

Flunitrazepam (Rohypnol), which produces diazepam-like effects, is becoming increasingly popular among young people as a drug of abuse. The drug is not marketed legally in the United States, but is smuggled in by traffickers.

Benzodiazepines are classified in the CSA as Schedule IV depressants. Repeated use of large doses or, in some cases, daily use of therapeutic doses of benzodiazepines is associated with physical dependence. The withdrawal syndrome is similar to that of alcohol withdrawal and is generally more unpleasant and longer lasting than narcotic withdrawal and frequently requires hospitalization. Abrupt cessation of benzodiazepines is not recommended, and tapering-down the dose eliminates many of the unpleasant symptoms.

Given the number of people who are prescribed benzodiapines, relatively few patients increase their dosage or engage in drug-seeking behavior. However, those individuals who do abuse benzodiazepines often maintain their drug supply by getting prescriptions from several doctors, forging prescriptions or buying diverted pharmaceutical products on the illicit market. Abuse is frequently associated with adolescents and young adults who take benzodiazepines to obtain a "high." This intoxicated state results in reduced inhibition and impaired judgement. Concurrent use of alcohol or other depressants with benzodiazepines can be life-threatening. Abuse of benzodiazepines is particularly high among heroin and cocaine abusers. Approximately 50 percent of people entering treatment for narcotic or cocaine addiction also report abusing benzodiazepines.

STIMULANTS

Stimulants are sometimes referred to as "uppers" and reverse the effects of fatigue on both mental and physical tasks. Two commonly used stimulants are nicotine, found in tobacco products, and caffeine, an active ingredient in coffee, tea, some soft drinks and many non-prescription medicines. Used in moderation, these substances tend to relieve malaise and increase alertness. Although the use of these products has been an accepted part of our culture, the recognition of their adverse effects has resulted in a proliferation of caffeine-free products and efforts to discourage cigarette smoking.

A number of stimulants, however, are under the regulatory control of the CSA. Some of these controlled substances are available by prescription for legitimate medical use in the treatment of obesity, narcolepsy and attention deficit hyperactivity disorders. As drugs of abuse, stimulants are frequently taken to produce a sense of exhilaration, enhance self esteem, improve mental and physical performance, increase activity, reduce appetite, produce prolonged wakefulness, and to "get high." They are recognized as among the most potent agents of reward and reinforcement that underlie the problem of dependence.

Stimulants are both diverted from legitimate channels and clandestinely manufactured exclusively for the illicit market. They are taken orally, sniffed, smoked and injected. Smoking, snorting or injecting stimulants produces a sudden sensation known as a "rush" or a "flash." Abuse is often associated with a pattern of binge use, that is, consuming large doses of stimulants sporadically. Heavy users may inject themselves every few hours, continuing until they have depleted their drug supply or reached a point of delirium, psychosis and physical exhaustion. During this period of heavy use, all other interests become secondary to recreating the initial euphoric rush. Tolerance can develop rapidly, and both physical and psychological dependence occur. Abrupt cessation, even after a weekend binge, is commonly followed by depression, anxiety, drug craving and extreme fatigue ("crash").

Therapeutic levels of stimulants can produce exhilaration, extended wakefulness and loss of appetite. These effects are greatly intensified when large doses of stimulants are taken. Physical side effects—including dizziness, tremor, headache, flushed skin, chest pain with palpitations, excessive sweating, vomiting and abdominal cramps—may occur as a result of taking too large a dose at one time or taking large doses over an extended period of time. Psychological effects include agitation, hostility, panic, aggression and suicidal or homicidal tendencies. Paranoia, sometimes accompanied by both auditory and visual hallucinations, may also occur. In overdose, unless there is medical intervention, high fever, convulsions and cardiovascular collapse may precede death. Because accidental death is partially due to the effects of stimulants on the body's cardiovascular and temperature-regulating systems, physical exertion increases the hazards of stimulant use.

Cocaine

Cocaine, the most potent stimulant of natural origin, is extracted from the leaves of the coca plant (Erythroxylon coca), which is indigenous to the Andean highlands of South America. Natives in this region chew or brew coca leaves into a tea for refreshment and to relieve fatigue similar to the customs of chewing tobacco and drinking tea or coffee.

Pure cocaine was first isolated in the 1880s and used as a local anesthetic in eye surgery. It was particulary useful in surgery of the nose and throat because of its ability to provide anesthesia as well as to constrict blood vessels and limit bleeding. Many of its therapeutic applications are now obsolete due to the development of safer drugs.

Illicit cocaine is usually distributed as a white crystaline powder or as an off-white chunky material. The powder, usually cocaine hydrochloride, is often diluted with a variety of substances, the most common of which are sugars such as lactose, inositol and mannitol, and local anesthetics such as lidocaine. The adulteration increases the volume and thus multiplies profits. Cocaine hydrochloride is generally snorted or dissolved in water and injected. It is rarely smoked.

"Crack," the chunk or "rock" form of cocaine, is a ready-to-use freebase. On the illicit market it is sold in small, inexpensive dosage units that are smoked. With crack came a dramatic increase in drug abuse problems and violence. Smoking delivers large quantities of cocaine to the lungs, producing effects comparable to intravenous injection; these effects are felt almost immediately after smoking, are very intense, and are quickly over. Once introduced in the mid-1980s, crack abuse spread rapidly and made the cocaine experience available to anyone with $10 and access to a dealer. In addition to other toxicities associated with cocaine abuse, cocaine smokers suffer from acute respiratory problems including cough, shortness of breath, and severe chest pains with lung trauma and bleeding.

The intensity of the psychological effects of cocaine, as with most psychoactive drugs, depends on the dose and rate of entry to the brain. Cocaine reaches the brain through the snorting method in three to five minutes. Intravenous injection of cocaine produces a rush in 15 to 30 seconds and smoking produces an almost immediate intense experience. The euphoric effects of cocaine are almost indistinguishable from those of amphetamine, although they do not last as long. These intense effects can be followed by a dysphoric crash. To avoid the fatigue and the depression of "coming down", frequent repeated doses are taken. Excessive doses of cocaine may lead to seizures and death from respiratory failure, stroke, cerebral hemorrhage or heart failure. There is no specific antidote for cocaine overdose.

According to the 1993 Household Drug Survey, the number of Americans who used cocaine within the preceding month of the survey numbered about 1.3 million; occasional users (those who used cocaine less often than monthly) numbered at approximately 3 million, down from 8.1 million in 1985. The number of weekly users has remained steady at around a half million since 1983.

Amphetamines

Amphetamine, dextroamphetamine, and methamphetamine are collectively referred to as amphetamines. Their chemical properties and actions are so similar that even experienced users have difficulty knowing which drug they have taken.

Amphetamine was first marketed in the 1930s as Benzedrine in an over-the-counter inhaler to treat nasal congestion. By 1937, amphetamine was available by prescription in tablet form and was used in the treatment of the sleeping disorder narcolepsy and the behavioral syndrome called minimal brain dysfunction (MBD), which today is called attention deficit hyperactivity disorder (ADHD). During World War II, amphetamine was widely used to keep the fighting men going; both dextroamphetamine (Dexedrine) and methamphetamine (Methedrine) became readily available.

As use of amphetamines spread, so did their abuse. Amphetamines became a cure-all for helping truckers to complete their long routes without falling asleep, for weight control, for helping athletes perform better and train longer, and for treating mild depression. Intravenous amphetamine abuse spread among a subculture known as "speed freaks". With experience, it became evident that the dangers of abuse of these drugs outweighed most of their therapeutic uses.

Increased control measures were initiated in 1965 with amendments to the federal food and drug laws to curb the black market in amphetamines. Many pharmaeutical amphetamine products were removed from the market and doctors prescribed those that remained less freely. In order to meet the ever-increasing black market demand for amphetamines, clandestine laboratory production mushroomed, especially methamphetamine laboratories on the West Coast. Today, most amphetamines distributed to the black market are produced in clandestine laboratories.

Amphetamines are generally taken orally or injected. However, the addition of "ice," the slang name for crystallized methamphetamine hydrochloride, has promoted smoking as another mode of administration. Just as "crack" is smokable cocaine, "ice" is smokable methamphetamine. Both drugs are highly addictive and toxic.

The effects of amphetamines, especially methamphetamine, are similar to cocaine, but their onset is slower and their duration is longer. In general, chronic abuse produces a psychosis that resembles schizophrenia and is characterized by paranoia, picking at the skin, preoccupation with one's own thoughts, and auditory and visual hallucinations. Violent and erratic behavior is frequently seen among chronic abusers of amphetamines.

Methcathinone

Methcathinone is one of the more recent drugs of abuse in the United States and was placed into Schedule I of the CSA in 1993. Known on the streets as "Cat," it is a structural analogue of methamphetamine and cathinone. Clandestinely manufactured, methcathinone is almost exclusively sold in the stable and highly water soluble hydrochloride salt form. It is most commonly snorted, although it can be taken orally by mixing it with a beverage or diluted in water and injected intravenously.

Methcathinone has an abuse potential equivalent to methamphetamine, and produces amphetamine-like activity including superabundant energy, hyperactivity, extended wakefulness and loss of appetite. Pleasant effects include a burst of energy, speeding of the mind, increased feelings of invincibility and euphoria. Unpleasant effects include anxiety, tremor, insomnia, weight loss, dehydration, sweating, stomach pains, pounding heart, nose bleeds and body aches. Toxic levels may produce convulsions, paranoia, and hallucinations. Like other CNS stimulants, binges are usually followed by a "crash" with periods of variable depression.

Khat

For centuries, khat, the fresh young leaves of the "Catha edulis" shrub, have been consumed where the plant is cultivated, primarily in East Africa and the Arabian peninsula. There, chewing khat predates the use of coffee and is used in a similar social context. Chewed in moderation, khat alleviates fatigue and reduces appetite. Compulsive use may result in manic behavior with grandiose delusions or in a paranoid type of illness, sometimes accompanied by hallucinations.

Khat has been brought into the United States and other countries for use by emigrants from the source countries. It contains a number of chemicals among which are two controlled substances, cathinone (Schedule I) and cathine (Schedule IV). As the leaves mature or dry, cathinone is converted to cathine, which significantly reduces its stimulatory properties.

Methylphenidate (Ritalin)

The primary, legitmate medical use of methylphenidate (Ritalin) is to treat attention deficit disorders in children. As with other Schedule II stimulants, the abuse of methylphenidate may produce the same effects as the abuse of cocaine or the amphetamines. It has been reported that the psychosis of chronic methylphenidate intoxication is identical to the paranoid psychosis of amphetamine intoxication.

Unlike other stimulants, however, methylphenidate has not been clandestinely produced, although abuse of this substance has been well documented among narcotic addicts who dissolve the tablets in water and inject the mixture. Complications arising from this practice are common due to the insoluble fillers used in the tablets. When injected, these materials block small blood vessels, causing serious damage to the lungs and retina of the eye.

Anorectic Drugs

A number of drugs have been developed and marketed to replace amphetamines as appetite suppressants. These anorectic drugs include benzphetamine (Didrex), diethylproprion (Tenuate, Tepanil), fenfluramine (Pondimin), mazindol (Sanorex, Mazanor), phendimetrazine (Bontril, Prelu-2, Plegine) and phentermine (Ionamin, AdipexP).

They produce many of the effects of the amphetamines, but are generally less potent. All are controlled under the CSA because of the similarity of their effects to those of the amphetamines.

CANNABIS

Cannabis sativa L., the hemp plant, grows wild throughout most of the tropic and temperate regions of the world. Prior to the advent of synthetic fibers, the cannabis plant was cultivated for the tough fiber of its stem. In the United States, cannabis is legitimately grown only for scientific research. In fact, since 1980, the United States has been the only country where cannabis is licitly cultivated for scientific research.

Cannabis contains chemicals called cannabinoids that are unique to the cannabis plant. Among the cannabinoids synthesized by the plant are cannabinol, cannabidiol, cannabinolidic acids, cannabigerol, cannabichromene, and several isomers of tetrahydrocannabinol. One of these, delta-9-tetrahydrocannabinol (THC), is believed to be responsible for most of the characteristic psychoactive effects of cannabis. Research has resulted in development and marketing of dronabinol (Marinol), a product containing synthetic THC, for the control of nausea and vomiting caused by chemotherapeutic agents used in the treatment of cancer, and to stimulate appetite in AIDS patients.

Cannabis products are usually smoked. Their effects are felt within minutes, reach their peak in 10 to 30 minutes, and may linger for two or three hours. The effects experienced often depend upon the experience and expectations of the individual user, as well as the activity of the drug itself. Low doses tend to induce a sense of well-being and a dreamy state of relaxation, which may be accompanied by a more vivid sense of sight, smell, taste, and hearing as well as by subtle alterations in thought formation and expression. This state of intoxication may not be noticeable to an observer. However, driving, occupational or household accidents may result from a distortion of time and space relationships and impaired coordination. Stronger doses intensify reactions. The individual may experience shifting sensory imagery, rapidly fluctuating emotions, a flight of fragmentary thoughts with disturbed associations, an altered sense of self-identity, impaired memory, and a dulling of attention despite an illusion of heightened insight. High doses may result in image distortion, a loss of personal identity, and fantasies and hallucinations.

Three drugs that come from cannabis—marijuana, hashish, and hashish oil—are currently distributed on the U.S. illicit market. Having no currently accepted medical use in treatment in the United States, they remain under Schedule I of the CSA. Today, cannabis is carefully illicitly cultivated, both indoors and out, to maximize its THC content, thereby producing the greatest possible psychoactive effect.

Marijuana

Marijuana is the most commonly used illicit drug in America today. The term marijuana, as commonly used, refers to the leaves and flowering tops of the cannabis plant.

A tobacco-like substance produced by drying the leaves and flowering tops of the cannabis plant, marijuana varies significantly in its potency, depending on the source and selection of plant materials used. The form of marijuana known as sinsemilla (Spanish, "sin semilla": without seed), derived from the unpollinated female cannabis plant, is preferred for its high THC content.

Marijuana is usually smoked in the form of loosely rolled cigarettes called joints or hollowed out commercial cigars called blunts. Joints and blunts may be laced with a number of adulterants including phencyclidine (PCP), substantially altering the effects and toxicity of these products. Street names for marijuana include pot, grass, weed, Mary Jane, Acupulco Gold, and reefer

Although marijuana grown in the United States was once considered inferior because of a low concentration of THC, advancements in plant selection and cultivation have resulted in highly potent domestic marijuana. In 1974, the average THC content of illicit marijuana was less than one percent; in early 1994, potency averged 5 percent. The THC of today's sinsemilla ranges up to 17 percent.

Marijuana contains known toxins and cancer-causing chemicals which are stored in fat cells for as long as several months. Marijuana users experience the same health problems as tobacco smokers, such as bronchitis, emphysema and bronchial asthma. Some of the effects of marijuana use also include increased heart rate, dryness of the mouth, reddening of the eyes, impaired motor skills and concentration, and frequently hunger and an increased desire for sweets. Extended use increases risk to the lungs and reproductive system, as well as suppression of the immune system. Occasionally, hallucinations, fantasies and paranoia are reported.

Hashish

Hashish consists of the THC-rich resinous material of the cannabis plant, which is collected, dried, and then compressed into a variety of forms, such as balls, cakes, or cookie-like sheets. Pieces are then broken off, placed in pipes and smoked. The Middle East, North Africa, and Pakistan/Afghanistan are the main sources of hashish. The THC content of hashish that reached the United States, where demand is limited, averaged 6 percent in the 1990s.

Hash Oil

The term hash oil is used by illicit drug users and dealers, but is a misnomer in suggesting any resemblance to hashish. Hash oil is produced by extracting the cannabinoids from plant material with a solvent. The color and odor of the resulting extract will vary, depending on the type of solvent used. Current samples of hash oil, a viscous liquid ranging from amber to dark brown in color, averge about 15 percent THC. In terms of its psychoactive effect, a drop or two of this liquid on a cigarette is equal to a single "joint"of marijuana.

HALLUCINOGENS

Hallucinogens are among the oldest known group of drugs that have been used for their ability to alter human perception and mood. For centuries, many of the naturally occurring hallucinogens found in plants and fungi have been used for medical, social, and religious practices. In more recent years, a number of synthetic hallucinogens have been produced, some of which are much more potent than their naturally occurring counterparts.

The biochemical, pharmacological and physiological basis for hallucinogenic activity is not well understood. Even the name for this class of drugs is not ideal, since hallucinogens do not always produce hallucinations. However, taken in non-toxic dosages, these substances produce changes in perception, thought and mood. Physiological effects include elevated heart rate, increased blood pressure and dilated pupils. Sensory effects include perceptual distortions that vary with dose, setting and mood. Psychic effects include disorders of thought associated with time and space. Time may appear to stand still and forms and colors seem to change and take on new significance. This experience may be pleasurable or extremely frightening. It needs to be stressed that the effects of hallucinogens are unpredictable each time they are used.

Weeks or even months after some hallucinogens have been taken, the user may experience flashbacks—fragmentary recurrences of certain aspects of the drug experience in the absence of actually taking the drug. The occurrence of a flashback is unpredictable, but is more likely to occur during times of stress and seem to occur more frequently in younger individuals. With time, these episodes diminish and become less intense.

The abuse of hallucinogens in the United States reached a peak in the late 1960s. A subsequent decline in their use may be attributed to real or perceived hazards associated with taking these drugs. However, a resurgence of use of hallucinogens in the 1990s, especially at the junior high school level, is cause for concern.

There is a considerable body of literature that links the use of some of the hallucinogenic substances to neuronal damage in animals; however, there is no conclusive scientific data that links brain or chromosomal damage to the use of hallucinogens in humans. The most common danger of hallucinogen use is impaired judgement that often leads to rash decisions and accidents.

Peyote & Mescaline

Peyote is a small, spineless cactus, "Lophophora williamsii," whose principal active ingredient is the hallucinogen mescaline. From earliest recorded time, peyote has been used by natives in northern Mexico and the southwestern United States as a part of traditional religious rites.

The top of the cactus above ground—also referred to as the crown—consists of disc-shaped buttons that are cut from the roots and dried. These buttons are generally chewed or soaked in water to produce an intoxicating liquid. The hallucinogenic dose for mescaline is about 0.3 to 0.5

grams (equivalent to about 5 grams of dried peyote) and lasts about 12 hours. While peyote produced rich visual hallucinations which were important to the native peyote cults, the full spectrum of effects served as a chemically induced model of mental illness. Mescaline can be extracted from peyote or produced synthetically.

Dimethyltryptamine (DMT)

Dimethyltryptamine (DMT) has a long history of use worldwide as it is found in a variety of plants and seeds, and can also be produced synthetically. It is ineffective when taken orally unless combined with another drug that inhibits its metabolism. Generally it is sniffed, smoked or injected. The effective hallucinogenic dose in humans is about 50 to 100 milligrams and lasts for about 45 to 60 minutes. Because the effects last only about an hour, the experience was called a "businessman's trip".

A number of other hallucinogens have very similar structures and properties to those of DMT, Diethyltryptamine (DET), for example, is an analogue of DMT and produces the same pharmacological effects but is somewhat less potent than DMT.

Alpha-ethyltryptamine (AET) is another tryptamine hallucinogen recently added to the list of Schedule I substances in the CSA.

LSD

Lysergic acid diethylamide (LSD) is the most potent and highly studied hallucinogen known to man. It was originally synthesized in 1938 by Dr. Albert Hoffman, but its hallucinogenic effects were unknown until 1943 when Hoffman accidently consumed some LSD. It was later found that an oral dose of as little as 0.025 mg (or 25 micrograms, equal to a few grains of salt) was capable of producing rich and vivid hallucinations.

Because of its structural similarity to a chemical present in the brain and its similarity in effects to certain aspects of psychosis, LSD was used as a research tool to study mental illness. Although there was a decline in its illicit use from its initial popularity in the 1960s, LSD is making a comeback in the 1990s. The average effective oral dose is from 20 to 80 micrograms with the effects of higher doses lasting for 10 to 12 hours. LSD is usually sold in the form of impregnated paper (blotter acid), tablets (microdots), or thin squares of gelatin (window panes).

Physical reactions may include dilated pupils, lowered body temperature, nausea, "goose bumps", profuse perspiration, increased blood sugar and rapid heart rate. During the first hour after ingestion, the user may experience visual changes with extreme changes in mood. In the hallucinatory state, the user may suffer impaired depth and time perception, accompanied by distorted perception of the size and shape of objects, movements, color, sound, touch and the user's own body image. During this period, the user's ability to perceive objects through the senses is distorted. He may describe "hearing colors" and "seeing sounds". The ability to make sensible judgements and see common dangers is impaired, making the user susceptible to personal injury. He may also injure others by attempting to drive a car or by operating machinery.

After an LSD "trip" the user may suffer acute anxiety or depression for a variable period of time. Flashbacks have been reported days or even months after taking the last dose.

DOM, DOB, MDA, MDMA & 2C-B

Many chemical variations of mescaline and amphetamine have been synthesized for their "feel good" effects. 4-Methyl-2,5-dimethoxyamphetamine (DOM) was introduced into the San Francisco drug scene in the late 1960s, and was nicknamed STP, an acronym for "Serenity, Tranquility, and Peace." Doses of 1 to 3 miligrams generally produce mood alterations and minor perceptual alterations, while larger doses can produce pronounced hallucinations that last from 8 to 10 hours.

Other illicitly manufactured analogues include 4-bromo-2, 5-dimethoxyamphetamine (DOB), 3, 4-methylenedioxyamphetamine (MDA), 3, 4-methylenedioxymeth-amphetamine (MDMA, also referred to as Ecstasy or XTC) and 4-bromo-2, 5dimethoxyhenethylamine (2C-B, NEXUS). These drugs differ from one another in their potency, speed of onset, duration of action and their capacity to modify mood with or without producing overt hallucinations. These drugs are widely used at "raves." (Raves are large all-night dance parties held in unusual settings, such a warehouses or railroad yards, that feature computer-generated, high volume, pulsating music.) The drugs are usually taken orally, sometimes snorted and rarely injected. Because they are produced in clandestine laboratories, they are seldom pure and the amount in a capsule or tablet is likely to vary considerably.

Phencyclidine (PCP) & Related Drugs

In the 1950s, phencyclidine was investigated as an anesthetic but, due to the side efffects of confusion and delirium, its development for human use was discontinued. It became commercially available for use as a veterinary anesthetic in the 1960s under the trade name of Sernylan and was placed in Schedule III of the CSA. In 1978, due to considerable abuse of phencyclidine, it was transferred to Schedule II of the CSA and manufacturing of Sernylan was discontinued. Today, virtually all of the phencyclidine encountered on the illicit market in the United States is produced in clandestine laboratories.

Phencyclidine, more commonly known as PCP, is illicitly marketed under a number of other names including Angel Dust, Supergrass, Killer Weed, Embalming Fluid, and Rocket Fuel, reflecting the range of its bizarre and volatile effects. In its pure form, it is a white crystalline powder that readily dissolves in water. However, most PCP on the illicit market contains a number of contaminates as a result of makeshift manufacturing, causing the color to range from tan to brown, and the consistency from powder to a gummy mass. Although sold in tablets and capsules as well as in powder and liquid form, it is commonly applied to a leafy material, such as parsley, mint, oregano or marijuana, and smoked.

The drug's effects are as varied as its appearance. A moderate amount of PCP often causes the user to feel detached, distant and estranged from his surroundings. Numbness, slurred speech and loss of coordination may be accompanied by a sense of strength and invulnerability. A blank stare, rapid and involuntary eye movements, and an exaggerated gait are among the more observable effects. Auditory hallucinations, image distortion, severe mood disorders, and amnesia may also occur. In some users, PCP may cause acute anxiety and a feeling of impending doom, in others, paranoia and violent hostility, and in some it may produce a psychoses indistinguishable from schizophrenia. PCP use is associated with a number of risks and many believe it to be one of the most dangerous drugs of abuse.

Modification of the manufacturing process may yield chemically related ananogues capable of producing psychic effects similar to PCP. Four of these substances (N-ethyl-l-phenylcyclohexylamine or PCE, l-(phenylcyclohexyl)-pyrrolidine or PCPy, l-l-(2-thienyl)-cyclohexyl]-piperdine or TCP, and l-[l-(2-thienyl)cyclohexyl]cyclohexyl]-pyrrolidine or TCPy have been encountered on the illicit market and have been placed in Schedule I of the CSA. LSD is also a Schedule I hallucinogen.

CLANDESTINE LABS

Drugs of abuse in the United States come from a variety of sources. Heroin and cocaine, for example, are produced in foreign countries and smuggled into the United States. Marijuana is cultivated domestically or smuggled from foreign sources. Legitimate pharmaceuticals are diverted to the illicit market. Continuing efforts on the part of state and federal governments to reduce the amount of dangerous and illicit drugs available for abuse, combined with the demand for psychoactive substances, have contributed to the proliferation of clandestine laboratories.

Clandestine laboratories are illicit operations consisting of chemicals and equipment necessary to manufacture controlled substances. The types and numbers of laboratories seized, to a large degree, reflect regional and national trends in the types and amounts of illicit substances that are being manufactured, trafficked and abused. Clandestine laboratories have been found in remote locations like mountain cabins and rural farms. Laboratories are also being operated in single and multifamily residences in urban and suburban neighborhoods where their toxic and explosive fumes can pose a significant threat to the health and safety of local residents.

The production of some substances, such as methamphetamine , PCP. MDMA and methcathinone, requires little sophisticated equipment or knowledge of chemistry; the synthesis of other drugs, such as fentanyl and LSD, requires much higher levels of expertise and equipment. Some clandestine laboratory operators have little or no training in chemistry and follow underground recipes; others employ chemistry students or professionals as "cooks."

The clandestine production of all drugs is dependent on the availability of essential raw materials. The distribution, sale, import and export of certain chemicals which are important to the manufacture of common illicitly produced substances have been regulated since the enactment of the Chemical Diversion and Trafficking Act of 1988. Enforcement of this and similar state laws has had a significant impact on the availability of chemicals to the clandestine laboratory.

INHALANTS

Inhalants are a chemically diverse group of psychoactive substances composed of organic solvents and volatile substances commonly found in adhesives, lighter fluids, cleaning fluids and paint products. Their easy accessibility, low cost and ease of concealment make inhalants, for many, one of the first substances abused. While not regulated under the CSA, a few states place restrictions on the sale of these products to minors. Studies have indicated that between 5 percent and 15 percent of young people in the United States have tried inhalants, although the vast majority of these youngsters do not become chronic abusers.

Inhalants may be sniffed directly from an open container or "huffed" from a rag soaked in the substance and held to the face. Alternatively, the open container or soaked rag can be placed in a bag where the vapors can concentrate before being inhaled. Although inhalant abusers may prefer one particular substance because of odor or taste, a variety of substances may be used because of their similar effects, availability and cost. Once inhaled, the extensive capillary surface of the lungs allows rapid absorption of the substance, and blood levels peak rapidly. Entry into the brain is so fast that the effects of inhalation can resemble the intensity of effects produced by intravenous injection of other psychoactive drugs.

The effects of inhalant intoxication resemble those of alcohol inebriation, with stimulation and loss of inhibition followed by depression at high doses. Users report distortion in perceptions of time and space. Many users experience headache, nausea or vomiting, slurred speech, loss of motor coordination and wheezing. A characteristic "glue sniffer's rash" around the nose and mouth may be seen. An odor of paint or solvents on clothes, skin and breath is sometimes a sign of inhalant abuse.

The chronic use of inhalants has been associated with a number of serious health problems. Glue and paint thinner sniffing in particular produce kidney abnormalities, while the solvents, toluene and trichloroethylene, cause liver toxicity. Memory impairment, attention deficits and diminished non-verbal intelligence have been associated with the abuse of inhalants. Deaths resulting from heart failure, asphyxiation or aspiration have occurred.

Excerpts From the
EMERGENCY MANAGEMENT GUIDE FOR BUSINESS & INDUSTRY

A step-by-step approach to emergency planning, response and recovery for companies of all sizes. Sponsored by a Public-Private Partnership with the Federal Emergency Management Agency. Special thanks to the following organizations for supporting the development, promotion and distribution of the Emergency Management Guide for Business & Industry:

American Red Cross
American Insurance Association
American Textile Manufacturers Institute
Building Owners and Managers Association International
Chemical Manufacturers Association
Fertilizer Institute
National Association of Manufacturers
National Commercial Builders Council
of the National Association of Home Builders
National Coordinating Council on Emergency Management
National Emergency Management Association
National Industrial Council — State Associations Group
New Jersey Business & Industry Association
Pacific Bell
Pennsylvania Emergency Management Agency

PREFACE

The Emergency Management Guide for Business & Industry was produced by the Federal Emergency Management Agency (FEMA) and supported by a number of private companies and associations representing business and industry.

The approaches described in this guide are recommendations, not regulations. There are no reporting requirements, nor will following these principles ensure compliance with any Federal, State or local codes or regulations that may apply to your facility.

FEMA is not a regulatory agency. Specific regulatory issues should be addressed with the appropriate agencies such as the Occupational Safety and Health Administration (OSHA) and the Environmental Protection Agency (EPA).

Prepared under FEMA Contract EMW-90-C-3348 by:

Thomas Wahle, Gregg Beatty, Ogilvy Adams & Rinehart
Roy F. Weston, Inc.Washington, D.C.
Rockville, Maryland(202) 452-9419
(301) 646-6855

INTRODUCTION

About This Guide
What Is an Emergency?
What Is Emergency Management?
Making the "Case" for Emergency Management

SECTION 1: 4 STEPS IN THE PLANNING PROCESS

STEP 1 - ESTABLISH A PLANNING TEAM

Form the Team
Establish Authority
Issue a Mission Statement
Establish a Schedule and Budget

STEP 2 - ANALYZE CAPABILITIES AND HAZARDS

Where Do You Stand Right Now?
Review Internal Plans and Policies
Meet with Outside Groups
Identify Codes and Regulations
Identify Critical Products, Services and Operations
Identify Internal Resources and Capabilities
Identify External Resources
Do an Insurance Review
Conduct a Vulnerability Analysis

STEP 3 - DEVELOP THE PLAN

Plan Components
The Development Process

STEP 4 - IMPLEMENT THE PLAN

Integrate the Plan into Company Operations
Conduct Training

SECTION 2: EMERGENCY MANAGEMENT CONSIDERATIONS

Direction and Control
Communications
Life Safety
Property Protection
Community Outreach
Recovery and Restoration
Administration and Logistics

SECTION 3: HAZARD-SPECIFIC INFORMATION

Fire
Hazardous Materials Incidents
Floods and Flash floods
Hurricanes
Tornadoes
Severe Winter Storms
Earthquakes
Technological Emergencies

SECTION 4: INFORMATION SOURCES

Additional readings from FEMA
Sources: Ready-to-print brochures

INTRODUCTION

A hurricane blasts through South Florida causing more than $25 billion in damages. A fire at a food processing plant results in 25 deaths, a company out of business and a small town devastated. A bombing in the World Trade Center results in six deaths, hundreds of injuries and the evacuation of 40,000 people. A blizzard shuts down much of the East Coast for days. More than 150 lives are lost and millions of dollars in damages incurred.

Every year emergencies take their toll on business and industry — in lives and dollars. But something can be done. Business and industry can limit injuries and damages and return more quickly to normal operations if they plan ahead.

•About This Guide

This guide provides step-by-step advice on how to create and maintain a comprehensive emergency management program. It can be used by manufacturers, corporate offices, retailers, utilities or any organization where a sizable number of people work or gather. Whether you operate from a high-rise building or an industrial complex; whether you own, rent or lease your property; whether you are a large or small company; the concepts in this guide will apply.

To begin, you need not have in-depth knowledge of emergency management. What you need is the authority to create a plan and a commitment from the chief executive officer to make emergency management part of your corporate culture.

If you already have a plan, use this guide as a resource to assess and update your plan.

•What Is an Emergency?

An emergency is any unplanned event that can cause deaths or significant injuries to employees, customers or the public; or that can shut down your business, disrupt operations, cause physical or environmental damage, or threaten the facility's financial standing or public image. Obviously, numerous events can be "emergencies," including:

1. Fire
2. Hazardous materials incident
3. Flood or flash flood
4. Hurricane
5. Tornado
6. Winter storm
7. Earthquake
8. Communications failure
9. Radiological accident
10. Civil disturbance
11. Loss of key supplier or customer
12. Explosion

The term "disaster" has been left out of this document because it lends itself to a preconceived notion of a large-scale event, usually a "natural disaster." In fact, each event must be addressed within the context of the impact it has on the company and the community. What might constitute a nuisance to a large industrial facility could be a "disaster" to a small business.

•What Is Emergency Management?

Emergency management is the process of preparing for, mitigating, responding to and recovering from an emergency.

Emergency management is a dynamic process. Planning, though critical, is not the only component. Training, conducting drills, testing equipment and coordinating activities with the community are other important functions.

•Making the "Case" for Emergency Management

To be successful, emergency management requires upper management support. The chief executive sets the tone by authorizing planning to take place and directing senior management to get involved.

When presenting the "case" for emergency management, avoid dwelling on the negative effects of an emergency (e.g., deaths, fines, criminal prosecution) and emphasize the positive aspects of preparedness. For example:

1. It helps companies fulfill their moral responsibility to protect employees, the community and the environment.

2. It facilitates compliance with regulatory requirements of Federal, State and local agencies.

3. It enhances a company's ability to recover from financial losses, regulatory fines, loss of market share, damages to equipment or products or business interruption.

4. It reduces exposure to civil or criminal liability in the event of an incident.

5. It enhances a company's image and credibility with employees, customers, suppliers and the community.

6. It may reduce your insurance premiums.

SECTION 1 — 4 STEPS IN THE PLANNING PROCESS

• STEP 1 — ESTABLISH A PLANNING TEAM. There must be an individual or group in charge of developing the emergency management plan. The following is guidance for making the appointment.

1. Form the Team - The size of the planning team will depend on the facility's operations, requirements, and resources. Usually involving a group of people is best because:
   a. It encourages participation and gets more people invested in the process
   b. It increases the amount of time and energy participants are able to give
   c. It enhances the visibility and stature of the planning process
   d. It provides for a broad perspective on the issues

   Determine who can be an active member and who can serve in an advisory capacity. In most cases, one or two people will be doing the bulk of the work. At the very least, you should obtain input from all functional areas. Remember:
   a. Upper management
   b. Line management
   c. Labor
   d. Human Resources
   e. Engineering and maintenance
   f. Safety, health and environmental affairs
   g. Public information officer
   h. Security
   i. Community relations
   j. Sales and marketing
   k. Legal
   l. Finance and purchasing

   Have participants appointed in writing by upper management. Their job descriptions could also reflect this assignment.

2. Establish Authority - Demonstrate management's commitment and promote an atmosphere of cooperation by "authorizing" the planning group to take the steps necessary to develop a plan. The group should be led by the chief executive or the plant manager. Establish a clear line of authority between group members and the group leader, though not so rigid as to prevent the free flow of ideas.

3. Issue a Mission Statement - Have the chief executive or plant manager issue a mission statement to demonstrate the company's commitment to emergency management. The statement should:

   Define the purpose of the plan and indicate that it will involve the entire organization
   Define the authority and structure of the planning group

4. Establish a Schedule and Budget - Establish a work schedule and planning deadlines. Timelines can be modified as priorities become more clearly defined.

Develop an initial budget for such things as research, printing, seminars, consulting services and other expenses that may be necessary during the development process.

•STEP 2 — ANALYZE CAPABILITIES AND HAZARDS. This step entails gathering information about current capabilities and about possible hazards and emergencies, and then conducting a vulnerability analysis to determine the facility's capabilities for handling emergencies.

1. WHERE DO YOU STAND RIGHT NOW?

    Review Internal Plans and Policies Documents to look for include:
    a. Evacuation plan
    b. Fire protection plan
    c. Safety and health program
    d. Environmental policies
    e. Security procedures
    f. Insurance programs
    g. Finance and purchasing procedures
    h. Plant closing policy
    i. Employee manuals
    j. Hazardous materials plan
    k. Process safety assessment
    l. Risk management plan
    m. Capital improvement program
    n. Mutual aid agreements

2. Meet with Outside Groups - Meet with government agencies, community organizations and utilities. Ask about potential emergencies and about plans and available resources for responding to them. Sources of information include:
    a. Community emergency management office
    b. Mayor or Community Administrator's office
    c. Local Emergency Planning Committee (LEPC)
    d. Fire Department
    e. Police Department
    f. Emergency Medical Services organizations
    g. American Red Cross
    h. National Weather Service
    i. Public Works Department
    j. Planning Commission
    k. Telephone companies
    l. Electric utilities
    m. Neighboring businesses

    While researching potential emergencies, one facility discovered that a dam — 50 miles away — posed a threat to its community. The facility was able to plan accordingly.

3. Identify Codes and Regulations - Identify applicable Federal, State and local regulations such as:
    a. Occupational safety and health regulations
    b. Environmental regulations

    c. Fire codes
    d. Seismic safety codes
    e. Transportation regulations
    f. Zoning regulations
    g. Corporate policies

4. Identify Critical Products, Services and Operations - You'll need this information to assess the impact of potential emergencies and to determine the need for backup systems. Areas to review include:
    a. Company products and services and the facilities and equipment needed to produce them
    b. Products and services provided by suppliers, especially sole source vendors
    c. Lifeline services such as electrical power, water, sewer, gas, telecommunications and transportation
    d. Operations, equipment and personnel vital to the continued functioning of the facility

5. Identify Internal Resources and Capabilities - Resources and capabilities that could be needed in an emergency include:
    a. Personnel — fire brigade, hazardous materials response team, emergency medical services, security, emergency management group, evacuation team, public information officer
    b. Equipment — fire protection and suppression equipment, communications equipment, first aid supplies, emergency supplies, warning systems, emergency power equipment, decontamination equipment
    c. Facilities — emergency operating center, media briefing area, shelter areas, first-aid stations, sanitation facilities
    d. Organizational capabilities — training, evacuation plan, employee support system
    e. Backup systems — arrangements with other facilities to provide for:
        (1) Payroll
        (2) Communications
        (3) Production
        (4) Customer services
        (5) Shipping and receiving
        (6) Information systems support
        (7) Emergency power
        (8) Recovery support

One way to increase response capabilities is to identify employee skills (medical, engineering, communications, foreign language) that might be needed in an emergency.

6. Identify External Resources - There are many external resources that could be needed in an emergency. In some cases, formal agreements may be necessary to define the facility's relationship with the following:
    a. Local emergency management office
    b. Fire Department
    c. Hazardous materials response organization
    d. Emergency medical services
    e. Hospitals

    f. Local and State police
    g. Community service organizations
    h. Utilities
    i. Contractors
    j. Suppliers of emergency equipment
    k. Insurance carriers

7. Do an Insurance Review - Meet with insurance carriers to review all policies. (See Section 2: Recovery and Restoration.)

8. Conduct A Vulnerabilty Analysis - The next step is to assess the vulnerability of your facility — the probability and potential impact of each emergency. Use the Vulnerability Analysis Chart in the appendix section to guide the process, which entails assigning probabilities, estimating impact and assessing resources, using a numerical system. The lower the score the better.

9. List Potential Emergencies - In the first column of the chart, list all emergencies that could affect your facility, including those identified by your local emergency management office. Consider both:
    a. Emergencies that could occur within your facility
    b. Emergencies that could occur in your community

Below are some other factors to consider:

Historical — What types of emergencies have occurred in the community, at this facility and at other facilities in the area?

Fires	Severe weather	Hazardous material spills
Transportation accidents	Earthquakes	Hurricanes
Tornadoes	Terrorism	Utility outages

Geographic — What can happen as a result of the facility's location? Keep in mind:
    a. Proximity to flood plains, seismic faults and dams
    b. Proximity to companies that produce, store, use or transport hazardous materials
    c. Proximity to major transportation routes and airports
    d. Proximity to nuclear power plants

Technological — What could result from a process or system failure? Possibilities include:
    a. Fire, explosion, hazardous materials incident
    b. Safety system failure
    c. Telecommunications failure
    e. Computer system failure
    f. Power failure
    g. Heating/cooling system failure
    h. Emergency notification system failure

Human Error — What emergencies can be caused by employee error? Are employees trained to work safely? Do they know what to do in an emergency? Human error is the single largest cause of workplace emergencies and can result from:
    a. Poor training
    b. Poor maintenance
    c. Carelessness

d. Misconduct
e. Substance abuse
f. Fatigue

Physical — What types of emergencies could result from the design or construction of the facility? Does the physical facility enhance safety? Consider:
a. The physical construction of the facility
b. Hazardous processes or byproducts
c. Facilities for storing combustibles
d. Layout of equipment
e. Lighting
f. Evacuation routes and exits
g. Proximity of shelter areas

Regulatory — What emergencies or hazards are you regulated to deal with?

Analyze each potential emergency from beginning to end. Consider what could happen as a result of:
a. Prohibited access to the facility
b. Loss of electric power
c. Communication lines down
e. Ruptured gas mains
f. Water damage
g. Smoke damage
h. Structural damage
i. Air or water contamination
j. Explosion
k. Building collapse
l. Trapped persons
m. Chemical release

10. Estimate Probability - Rate the likelihood of each emergency's occurrence. This is a subjective, but useful consideration. Use a simple scale of 1 to 5 with 1 as the lowest probability and 5 as the highest.

11. Assess the Potential Human Impact - Analyze the potential human impact of each emergency — the possibility of death or injury. Assign a rating with 1 as the lowest impact and 5 as the highest.

12. Assess the Potential Property Impact - Consider the potential property for losses and damages. Again, assign a rating, 1 being the lowest impact and 5 being the highest.

Consider:
a. Cost to replace
b. Cost to set up temporary replacement
c. Cost to repair

A bank's vulnerability analysis concluded that a "small" fire could be as catastrophic to the business as a computer system failure. The planning group discovered that bank employees did not know how to use fire extinguishers, and that the bank lacked any kind of evacuation or emergency response system.

13. Assess the Potential Business Impact - Consider the potential loss of market share. Assign a rating. Again, 1 is the lowest impact and 5 is the highest.

    Assess the impact of:
    a. Business interruption
    b. Employees unable to report to work
    c. Customers unable to reach facility
    d. Company in violation of contractual agreements
    e. Imposition of fines and penalties or legal costs
    f. Interruption of critical supplies
    g. Interruption of product distribution

14. Assess Internal and External Resources - Next assess your resources and ability to respond. Assign a score to your Internal Resources and External Resources. The lower the score the better. To help you do this, consider each potential emergency from beginning to end and each resource that would be needed to respond. For each emergency ask these questions:

    Do we have the needed resources and capabilities to respond?

    Will external resources be able to respond to us for this emergency as quickly as we may need them, or will they have other priority areas to serve?

    If the answers are yes, move on to the next assessment. If the answers are no, identify what can be done to correct the problem. For example, you may need to:
    a. Develop additional emergency procedures
    b. Conduct additional training
    c. Acquire additional equipment
    d. Establish mutual aid agreements
    e. Establish agreements with specialized contractors

15. Total the scores for each emergency by adding the numerical values for each emergency. The lower the score the better. While this is a subjective rating, the comparisons will help determine planning and resource priorities — the subject of the pages to follow.

When assessing resources, remember that community emergency workers — police, paramedics, firefighters — will focus their response where the need is greatest. Or they may be victims themselves and be unable to respond immediately. That means response to your facility may be delayed.

B-11

•STEP 3 — DEVELOP THE PLAN
You are now ready to develop an emergency management plan. This section describes how.

PLAN COMPONENTS - Your plan should include the following basic components.

1. Executive Summary - The executive summary gives management a brief overview of: the purpose of the plan; the facility's emergency management policy; authorities and responsibilities of key personnel; the types of emergencies that could occur; and where response operations will be managed.

2. Emergency Management Elements - This section of the plan briefly describes the facility's approach to the core elements of emergency management, which are:
   a. Direction and control
   b. Communications
   c. Life safety
   d. Property protection
   e. Community outreach
   f. Recovery and restoration
   g. Administration and logistics

   These elements, which are described in detail in Section 2, are the foundation for the emergency procedures that your facility will follow to protect personnel and equipment and resume operations.

3. Emergency Response Procedures - The procedures spell out how the facility will respond to emergencies. Whenever possible, develop them as a series of checklists that can be quickly accessed by senior management, department heads, response personnel and employees.

   Determine what actions would be necessary to:
   a. Assess the situation
   b. Protect employees, customers, visitors, equipment, vital records and other assets, particularly during the first three days
   c. Get the business back up and running.

   Specific procedures might be needed for any number of situations such as bomb threats or tornadoes, and for such functions as:
   a. Warning employees and customers
   b. Communicating with personnel and community responders
   c. Conducting an evacuation and accounting for all persons in the facility
   d. Managing response activities
   e. Activating and operating an emergency operations center
   f. Fighting fires
   g. Shutting down operations
   h. Protecting vital records
   i. Restoring operations

4. Support Documents - Documents that could be needed in an emergency include:

Emergency call lists — lists (wallet size if possible) of all persons on and off site who would be involved in responding to an emergency, their responsibilities and their 24-hour telephone numbers

Building and site maps that indicate:

a. Utility shutoffs
b. Water hydrants
c. Water main valves
d. Water lines
e. Gas main valves
f. Gas lines
g. Electrical cutoffs
h. Electrical substations
i. Storm drains
j. Location of each building (include name of building, street name and number)
k. Sewer lines
l. Floor plans
m. Alarm and enunciators
n. Fire extinguishers
o. Fire systems
p. Exits
q. Stairways
r. Designated escape routes
s. Restricted areas
t. Hazardous materials (including cleaning supplies and chemicals)
u. High-value items

5. Resource lists — lists of major resources (equipment, supplies, services) that could be needed in an emergency; mutual aid agreements with other companies and government agencies.

In an emergency, all personnel should know:

1. What is my role?
2. Where should I go?

Some facilities are required to develop:

1. Emergency escape procedures and routes
2. Procedures for employees who perform or shut down critical operations before an evacuation
3. Procedures to account for all employees, visitors and contractors after an evacuation is completed
4. Rescue and medical duties for assigned employees
5. Procedures for reporting emergencies
6. Names of persons or departments to be contacted for information regarding the plan

THE DEVELOPMENT PROCESS - The following is guidance for developing the plan.
1. Identify Challenges and Prioritize Activities - Determine specific goals and milestones. Make a list of tasks to be performed, by whom and when. Determine how you will address the problem areas and resource shortfalls that were identified in the vulnerability analysis.
2. Write the Plan - Assign each member of the planning group a section to write. Determine the most appropriate format for each section.
Establish an aggressive timeline with specific goals. Provide enough time for completion of work, but not so much as to allow assignments to linger. Establish a schedule for:

a. First draft   b. Review   c. Second draft   d. Tabletop exercise
e. Final draft   f. Printing   g. Distribution

B-13

3. Establish a Training Schedule - Have one person or department responsible for developing a training schedule for your facility. For specific ideas about training, refer to Step 4.

4. Coordinate with Outside Organizations - Meet periodically with local government agencies and community organizations. Inform appropriate government agencies that you are creating an emergency management plan. While their official approval may not be required, they will likely have valuable insights and information to offer.

   Determine State and local requirements for reporting emergencies, and incorporate them into your procedures.

   Determine protocols for turning control of a response over to outside agencies. Some details that may need to be worked out are:
   a. Which gate or entrance will responding units use?
   b. Where and to whom will they report?
   c. How will they be identified?
   d. How will facility personnel communicate with outside responders?
   e. Who will be in charge of response activities?

   Determine what kind of identification authorities will require to allow your key personnel into your facility during an emergency.

   Determine the needs of disabled persons and non-English-speaking personnel. For example, a blind employee could be assigned a partner in case an evacuation is necessary.

   The Americans with Disabilities Act (ADA) defines a disabled person as anyone who has a physical or mental impairment that substantially limits one or more major life activities, such as seeing, hearing, walking, breathing, performing manual tasks, learning, caring for oneself or working.

   Your emergency planning priorities may be influenced by government regulation. To remain in compliance you may be required to address specific emergency management functions that might otherwise be a lower priority activity for that given year.

5. Maintain Contact with Other Corporate Offices - Communicate with other offices and divisions in your company to learn:
   a. Their emergency notification requirements
   b. The conditions where mutual assistance would be necessary
   c. How offices will support each other in an emergency
   d. Names, telephone numbers and pager numbers of key personnel

   Incorporate this information into your procedures.

6. Review, Conduct Training and Revise - Distribute the first draft to group members for review. Revise as needed.

   For a second review, conduct a tabletop exercise with management and personnel who have a key emergency management responsibility. In a conference room setting, describe an emergency scenario and have participants discuss their responsibilities and how they would react to the situation. Based on this discussion, identify areas of confusion and overlap, and modify the plan accordingly.

7. Seek Final Approval - Arrange a briefing for the chief executive officer and senior management and obtain written approval.

8. Distribute the Plan - Place the final plan in three-ring binders and number all copies and pages. Each individual who receives a copy should be required to sign for it and be responsible for posting subsequent changes. Determine which sections of the plan would be appropriate to show to government agencies (some sections may refer to corporate secrets or include private listings of names, telephone numbers or radio frequencies). Distribute the final plan to:
   a. Chief executive and senior managers
   b. Key members of the company's emergency response organization
   c. Company headquarters
   d. Community emergency response agencies (appropriate sections)

Have key personnel keep a copy of the plan in their homes. Inform employees about the plan and training schedule.

> Consolidate emergency plans for better coordination. Stand-alone plans, such as a Spill Prevention Control and Countermeasures (SPCC) plan, fire protection plan or safety and health plan, should be incorporated into one comprehensive plan.

STEP 4 — IMPLEMENT THE PLAN

Implementation means more than simply exercising the plan during an emergency. It means acting on recommendations made during the vulnerability analysis, integrating the plan into company operations, training employees and evaluating the plan.

INTEGRATE THE PLAN INTO COMPANY OPERATIONS

Emergency planning must become part of the corporate culture. Look for opportunities to build awareness; to educate and train personnel; to test procedures; to involve all levels of management, all departments and the community in the planning process; and to make emergency management part of what personnel do on a day-to-day basis.

Test How Completely The Plan Has Been Integrated By Asking:
   a. How well does senior management support the responsibilities outlined in the plan?
   b. Have emergency planning concepts been fully incorporated into the facility's accounting, personnel and financial procedures?
   c. How can the facility's processes for evaluating employees and defining job classifications better address emergency management responsibilities?
   d. Are there opportunities for distributing emergency preparedness information through corporate newsletters, employee manuals or employee mailings?
   e. What kinds of safety posters or other visible reminders would be helpful?
   f. Do personnel know what they should do in an emergency?
   g. How can all levels of the organization be involved in evaluating and updating the plan?

CONDUCT TRAINING, DRILLS AND EXERCISES - Everyone who works at or visits the facility requires some form of training. This could include periodic employee discussion sessions to review procedures, technical training in equipment use for emergency responders, evacuation drills and full-scale exercises. Below are basic considerations for developing a training plan.

1. Planning Considerations

    Assign responsibility for developing a training plan. Consider the training and information needs for employees, contractors, visitors, managers and those with an emergency response role identified in the plan. Determine for a 12 month period:
    a. Who will be trained?
    b. Who will do the training?
    c. What training activities will be used?
    d. When and where each session will take place?
    e. How the session will be evaluated and documented?

    Create a Training Drill and Exercise Chart. Consider how to involve community responders in training activities. Conduct reviews after each training activity. Involve both personnel and community responders in the evaluation process.

2. Training Activities - Training can take many forms:
    a. Orientation and Education Sessions — These are regularly scheduled discussion sessions to provide information, answer questions and identify needs and concerns.
    b. Tabletop Exercise — Members of the emergency management group meet in a conference room setting to discuss their responsibilities and how they would react to emergency scenarios. This is a cost-effective and efficient way to identify areas of overlap and confusion before conducting more demanding training activities.
    c. Walk-through Drill — The emergency management group and response teams actually perform their emergency response functions. This activity generally involves more people and is more thorough than a tabletop exercise.
    d. Functional Drills — These drills test specific functions such as medical response, emergency notifications, warning and communications procedures and equipment, though not necessarily at the same time. Personnel are asked to evaluate the systems and identify problem areas.
    e. Evacuation Drill — Personnel walk the evacuation route to a designated area where procedures for accounting for all personnel are tested. Participants are asked to make notes as they go along of what might become a hazard during an emergency, e.g., stairways cluttered with debris, smoke in the hallways. Plans are modified accordingly.
    f. Full-scale Exercise — A real-life emergency situation is simulated as closely as possible. This exercise involves company emergency response personnel, employees, management and community response organizations.

3. Employee Training - General training for all employees should address:
    a. Individual roles and responsibilities
    b. Information about threats, hazards and protective actions
    c. Notification, warning and communications procedures
    d. Means for locating family members in an emergency
    e. Emergency response procedures
    f. Evacuation, shelter and accountability procedures
    g. Location and use of common emergency equipment
    h. Emergency shutdown procedures

The scenarios developed during the vulnerability analysis can serve as the basis for training events.

OSHA training requirements are a minimum standard for many facilities that have a fire brigade, hazardous materials team, rescue team or emergency medical response team.

4. Evaluate and Modify the Plan - Conduct a formal audit of the entire plan at least once a year. Among the issues to consider are:
    a. How can you involve all levels of management in evaluating and updating the plan?
    b. Are the problem areas and resource shortfalls identified in the vulnerability analysis being sufficiently addressed?
    c. Does the plan reflect lessons learned from drills and actual events?
    d. Do members of the emergency management group and emergency response team understand their respective responsibilities? Have new members been trained?
    e. Does the plan reflect changes in the physical layout of the facility? Does it reflect new facility processes?
    f. Are photographs and other records of facility assets up to date?
    g. Is the facility attaining its training objectives?
    h. Have the hazards in the facility changed?
    i. Are the names, titles and telephone numbers in the plan current?
    j. Are steps being taken to incorporate emergency management into other facility processes?

Have community agencies and organizations been briefed on the plan? Are they involved in evaluating the plan?

In addition to a yearly audit, evaluate and modify the plan at these times:
    a. After each training drill or exercise
    b. After each emergency
    c. When personnel or their responsibilities change
    d. When the layout or design of the facility changes
    e. When policies or procedures change
    f. Remember to brief personnel on changes to the plan

Conduct a formal audit of the entire plan at least once a year.

SECTION 2 — EMERGENCY MANAGEMENT CONSIDERATIONS

•FUNCTION: DIRECTION AND CONTROL.

Someone must be in charge in an emergency. The system for managing resources, analyzing information and making decisions in an emergency is called direction and control.

The direction and control system described below assumes a facility of sufficient size. Your facility may require a less sophisticated system, though the principles described here will still apply.

The configuration of your system will depend on many factors. Larger industries may have their own fire team, emergency medical technicians or hazardous materials team, while smaller organizations may need to rely on mutual aid agreements. They may also be able to consolidate positions or combine responsibilities. Tenants of office buildings or industrial parks may be part of an emergency management program for the entire facility.

1. **Emergency Management Group (EMG)**

   The EMG is the team responsible for the big picture. It controls all incident-related activities. The Incident Commander (IC) oversees the technical aspects of the response.

   The EMG supports the IC by allocating resources and by interfacing with the community, the media, outside response organizations and regulatory agencies.

   The EMG is headed by the Emergency Director (ED), who should be the facility manager. The ED is in command and control of all aspects of the emergency. Other EMG members should be senior managers who have the authority to:
   a. Determine the short- and long- term effects of an emergency
   b. Order the evacuation or shutdown of the facility
   c. Interface with outside organizations and the media
   d. Issue press releases

2. **Incident Command System (ICS)**

   The ICS was developed specifically for the fire service, but its principles can be applied to all emergencies. The ICS provides for coordinated response and a clear chain of command and safe operations.

   The Incident Commander (IC) is responsible for front-line management of the incident, for tactical planning and execution, for determining whether outside assistance is needed and for relaying requests for internal resources or outside assistance through the Emergency Operations Center (EOC).

   The IC can be any employee, but a member of management with the authority to make decisions is usually the best choice. The IC must have the capability and authority to:
   a. Assume command
   b. Assess the situation
   c. Implement the emergency management plan
   d. Determine response strategies

    e. Activate resources

    f. Order an evacuation

    g. Oversee all incident response activities

    h. Declare that the incident is "over"

3. **Emergency Operations Center (EOC)**

The EOC serves as a centralized management center for emergency operations. Here, decisions are made by the EMG based upon information provided by the IC and other personnel. Regardless of size or process, every facility should designate an area where decision makers can gather during an emergency.

The EOC should be located in an area of the facility not likely to be involved in an incident, perhaps the security department, the manager's office, a conference room or the training center. An alternate EOC should be designated in the event that the primary location is not usable.

Each facility must determine its requirements for an EOC based upon the functions to be performed and the number of people involved. Ideally, the EOC is a dedicated area equipped with communications equipment, reference materials, activity logs and all the tools necessary to respond quickly and appropriately to an emergency.

> In a hazardous materials accident, an off-site medic was exposed to the spilled material and required hospitalization. It was determined that the person was able to enter the hazardous area unprotected because no one was "in charge" at the scene.

> EOC Resources:
> Communications equipment
> A copy of the emergency management plan and EOC procedures
> Blueprints, maps, status boards
> A list of EOC personnel and descriptions of their duties
> Technical information and data for advising responders
> Building security system information
> Information and data management capabilities
> Telephone directories
> Backup power, communications and lighting
> Emergency supplies

4. **Planning Considerations**

To develop a direction and control system:

    a. Define the duties of personnel with an assigned role. Establish procedures for each position. Prepare checklists for all procedures

    b. Define procedures and responsibilities for fire fighting, medical and health, and engineering

    c. Determine lines of succession to ensure continuous leadership, authority and responsibility in key positions

    d. Determine equipment and supply needs for each response function

At a minimum, assign all personnel responsibility for:
a. Recognizing and reporting an emergency
b. Warning other employees in the area
c. Taking security and safety measures
d. Evacuating safely
e. Provide training

5. **Security**

Isolation of the incident scene must begin when the emergency is discovered. If possible, the discoverer should attempt to secure the scene and control access, but no one should be placed in physical danger to perform these functions. Basic security measures include:

Closing doors or windows
Establishing temporary barriers with furniture after people have safely evacuated
Dropping containment materials (sorbent pads, etc.) in the path of leaking materials
Closing file cabinets or desk drawers

Only trained personnel should be allowed to perform advanced security measures. Access to the facility, the EOC and the incident scene should be limited to persons directly involved in the response.

6. **Coordination of Outside Response**

In some cases, laws, codes, prior agreements or the very nature of the emergency require the IC to turn operations over to an outside response organization. When this happens, the protocols established between the facility and outside response organizations are implemented. The facility's IC provides the community's IC a complete report on the situation.

The facility IC keeps track of which organizations are on-site and how the response is being coordinated. This helps increase personnel safety and accountability, and prevents duplication of effort.

Keep detailed logs of actions taken during an emergency. Describe what happened, decisions made and any deviations from policy. Log the time for each event.

7. **FUNCTION: COMMUNICATIONS.**

Communications are essential to any business operation. A communications failure can be a disaster in itself, cutting off vital business activities.

Communications are needed to report emergencies, to warn personnel of the danger, to keep families and off-duty employees informed about what's happening at the facility to coordinate response actions and to keep in contact with customers and suppliers.

8. **Contingency Planning**

Plan for all possible contingencies from a temporary or short- term disruption to a total communications failure. Consider the everyday functions performed by your facility and the communications, both voice and data, used to support them.

Consider the business impact if your communications were inoperable. How would this impact your emergency operations?

Prioritize all facility communications. Determine which should be restored first in an emergency.

Establish procedures for restoring communications systems.

Talk to your communications vendors about their emergency response capabilities. Establish procedures for restoring services.

Determine needs for backup communications for each business function. Options include messengers, telephones, portable microwave, amateur radios, point-to-point private lines, satellite, high-frequency radio.

9. **Emergency Communications**

Consider the functions your facility might need to perform in an emergency and the communications systems needed to support them. Consider communications between:
a. Emergency responders
b. Responders and the Incident Commander (IC)
c. The IC and the Emergency Operations Center (EOC)
d. The IC and employees
e. The EOC and outside response organizations
f. The EOC and neighboring businesses
g. The EOC and employees' families
h. The EOC and customers
i. The EOC and media

Methods of communication include:
a. Messenger
b. Telephone
c. Two-way radio
d. FAX machine
e. Microwave
f. Satellite
g. Dial-up modems
h. Local area networks
i. Hand signals

10. **Family Communications**

In an emergency, personnel will need to know whether their families are okay. Taking care of one's loved ones is always a first priority.

Make plans for communicating with employees' families in an emergency. Also, encourage employees to:

Consider how they would communicate with their families in case they are separated from one another or injured in an emergency.

Arrange for an out-of-town contact for all family members to call in an emergency.

Designate a place to meet family members in case they cannot get home in an emergency.

11. **Notification**

Establish procedures for employees to report an emergency. Inform employees of procedures. Train personnel assigned specific notification tasks.

Post emergency telephone numbers near each telephone, on employee bulletin boards and in other prominent locations.

Maintain an updated list of addresses and telephone and pager numbers of key emergency response personnel (from within and outside the facility).

Listen for tornado, hurricane and other severe weather warnings issued by the National Weather Service.

Determine government agencies' notification requirements in advance. Notification must be made immediately to local government agencies when an emergency has the potential to affect public health and safety.

Prepare announcements that could be made over public address systems.

12. **Warning**

Establish a system for warning personnel of an emergency. The system should:
a. Be audible or within view by all people in the facility
b. Have an auxiliary power supply
c. Have a distinct and recognizable signal

Make plans for warning persons with disabilities. For instance, a flashing strobe light can be used to warn hearing-impaired people.

Familiarize personnel with procedures for responding when the warning system is activated.

Establish procedures for warning customers, contractors, visitors and others who may not be familiar with the facility's warning system.

Test your facility's warning system at least monthly.

Test communications often. A research firm discovered in a drill that its two-way radio system did not work, limiting communications between the Emergency Operating Center (EOC) and the Incident Commander (IC) to a single telephone line. The Emergency Management Group had failed to provide a backup radio for the EOC. Fortunately, this was discovered during training.

Test alarm systems monthly. One company conducted its first test of a sophisticated alarm system 21 years after the system was installed. Rather than alarm bells, the system played Christmas music.

FUNCTION: LIFE SAFETY.

Protecting the health and safety of everyone in the facility is the first priority during an emergency.

1. **Evacuation Planning**

   One common means of protection is evacuation. In the case of fire, an immediate evacuation to a predetermined area away from the facility may be necessary. In a hurricane, evacuation could involve the entire community and take place over a period of days.

   To develop an evacuation policy and procedure:
   a. Determine the conditions under which an evacuation would be necessary
   b. Establish a clear chain of command. Identify personnel with the authority to order an evacuation; designate "evacuation wardens" to assist others in an evacuation and to account for personnel
   c. Establish specific evacuation procedures, establish a system for accounting for personnel, consider employees' transportation needs for community-wide evacuations
   d. Establish procedures for assisting persons with disabilities and those who do not speak English
   e. Post evacuation procedures
   f. Designate personnel to continue or shut down critical operations while an evacuation is underway; they must be capable of recognizing when to abandon the operation and evacuate themselves
   g. Coordinate plans with the local emergency management office

2. **Evacuation Routes and Exits**

   Designate primary and secondary evacuation routes and exits. Have them clearly marked and well lit.

   Post signs.

   Install emergency lighting in case a power outage occurs during an evacuation.

   Ensure that evacuation routes and emergency exits are:
   a. Wide enough to accommodate the number of evacuating personnel
   b. Clear and unobstructed at all times
   c. Unlikely to expose evacuating personnel to additional hazards
   d. Have evacuation routes evaluated by someone not in your organization.

   Consider how you would access important personal information about employees (home phone, next-of-kin, medical) in an emergency. Storing information on computer disks or in sealed envelopes are two options.

3. **Assembly Areas and Accountability**

   Obtaining an accurate account of personnel after a site evacuation requires planning and practice.

   Designate assembly areas where personnel should gather after evacuating.

Take a head count after the evacuation. The names and last known locations of personnel not accounted for should be determined and given to the EOC. (Confusion in the assembly areas can lead to unnecessary and dangerous search and rescue operations.)

Establish a method for accounting for non-employees such as suppliers and customers.

Establish procedures for further evacuation in case the incident expands. This may consist of sending employees home by normal means or providing them with transportation to an off-site location.

4. **Shelter**

In some emergencies, the best means of protection is to take shelter either within the facility or away from the facility in a public building.

Consider the conditions for taking shelter, e.g., tornado warning.

Identify shelter space in the facility and in the community. Establish procedures for sending personnel to shelter.

Determine needs for emergency supplies such as water, food and medical supplies.

Designate shelter managers, if appropriate.

Coordinate plans with local authorities.

5. **Training and Information**

Train employees in evacuation, shelter and other safety procedures. Conduct sessions at least annually or when:
a. Employees are hired
b. Evacuation wardens, shelter managers and others with special assignments are designated
c. New equipment, materials or processes are introduced
d. Procedures are updated or revised
e. Exercises show that employee performance must be improved

Provide emergency information such as checklists and evacuation maps.

Post evacuation maps in strategic locations.

Consider the information needs of customers and others who visit the facility.

6. **Family Preparedness**

Consider ways to help employees prepare their families for emergencies. This will increase their personal safety and help the facility get back up and running. Those who are prepared at home will be better able to carry out their responsibilities at work.

A gas explosion and fire in a nursing home caused the evacuation of all patients, most of whom were disabled. Because the staff had trained for this scenario, all patients were evacuated safely.

Search and rescue should be conducted only by properly trained and equipped professionals. Death or serious injury can occur when untrained employees reenter a damaged or contaminated facility.

FUNCTION: PROPERTY PROTECTION.

Protecting facilities, equipment and vital records is essential to restoring operations once an emergency has occurred.

1. **Planning Considerations** - Establish procedures for:
   a. Fighting fires
   b. Containing material spills
   c. Closing or barricading doors and windows
   d. Shutting down equipment
   e. Covering or securing equipment
   f. Moving equipment to a safe location

   Identify sources of backup equipment, parts and supplies.

   Designate personnel to authorize, supervise and perform a facility shutdown. Train them to recognize when to abandon the effort.

   Obtain materials to carry out protection procedures and keep them on hand for use only in emergencies.

2. **Protection Systems**

   Determine needs for systems to detect abnormal situations, provide warning and protect property. Consider:
   a. Fire protection systems
   b. Lightning protection systems
   c. Water-level monitoring systems
   d. Overflow detection devices
   e. Automatic shutoffs
   f. Emergency power generation systems

   Consult your property insurer about special protective systems.

3. **Mitigation**

   Consider ways to reduce the effects of emergencies, such as moving or constructing facilities away from flood plains and fault zones. Also consider ways to reduce the chances of emergencies from occurring, such as changing processes or materials used to run the business.

   Consider physical retrofitting measures such as:
   a. Upgrading facilities to withstand the shaking of an earthquake or high winds
   b. "Floodproofing" facilities by constructing flood walls or other flood protection devices (see Section 3 for additional information)

c. Installing fire sprinkler systems
d. Installing fire-resistant materials and furnishing
e. Installing storm shutters for all exterior windows and doors

There are also non-structural mitigation measures to consider, including:
a. Installing fire-resistant materials and furnishing
b. Securing light fixtures and other items that could fall or shake loose in an emergency
c. Moving heavy or breakable objects to low shelves
d. Attaching cabinets and files to low walls or bolting them together
e. Placing Velcro strips under typewriters, tabletop computers and television monitors
f. Moving work stations away from large windows
g. Installing curtains or blinds that can be drawn over windows to prevent glass from shattering onto employees
h. Anchoring water heaters and bolting them to wall studs

Consult a structural engineer or architect and your community's building and zoning offices for additional information.

4. **Facility Shutdown**

   Facility shutdown is generally a last resort but always a possibility. Improper or disorganized shutdown can result in confusion, injury and property damage.

   Some facilities require only simple actions such as turning off equipment, locking doors and activating alarms. Others require complex shutdown procedures.

   Work with department heads to establish shutdown procedures. Include information about when and how to shut off utilities. Identify:
   a. The conditions that could necessitate a shutdown
   b. Who can order a shutdown
   c. Who will carry out shutdown procedures
   d. How a partial shutdown would affect other facility operations
   e. The length of time required for shutdown and restarting

   Train personnel in shutdown procedures. Post procedures.

5. **Records Preservation**

   Vital records may include:
   a. Financial and insurance information
   b. Engineering plans and drawings
   c. Product lists and specifications
   d. Employee, customer and supplier databases
   e. Formulas and trade secrets
   f. Personnel files

   Preserving vital records is essential to the quick restoration of operations. Analyzing vital records involves:
   a. Classifying operations into functional categories, e.g., finance, production, sales, administration

b. Determining essential functions for keeping the business up and running, such as finance, production, sales, etc.
c. Identifying the minimum information that must be readily accessible to perform essential functions, e.g., maintaining customer collections may require access to account statements
d. Identifying the records that contain the essential information and where they are located
e. Identifying the equipment and materials needed to access and use the information

Next, establish procedures for protecting and accessing vital records. Among the many approaches to consider are:
a. Labeling vital records
b. Backing up computer systems
c. Making copies of records
d. Storing tapes and disks in insulated containers
e. Storing data off-site where they would not likely be damaged by an event affecting your facility
f. Increasing security of computer facilities
g. Arranging for evacuation of records to backup facilities
h. Backing up systems handled by service bureaus
i. Arranging for backup power

FUNCTION: COMMUNITY OUTREACH.

Your facility's relationship with the community will influence your ability to protect personnel and property and return to normal operations.

1. **Involving the Community**

   Maintain a dialogue with community leaders, first responders, government agencies, community organizations and utilities, including:
   a. Fire, police and emergency medical services personnel
   b. Local Emergency Planning Committee (LEPC) members
   c. Emergency management director
   d. Public Works Department
   e. American Red Cross
   f. Hospitals
   g. Telephone company
   h. Electric utility
   i. Neighborhood groups

   Have regular meetings with community emergency personnel to review emergency plans and procedures. Talk about what you're doing to prepare for and prevent emergencies. Explain your concern for the community's welfare.

   Identify ways your facility could help the community in a community-wide emergency.

   Look for common interests and concerns. Identify opportunities for sharing resources and information.

Conduct confidence-building activities such as facility tours. Do a facility walk-through with community response groups.

Involve community fire, police and emergency management personnel in drills and exercises.

Meet with your neighbors to determine how you could assist each other in an emergency.

2. **Mutual Aid Agreements**

To avoid confusion and conflict in an emergency, establish mutual aid agreements with local response agencies and businesses. These agreements should:
a. Define the type of assistance
b. Identify the chain of command for activating the agreement
c. Define communications procedures

Include these agencies in facility training exercises whenever possible.

Mutual aid agreements can address any number of activities or resources that might be needed in an emergency. For example:
1. Providing for firefighting and HAZMAT response.
2. Providing shelter space, emergency storage, emergency supplies, medical support.
3. Businesses allowing neighbors to use their property to account for personnel after an evacuation.

3. **Community Service**

In community-wide emergencies, business and industry are often needed to assist the community with:
a. Personnel
b. Equipment
c. Shelter
d. Training
e. Storage
f. Feeding facilities
g. EOC facilities
h. Food, clothing, building materials
i. Funding
j. Transportation

While there is no way to predict what demands will be placed on your company's resources, give some thought to how the community's needs might influence your corporate responsibilities in an emergency. Also, consider the opportunities for community service before an emergency occurs.

4. **Public Information**

When site emergencies expand beyond the facility, the community will want to know the nature of the incident, whether the public's safety or health is in danger, what is being done to resolve the problem and what was done to prevent the situation from happening.

Determine the audiences that may be affected by an emergency and identify their information needs. Include:

a. The public
b. The media
c. Employees and retirees
d. Unions organizations

e. Contractors and suppliers
f. customers
g. Shareholders
h. Emergency response

i. Regulatory agencies
j. Appointed and elected officials
k. Special interest groups
l. Neighbors

The community wants to know:
1. What does the facility do?
2. What are the hazards?
3. What programs are in place to respond to emergencies?
4. How could a site emergency affect the community?
5. What assistance will be required from the community?

5. **Media Relations**

In an emergency, the media are the most important link to the public. Try to develop and maintain positive relations with media outlets in your area. Determine their particular needs and interests. Explain your plan for protecting personnel and preventing emergencies.

Determine how you would communicate important public information through the media in an emergency.

Designate a trained spokesperson and an alternate spokesperson.

Set up a media briefing area.

Establish security procedures.

Establish procedures for ensuring that information is complete, accurate and approved for public release.

Determine an appropriate and useful way of communicating technical information.

Prepare background information about the facility.

When providing information to the media during an emergency:

Do:

Give all media equal access to information.

When appropriate, conduct press briefings and interviews. Give local and national media equal time.

Try to observe media deadlines.

Escort media representatives to ensure safety.

Keep records of information released.

Provide press releases when possible.

Don't:

Do not speculate about the incident.

Do not permit unauthorized personnel to release information.

Do not cover up facts or mislead the media.

Do not place blame for the incident.

> Press releases about facility-generated emergencies should describe who is involved in the incident and what happened, including when, where, why and how.

6. **FUNCTION: RECOVERY AND RESTORATION.**

Business recovery and restoration, or business resumption, goes right to a facility's bottom line: keeping people employed and the business running.

7. **Planning Considerations**

Consider making contractual arrangements with vendors for such post-emergency services as records preservation, equipment repair, earthmoving or engineering.

Meet with your insurance carriers to discuss your property and business resumptions policies (see the next page for guidelines).

Determine critical operations and make plans for bringing those systems back on-line. The process may entail:
a. Repairing or replacing equipment
b. Relocating operations to an alternate location
c. Contracting operations on a temporary basis

Take photographs or videotape the facility to document company assets. Update these records regularly.

8. **Continuity of Management**

You can assume that not every key person will be readily available or physically at the facility after an emergency. Ensure that recovery decisions can be made without undue delay. Consult your legal department regarding laws and corporate bylaws governing continuity of management.

Establish procedures for:
a. Assuring the chain of command
b. Maintaining lines of succession for key personnel
c. Moving to alternate headquarters

Include these considerations in all exercise scenarios.

9. **Insurance**

Most companies discover that they are not properly insured only after they have suffered a loss. Lack of appropriate insurance can be financially devastating. Discuss the following topics with your insurance advisor to determine your individual needs.

a. How will my property be valued?

b. Does my policy cover the cost of required upgrades to code?

c. How much insurance am I required to carry to avoid becoming a co-insurer?

d. What perils or causes of loss does my policy cover?

e. What are my deductibles?

f. What does my policy require me to do in the event of a loss?

g. What types of records and documentation will my insurance company want to see? Are records in a safe place where they can be obtained after an emergency?

h. To what extent am I covered for loss due to interruption of power? Is coverage provided for both on- and off-premises power interruption?

i. Am I covered for lost income in the event of business interruption because of a loss? Do I have enough coverage? For how long is coverage provided? How long is my coverage for lost income if my business is closed by order of a civil authority?

j. To what extent am I covered for reduced income due to customers' not all immediately coming back once the business reopens?

k. How will my emergency management program affect my rates?

10. **Employee Support**

Since employees who will rely on you for support after an emergency are your most valuable asset, consider the range of services that you could provide or arrange for, including:

a. Cash advances   d. Reduced work hours   f. Care packages

b. Salary continuation   e. Crisis counseling   g. Day care

c. Flexible work hours

> After a site emergency, assess the impact of the event on business neighbors and the community and take appropriate action. How you handle this issue will have long-lasting consequences.

11. **Resuming Operations** — Immediately after an emergency:

Establish a recovery team, if necessary. Establish priorities for resuming operations.

Continue to ensure the safety of personnel on the property. Assess remaining hazards. Maintain security at the incident scene.

Conduct an employee briefing.

Keep detailed records. Consider audio recording all decisions. Photographs or videotape the damage.

Account for all damage-related costs. Establish special job order numbers and charge codes for purchases and repair work.

Follow notification procedures. Notify employees' families about the status of personnel on the property. Notify off-duty personnel about work status. Notify insurance carriers and appropriate government agencies.

Protect undamaged property. Close up building openings. Remove smoke, water and debris. Protect equipment against moisture. Restore sprinkler systems. Physically secure the property. Restore power.

Conduct an investigation. Coordinate actions with appropriate government agencies.

Conduct salvage operations. Segregate damaged from undamaged property. Keep damaged goods on hand until an insurance adjuster has visited the premises, but you can move material outside if it's seriously in the way and exposure to the elements won't make matters worse.

Take an inventory of damaged goods. This is usually done with the adjuster, or the adjuster's salvor if there is any appreciable amount of goods or value. If you release goods to the salvor, obtain a signed inventory stating the quantity and type of goods being removed.

Restore equipment and property. For major repair work, review restoration plans with the insurance adjuster and appropriate government agencies.

Assess the value of damaged property. Assess the impact of business interruption.

Maintain contact with customers and suppliers.

12. **FUNCTION: ADMINISTRATION AND LOGISTICS.**

Maintain complete and accurate records at all times to ensure a more efficient emergency response and recovery. Certain records may also be required by regulation or by your insurance carriers or prove invaluable in the case of legal action after an incident.

13. Administrative Actions

Administrative actions prior to an emergency include:
a. Establishing a written emergency management plan
b. Maintaining training records
c. Maintaining all written communications
d. Documenting drills and exercises and their critiques
e. Involving community emergency response organizations in planning activities

Administrative actions during and after an emergency include:
a. Maintaining telephone logs
b. Keeping a detailed record of events
c. Maintaining a record of injuries and follow-up actions
d. Accounting for personnel
e. Coordinating notification of family members
f. Issuing press releases

   g. Maintaining sampling records
   h. Managing finances
   i. Coordinating personnel services
   j. Documenting incident investigations and recovery operations

14. **Logistics**

Before an emergency, logistics may entail:
   a. Acquiring equipment
   b. Stockpiling supplies
   c. Designating emergency facilities
   d. Establishing training facilities
   e. Establishing mutual aid agreements
   f. Preparing a resource inventory

During an emergency, logistics may entail the provision of:
   a. Providing utility maps to emergency responders
   b. Providing material safety data sheets to employees
   c. Moving backup equipment in place
   d. Repairing parts
   e. Arranging for medical support, food and transportation
   f. Arranging for shelter facilities
   g. Providing for backup power
   h. Providing for backup communications

Emergency funding can be critical immediately following an emergency. Consider the need for pre-approved purchase requisitions and whether special funding authorities may be necessary.

SECTION 3 — HAZARD-SPECIFIC INFORMATION

1. **HAZARDS: FIRE.**

   Fire is the most common of all the hazards. Every year fires cause thousands of deaths and injuries and billions of dollars in property damage.

   Planning Considerations
   a. Meet with the fire department to talk about the community's fire response capabilities, talk about your operations, identify processes and materials that could cause or fuel a fire, or contaminate the environment in a fire
   b. Have your facility inspected for fire hazards; ask about fire codes and regulations
   c. Ask your insurance carrier to recommend fire prevention and protection measures, your carrier may also offer training
   d. Distribute fire safety information to employees: how to prevent fires in the workplace, how to contain a fire, how to evacuate the facility, where to report a fire
   e. Instruct personnel to use the stairs — not elevators — in a fire, instruct them to crawl on their hands and knees when escaping a hot or smoke-filled area
   f. Conduct evacuation drills, post maps of evacuation routes in prominent places, keep evacuation routes including stairways and doorways clear of debris
   g. Assign fire wardens for each area to monitor shutdown and evacuation procedures
   h. Establish procedures for the safe handling and storage of flammable liquids and gases
   i. Establish procedures to prevent the accumulation of combustible materials
   j. Provide for the safe disposal of smoking materials
   k. Establish a preventive maintenance schedule to keep equipment operating safely
   l. Place fire extinguishers in appropriate locations
   m Train employees in use of fire extinguishers
   n. Install smoke detectors, check smoke detectors once a month, change batteries at least once a year
   o. Establish a system for warning personnel of a fire, consider installing a fire alarm with automatic notification to the fire department
   p. Consider installing a sprinkler system, fire hoses and fire-resistant walls and doors
   q. Ensure that key personnel are familiar with all fire safety systems
   r. Identify and mark all utility shutoffs so that electrical power, gas or water can be shut off quickly by fire wardens or responding personnel

   Determine the level of response your facility will take if a fire occurs. Among the options are:

   Option 1 — Immediate evacuation of all personnel on alarm.

   Option 2 — All personnel are trained in fire extinguisher use. Personnel in the immediate area of a fire attempt to control it. If they cannot, the fire alarm is sounded and all personnel evacuate.

   Option 3 — Only designated personnel are trained in fire extinguisher use.

   Option 4 — A fire team is trained to fight incipient-stage fires that can be controlled without protective equipment or breathing apparatus. Beyond this level fire, the team evacuates.

Option 5 — A fire team is trained and equipped to fight structural fires using protective equipment and breathing apparatus.

2. HAZARDS: HAZARDOUS MATERIALS INCIDENTS.

Hazardous materials are substances that are either flammable or combustible, explosive, toxic, noxious, corrosive, oxidizable, an irritant or radioactive.

A hazardous material spill or release can pose a risk to life, health or property. An incident can result in the evacuation of a few people, a section of a facility or an entire neighborhood.

There are a number of Federal laws that regulate hazardous materials, including: the Superfund Amendments and Reauthorization Act of 1986 (SARA), the Resource Conservation and Recovery Act of 1976 (RCRA), the Hazardous Materials Transportation Act (HMTA), the Occupational Safety and Health Act (OSHA), the Toxic Substances Control Act (TSCA) and the Clean Air Act.

Title III of SARA regulates the packaging, labeling, handling, storage and transportation of hazardous materials. The law requires facilities to furnish information about the quantities and health effects of materials used at the facility, and to promptly notify local and State officials whenever a significant release of hazardous materials occurs.

In addition to on-site hazards, you should be aware of the potential for an off-site incident affecting your operations. You should also be aware of hazardous materials used in facility processes and in the construction of the physical plant.Detailed definitions as well as lists of hazardous materials can be obtained from the Environmental Protection Agency (EPA) and the Occupational Safety and Health Administration (OSHA).

Planning Considerations. Consider the following when developing your plan:
a. Identify and label all hazardous materials stored, handled, produced and disposed of by your facility, follow government regulations that apply to your facility, obtain material safety data sheets (MSDS) for all hazardous materials at your location
b. Ask the local fire department for assistance in developing appropriate response procedures
c. Train employees to recognize and report hazardous material spills and releases, train employees in proper handling and storage
d. Establish a hazardous material response plan:
    (1) Establish procedures to notify management and emergency response organizations of an incident
    (2) Establish procedures to warn employees of an incident
    (3) Establish evacuation procedures
e. Depending on your operations, organize and train an emergency response team to confine and control hazardous material spills in accordance with applicable regulations
f. Identify other facilities in your area that use hazardous materials, determine whether an incident could affect your facility
g. Identify highways, railroads and waterways near your facility used for the transportation of hazardous materials, determine how a transportation accident near your facility could affect your operations

3. **HAZARDS: FLOODS AND FLASH FLOODS.**

Floods are the most common and widespread of all natural disasters. Most communities in the United States can experience some degree of flooding after spring rains, heavy thunderstorms or winter snow thaws.

Most floods develop slowly over a period of days. Flash floods, however, are like walls of water that develop in a matter of minutes. Flash floods can be caused by intense storms or dam failure.

Planning Considerations. Consider the following when preparing for floods:
a. Ask your local emergency management office whether your facility is located in a flood plain, learn the history of flooding in your area, learn the elevation of your facility in relation to steams, rivers and dams
b. Review the community's emergency plan, learn the community's evacuation routes, know where to find higher ground in case of a flood
c. Establish warning and evacuation procedures for the facility, make plans for assisting employees who may need transportation
d. Inspect areas in your facility subject to flooding, identify records and equipment that can be moved to a higher location, make plans to move records and equipment in case of flood
e. Purchase a NOAA Weather Radio with a warning alarm tone and battery backup, listen for flood watches and warnings
f. Flood Watch — Flooding is possible, stay tuned to NOAA radio, be prepared to evacuate, tune to local radio and television stations for additional information
g. Flood Warning — Flooding is already occurring or will occur soon, take precautions at once, be prepared to go to higher ground, if advised, evacuate immediately
h. Ask your insurance carrier for information about flood insurance, regular property and casualty insurance does not cover flooding
i. Consider the feasibility of floodproofing your facility, there are three basic types of methods

Permanent floodproofing measures are taken before a flood occurs and require no human intervention when flood waters rise. They include:
a. Filling windows, doors or other openings with water-resistant materials such as concrete blocks or bricks; this approach assumes the structure is strong enough to withstand flood waters
b. Installing check valves to prevent water from entering where utility and sewer lines enter the facility
c. Reinforcing walls to resist water pressure, sealing walls to prevent or reduce seepage
d. Building watertight walls around equipment or work areas within the facility that are particularly susceptible to flood damage
e. Constructing floodwalls or levees outside the facility to keep flood waters away
f. Elevating the facility on walls, columns or compacted fill; this approach is most applicable to new construction, though many types of buildings can be elevated

Contingent floodproofing measures are also taken before a flood but require some additional action when flooding occurs. These measures include:
a. Installing watertight barriers called flood shields to prevent the passage of water through doors, windows, ventilation shafts or other openings
b. Installing permanent watertight doors

    c. Constructing movable floodwalls

    d. Installing permanent pumps to remove flood waters

Emergency floodproofing measures are generally less expensive than those listed above, though they require substantial advance warning and do not satisfy the minimum requirements for watertight floodproofing as set forth by the National Flood Insurance Program (NFIP). They include:

    a. Building walls with sandbags

    b. Constructing a double row of walls with boards and posts to create a "crib," then filling the crib with soil

    c. Constructing a single wall by stacking small beams or planks on top of each other

    d. Consider the need for backup systems:

        (1) Portable pumps to remove flood water

        (2) Alternate power sources such as generators or gasoline-powered pumps

        (3) Battery-powered emergency lighting

    e. Participate in community flood control projects

4. HAZARDS: HURRICANES.

Hurricanes are severe tropical storms with sustained winds of 74 miles per hour or greater.

Hurricane winds can reach 160 miles per hour and extend inland for hundreds of miles.

Hurricanes bring torrential rains and a storm surge of ocean water that crashes into land as the storm approaches. Hurricanes also spawn tornadoes.

Hurricane advisories are issued by the National Weather Service as soon as a hurricane appears to be a threat. The hurricane season lasts from June through November.

Planning Considerations

    a. Ask your local emergency management office about community evacuation plans

    b. Establish facility shutdown procedures, establish warning and evacuation procedures, make plans for assisting employees who may need transportation

    c. Make plans for communicating with employees' families before and after a hurricane

    d. Purchase a NOAA Weather Radio with a warning alarm tone and battery backup

    e. Listen for hurricane watches and warnings

    f. Hurricane Watch — A hurricane is possible within 24 to 36 hours, stay tuned for additional advisories, tune to local radio and television stations for additional information; an evacuation may be necessary

    g. Hurricane Warning — A hurricane will hit land within 24 hours; take precautions at once, if advised, evacuate immediately

    h. Survey your facility, make plans to protect outside equipment and structures

    i. Make plans to protect windows, permanent storm shutters offer the best protection

    j. Covering windows with 5/8" marine plywood is a second option

Consider the need for backup systems:

    Portable pumps to remove flood water

    Alternate power sources such as generators or gasoline-powered pumps

    Battery-powered emergency lighting

Prepare to move records, computers and other items within your facility or to another location.

5. HAZARDS: TORNADOES.

Tornadoes are incredibly violent local storms that extend to the ground with whirling winds that can reach 300 mph.

Spawned from powerful thunderstorms, tornadoes can uproot trees and buildings and turn harmless objects into deadly missiles in a matter of seconds. Damage paths can be in excess of one mile wide and 50 miles long.

Tornadoes can occur in any state but occur more frequently in the Midwest, Southeast and Southwest. They occur with little or no warning.

Planning Considerations:
a. Ask your local emergency management office about the community's tornado warning system
b. Purchase a NOAA Weather Radio with a warning alarm tone and battery backup, listen for tornado watches and warnings
c. Tornado Watch — Tornadoes are likely, be ready to take shelter, stay tuned to radio and television stations for additional information
d. Tornado Warning — A tornado has been sighted in the area or is indicated by radar; take shelter immediately
e. Establish procedures to inform personnel when tornado warnings are posted, consider the need for spotters to be responsible for looking out for approaching storms
f. Work with a structural engineer or architect to designate shelter areas in your facility, ask your local emergency management office or National Weather Service office for guidance
g. Consider the amount of space you will need; adults require about six square feet of space, nursing home and hospital patients require more.
h. The best protection in a tornado is usually an underground area. If an underground area is not available, consider:
    (1) Small interior rooms on the lowest floor and without windows
    (2) Hallways on the lowest floor away from doors and windows
    (3) Rooms constructed with reinforced concrete, brick or block with no windows and a heavy concrete floor or roof system overhead
    (4) Protected areas away from doors and windows

Note: Auditoriums, cafeterias and gymnasiums that are covered with a flat, wide-span roof are not considered safe.
i. Make plans for evacuating personnel away from lightweight modular offices or mobile home-size buildings; these structures offer no protection from tornadoes
j. Conduct tornado drills
k. Once in the shelter, personnel should protect their heads with their arms and crouch down

6. **HAZARDS: SEVERE WINTER STORMS.**

Severe winter storms bring heavy snow, ice, strong winds and freezing rain. Winter storms can prevent employees and customers from reaching the facility, leading to a temporary shutdown until roads are cleared. Heavy snow and ice can also cause structural damage and power outages.

Planning Considerations:
a. Listen to NOAA Weather Radio and local radio and television stations for weather information
b. Winter Storm Watch — Severe winter weather is possible
c. Winter Storm Warning — Severe winter weather is expected
d. Blizzard Warning — Severe winter weather with sustained winds of at least 35 mph is expected
e. Traveler's Advisory — Severe winter conditions may make driving difficult or dangerous
f. Establish procedures for facility shutdown and early release of employees
g. Store food, water, blankets, battery-powered radios with extra batteries and other emergency supplies for employees who become stranded at the facility
h. Provide a backup power source for critical operations
i. Arrange for snow and ice removal from parking lots, walkways, loading docks, etc.

7. **HAZARDS: EARTHQUAKES.**

Earthquakes occur most frequently west of the Rocky Mountains, although historically the most violent earthquakes have occurred in the central United States. Earthquakes occur suddenly and without warning.

Earthquakes can seriously damage buildings and their contents; disrupt gas, electric and telephone services; and trigger landslides, avalanches, flash floods, fires and huge ocean waves called tsunamis. Aftershocks can occur for weeks following an earthquake.In many buildings, the greatest danger to people in an earthquake is when equipment and non-structural elements such as ceilings, partitions, windows and lighting fixtures shake loose.

Planning Considerations:
a. Assess your facility's vulnerability to earthquakes, ask local government agencies for seismic information for your area
b. Have your facility inspected by a structural engineer, develop and prioritize strengthening measures. These may include:
   (1) Adding steel bracing to frames
   (2) Adding sheer walls to frames
   (3) Strengthening columns and building foundations
   (4) Replacing unreinforced brick filler walls
c. Follow safety codes when constructing a facility or making major renovations
d. Inspect non-structural systems such as air conditioning, communications and pollution control systems; assess the potential for damage; prioritize measures to prevent damages
e. Inspect your facility for any item that could fall, spill, break or move during an earthquake, take steps to reduce these hazards
f. Move large and heavy objects to lower shelves or the floor, hang heavy items away from where people work

g. Secure shelves, filing cabinets, tall furniture, desktop equipment, computers, printers, copiers and light fixtures
h. Secure fixed equipment and heavy machinery to the floor, larger equipment can be placed on casters and attached to tethers which attach to the wall
i. Add bracing to suspended ceilings, if necessary
j. Install safety glass where appropriate
k. Secure large utility and process piping
l. Keep copies of design drawings of the facility to be used in assessing the facility's safety after an earthquake
m. Review processes for handling and storing hazardous materials; have incompatible chemicals stored separately
n. Ask your insurance carrier about earthquake insurance and mitigation techniques
o. Establish procedures to determine whether an evacuation is necessary after an earthquake
p. Designate areas in the facility away from exterior walls and windows where occupants should gather after an earthquake if an evacuation is not necessary
q. Conduct earthquake drills; provide personnel with the following safety information
r. In an earthquake, if indoors, stay there; take cover under a sturdy piece of furniture or counter, or brace yourself against an inside wall; protect your head and neck
s. If outdoors, move into the open, away from buildings, street lights and utility wires
t. After an earthquake, stay away from windows, skylights and items that could fall; do not use the elevators
u. Use stairways to leave the building if it is determined that a building evacuation is necessary

8. **HAZARDS: TECHNOLOGICAL EMERGENCIES.**

Technological emergencies include any interruption or loss of a utility service, power source, life support system, information system or equipment needed to keep the business in operation.

Planning Considerations:

Identify all critical operations, including:
a. Utilities including electric power, gas, water, hydraulics, compressed air, municipal and internal sewer systems, wastewater treatment services
b. Security and alarm systems, elevators, lighting, life support systems, heating, ventilation and air conditioning systems, electrical distribution system
c. Manufacturing equipment, pollution control equipment
d. Communication systems, both data and voice computer networks
e. Transportation systems including air, highway, railroad and waterway

Determine the impact of service disruption.

Ensure that key safety and maintenance personnel are thoroughly familiar with all building systems.

Establish procedures for restoring systems. Determine need for backup systems.

Establish preventive maintenance schedules for all systems and equipment.

SECTION 4 — INFORMATION SOURCES

1. **SOURCES: ADDITIONAL READINGS FROM FEMA.**

   These publications can be obtained from FEMA, Publications, P.O. Box 70274, Washington, DC 20024.

   Disaster Mitigation Guide for Business and Industry (FEMA 190) —Technical planning information for building owners and industrial facilities on how to reduce the impact of natural disasters and man-made emergencies.

   Principal Threats Facing Communities and Local Emergency Management Coordinators (FEMA 191) — Statistics and analyses of natural disasters and man-made threats in the U.S.

   Floodproofing Non-Residential Structures (FEMA 102) — Technical information for building owners, designers and contractors on floodproofing techniques (200 pages).

   Non-Residential Flood-proofing — Requirements and Certification for Buildings Located in Flood Hazard Areas in Accordance with the National Flood Insurance Program (FIA-TB-3) — Planning and engineering considerations for floodproofing new commercial buildings.

   Building Performance: Hurricane Andrew in Florida (FIA 22) — Technical guidance for enhancing the performance of buildings in hurricanes.

   Building Performance: Hurricane Iniki in Hawaii (FIA 23) — Technical guidance for reducing hurricane and flood damage.

   Answers to Questions About Substantially Damaged Buildings (FEMA 213)—Regulations and policies of the National Flood Insurance Program regarding substantially damaged buildings (25 pages).

   Design Guidelines for Flood Damage Reduction (FEMA 15) — A study on land use, watershed management, design and construction practices in flood- prone areas.

   Comprehensive Earthquake Preparedness Planning Guidelines: Corporate FEMA 71) — Earthquake planning guidance for corporate safety officers and managers.

2. **SOURCES: READY-TO-PRINT BROCHURES**

   Ready-to-Print Brochure Mechanicals for Your Employee Safety Program. Life-saving information from FEMA and the American Red Cross. Available at no charge is ready-to-print artwork for a series of brochures on disaster preparedness and family safety.

   For camera-ready materials, printing instructions and ideas for adding your logo or sponsor message. Write to: Camera-ready Requests, FEMA Publications, 500 C Street, SW, Washington, DC 20472.

   Your Family Disaster Plan — A 4-step plan for individuals and families on how to prepare for any type of disaster.

B-41

Emergency Preparedness Checklist—A checklist on home safety, evacuation and disaster preparedness.

Your Family Disaster Supplies Kit — A checklist of emergency supplies for the home and car.

Helping Children Cope With Disaster — Practical advice on how to help children deal with the stress of disaster.

Foreword

Bombing and the threat of being bombed are harsh realities in today's world. The public is becoming more aware of those incidents of violence that are perpetrated by vicious, nefarious segments of our society through the illegal use of explosives. Law enforcement agencies are charged with providing protection for life and property, but law enforcement alone cannot be held responsible. Every citizen must do his or her part to ensure a safe environment.

The following information is designed to help both the public and private sectors prepare for the potential threat of explosives-related violence. While the ideas set forth herein are applicable in most cases, they are intended only as a guide. The information provided is compiled from a wide range of sources, including the actual experiences of special agents of the Bureau of Alcohol, Tobacco and Firearms (ATF).

If there is one point that cannot be overemphasized, it is the value of being prepared. Do not allow a bomb incident to catch you by surprise. By developing a bomb incident plan and considering possible bomb incidents in your physical security plan, you can reduce the potential for personal injury and property damage.

In making this information available to you, we hope to help you better prepare to deal with bomb threats and the illegal use of explosives.

Bombs

Bombs can be constructed to look like almost anything and can be placed or delivered in any number of ways. The probability of finding a bomb that looks like the stereotypical bomb is almost nonexistent. The only common denominator that exists among bombs is that they are designed or intended to explode.

Most bombs are homemade and are limited in their design only by the imagination of, and resources available to, the bomber. Remember, when searching for a bomb, suspect anything that looks unusual. Let the trained bomb technician determine what is or is not a bomb.

Bomb threats

Bomb threats are delivered in a variety of ways. The majority of threats are called in to the target. Occasionally these calls are through a third party. Sometimes a threat is communicated in writing or by a recording.

Two logical explanations for reporting a bomb threat are:

1. The caller has definite knowledge or believes that an explosive or incendiary bomb has been or will be placed and he/she wants to minimize personal injury or property damage. The caller may be the person who placed the device or someone who has become aware of such information.

2. The caller wants to create an atmosphere of anxiety and panic which will, in turn, result in a disruption of the normal activities at the facility where the device is purportedly placed.

Whatever the reason for the report, there will certainly be a reaction to it. Through proper planning, the wide variety of potentially uncontrollable reactions can be greatly reduced.

Why Prepare

If you accept the two aforementioned explanations for reporting that a bomb is about to go off, you can better prepare to foil the bomber or threat maker.

Through proper preparation, you can reduce the accessibility of your business or building and identify those areas that can be "hardened" against the potential bomber. This will limit the amount of time lost to searching, if you determine a search is necessary. If a bomb incident occurs, proper planning will instill confidence in the leadership, reinforce the notion that those in charge do care, and reduce the potential for personal injury and property loss.

Proper planning can also reduce the threat of panic, the most contagious of all human emotions. Panic is sudden, excessive, unreasoning, infectious terror. Once a state of panic has been reached, the potential for injury and property damage is greatly increased. In the context of a bomb threat, panic is the ultimate achievement of the caller.

Be prepared! There is no excuse for not taking every step necessary to meet the threat.

How to Prepare

In preparing to cope with a bomb incident, it is necessary to develop two separate but interdependent plans, namely a physical security plan and a bomb incident plan.

Physical security provides for the protection of property, personnel, facilities, and material against unauthorized entry, trespass, damage, sabotage, or other illegal or criminal acts. The physical security plan deals with prevention and control of access to the building. In most instances, some form of physical security may be already in existence, although not necessarily intended to prevent a bomb attack.

The bomb incident plan provides detailed procedures to be implemented when a bombing attack is executed or threatened. In planning for the bomb incident, a definite chain of command or line of authority must be established. Only by using an established organization and procedures can the bomb incident be handled with the least risk to all concerned. A clearly defined line of authority will instill confidence and avoid panic.

Establishing a chain of command is easy if there is a simple office structure, one business, one building. However, if a complex situation exists, a multi-occupant building for example, a representative from each occupant entity should attend the planning conference. A leader should be appointed and a clear line of succession delineated. This chain of command should be printed and circulated to all concerned parties.

In planning, you should designate a command center to be located in the switchboard room or other focal point of telephone or radio communications. The management personnel assigned to operate the center should have the authority to decide whatever action should be taken during the threat. Only those with assigned duties should be permitted in the center. Make some provision for alternates in the event someone is absent when a threat is received. Obtain an updated blueprint or floor plan of your building and maintain it in the command center.

Contact the police department, fire department, or local government agencies to determine if any assistance is available to you for developing your physical security plan or bomb incident plan. If possible, have police and/or fire department representatives and members of your staff inspect the building for areas where explosives are likely to be concealed. (Make a checklist of these areas for inclusion in command center materials.) Determine whether there is a bomb disposal unit available, how to contact the unit, and under what conditions it is activated. In developing your bomb incident plan, you must also ascertain whether the bomb disposal unit, in addition to disarming and removing the explosives, will assist in searching the building in the event of a threat.

Training is essential to deal properly with a bomb threat incident. Instruct all personnel, especially those at the telephone switchboard, in what to do if a bomb threat is received. Be absolutely certain that all personnel assigned to the command center are aware of their duties. The positive aspects of planning will be lost if the leadership is not apparent. It is also very important to organize and train an evacuation unit which will be responsive to the command center and has a clear understanding of the importance of its role.

We have suggested that the command center be located near the switchboard or focal point of communications. It is critical that lines of communication be established between the command center and the search or evacuation teams. The center must have the flexibility to keep up with the search team progress. In a large facility, if the teams go beyond the communications network, the command center must have the mobility to maintain contact and track search or evacuation efforts.

Security Against Bomb Incidents

We mentioned earlier that, in dealing with bomb incidents or potential bomb incidents, two interrelated plans must be developed, the bomb incident plan and the physical security plan. Heretofore, we have primarily addressed the bomb incident plan. Now, before continuing with that plan, we will discuss security measures as they apply to "hardening" against the bomb attack.

Most commercial structures and individual residences already have some security in place, planned or unplanned, realized or not. Locks on windows and doors, outside lights, etc., are all designed and installed to contribute toward the security of a facility and the protection of its occupants.

In considering measures to increase security for your building or office, it is highly recommended that you contact your local police department for guidance regarding a specific plan for your facility. There is no single security plan that is adaptable to all situations. The following recommendations are offered because they may contribute to reducing your vulnerability to bomb attacks.

The exterior configuration of a building or facility is very important. Unfortunately, in most instances, the architect has given little or no consideration to security, particularly toward thwarting or discouraging a bomb attack.

However, by the addition of fencing and lighting, and by controlling access, the vulnerability of a facility to a bomb attack can be reduced significantly.

C-3

Bombs being delivered by car or left in a car are a grave reality. Parking should be restricted, if possible, to 300 feet from your building or any building in a complex. If restricted parking is not feasible, properly identified employee vehicles should be parked closest to your facility and visitor vehicles parked at a distance.

Heavy shrubs and vines should be kept close to the ground to reduce their potential to conceal criminals or bombs. Window boxes and planters are perfect receptacles for the bomber. Unless there is an absolute requirement for such ornamentation, window boxes and planters are better removed. If they must remain, a security patrol should be employed to check them regularly.

A highly visible security patrol can be significant deterrent. Even if this "patrol" is only one security guard/night guard, he/she is optimally utilized outside the building. If an interior guard is utilized, consider the installation of closed-circuit television cameras that cover exterior building perimeters.

Have an adequate burglar alarm system installed by a reputable company that can service and properly maintain the equipment. Post signs indicating that such a system is in place.

Entrance/exit doors with hinges and hinge pins on the inside to prevent removal should be installed. Solid wood or sheet metal faced doors provide extra integrity that a hollow-core wooden door cannot provide. A steel door frame that properly fits the door is as important as the construction of the door.

The ideal security situation is a building with no windows. However, bars, grates, heavy mesh screens, or steel shutters over windows offer good protection from otherwise unwanted entry. It is important that the openings in the protective coverings are not too large. Otherwise, a bomb may be introduced into the building while the bomber remains outside. Floor vents, transoms, and skylights should also be covered. Please note that fire safety considerations preclude the use of certain window coverings. Municipal ordinances should be researched and safety considered before any of these renovations are undertaken.

Controls should be established for positively identifying personnel who are authorized access to critical areas and for denying access to unauthorized personnel. These controls should extend to the inspection of all packages and materials being taken into critical areas.

Security and maintenance personnel should be alert for people who act in a suspicious manner, as well as objects, items, or parcels which look out of place or suspicious. Surveillance should be established to include potential hiding places (e.g., stairwells, rest rooms, and any vacant office space) for unwanted individuals.

Doors or access ways to such areas as boiler rooms, mail rooms, computer areas, switchboards, and elevator control rooms should remain locked when not in use. It is important to establish a procedure for the accountability of keys. If keys cannot be accounted for, locks should be changed.

Good housekeeping is also vital. Trash or dumpster areas should remain free of debris. A bomb or device can easily be concealed in the trash. Combustible materials should be properly disposed of, or protected if further use is anticipated.

Install detection devices at all entrances and closed-circuit television in those areas previously identified as likely places where a bomb may be placed. This, coupled with the posting of signs indicating such measures are in place, is a good deterrent.

We in ATF recognize the necessity for businesses to maintain good public relations. Corporate responsibility however, also encompasses the safety and protection of the public. The threatened use of explosives necessitates that in the interest of safety and security, some inconvenience may have to be imposed on visitors to public buildings. The public is becoming more accustomed to routine security checks and will readily accept these minor inconveniences.

Perhaps entrances and exits can be modified with a minimal expenditure to channel all visitors through someone at a reception desk. Individuals entering the building would be required to sign a register indicating the name and room number of the person whom they wish to visit. Employees at these reception desks could contact the person to be visited and advise him/her that a visitor, by name, is in the lobby. The person to be visited may decide to come to the lobby to ascertain that the purpose of the visit is valid. A system for signing out when the individual departs could be integrated into this procedure.

Such a procedure may result in complaints from the public. If the reception desk clerk explains to the visitor that these procedures were implemented in his/her best interest and safety, the complaints would be reduced. The placement of a sign at the reception desk informing visitors of the need for safety is another option.

Responding to Bomb Threats

Instruct all personnel, especially those at the telephone switchboard, in what to do if a bomb threat call is received.

It is always desirable that more than one person listen in on the call. To do this, a covert signaling system should be implemented, perhaps by using a coded buzzer signal to a second reception point.

A calm response to the bomb threat caller could result in obtaining additional information. This is especially true if the caller wishes to avoid injuries or deaths. If told that the building is occupied or cannot be evacuated in time, the bomber may be willing to give more specific information on the bomb's location, components, or method of initiation.

The bomb threat caller is the best source of information about the bomb. When a bomb threat is called in:
- Keep the caller on the line as long as possible. Ask him/her to repeat the message. Record every word spoken by the person.
- If the caller does not indicate the location of the bomb or the time of possible detonation, ask him/her for this information.
- Inform the caller that the building is occupied and the detonation of a bomb could result in death or serious injury to many innocent people.
- Pay particular attention to background noises, such as motors running, music playing, and any other noise which maygive a clue as to the location of the caller.
- Listen closely to the voice (male, female), voice quality (calm, excited), accents, and speech impediments. Immediately after the caller hangs up, report the threat to the person designated by management to receive such information.

- Report the information immediately to the police department, fire department, ATF, FBI, and other appropriate agencies. The sequence of notification should be established in the bomb incident plan.
- Remain available, as law enforcement personnel will want to interview you.

When a written threat is received, save all materials, including any envelope or container. Once the message is recognized as a bomb threat, further unnecessary handling should be avoided. Every possible effort must be made to retain evidence such as fingerprints, handwriting or typewriting, paper, and postal marks. These will prove essential in tracing the threat and identifying the writer.

While written messages are usually associated with generalized threats and extortion attempts, a written warning of a specific device may occasionally be received. It should never be ignored.

Decision Time

The most serious of all decisions to be made by management in the event of a bomb threat is whether to evacuate the building. In many cases, this decision may have already been made during the development of the bomb incident plan. Management may pronounce a carte blanche policy that, in the event of a bomb threat, total evacuation will be effective immediately. This decision circumvents the calculated risk and demonstrates a deep concern for the safety of personnel in the building. However, such a decision can result in costly loss of time.

Essentially, there are three alternatives when faced with a bomb threat:

1. Ignore the threat.

2. Evacuate immediately.

3. Search and evacuate if warranted.

Ignoring the threat completely can result in some problems. While a statistical argument can be made that very few bomb threats are real, it cannot be overlooked that bombs have been located in connection with threats. If employees learn that bomb threats have been received and ignored, it could result in morale problems and have a long-term adverse effect on your business. Also, there is the possibility that if the bomb threat caller feels that he/she is being ignored, he/she may go beyond the threat and actually plant a bomb.

Evacuating immediately on every bomb threat is an alternative that on face value appears to be the preferred approach. However, the negative factors inherent in this approach must be considered. The obvious result of immediate evacuation is the disruptive effect on your business. If the bomb threat caller knows that your policy is to evacuate each time a call is made, he/she can continually call and force your business to a standstill. An employee, knowing that the policy is to evacuate immediately, may make a threat in order to get out of work. A student may use a bomb threat to avoid a class or miss a test. Also, a bomber wishing to cause personal injuries could place a bomb near an exit normally used to evacuate and then call in the threat.

Initiating a search after a threat is received and evacuating a building after a suspicious package or device is found is the third, and perhaps most desired, approach. It is certainly not as disruptive as an immediate evacuation and will satisfy the requirement to do something when a threat is received. If a device is found, the evacuation can be accomplished expeditiously while at the same time avoiding the potential danger areas of the bomb.

Evacuation

An evacuation unit consisting of management personnel should be organized and trained. The organization and training of this unit should be coordinated with the development of the bomb incident plan, as well as with all tenants of a building.

The evacuation unit should be trained in how to evacuate the building during a bomb threat. You should consider priority of evacuation, e.g., evacuation by floor level. Evacuate the floor levels above and below the danger area in order to remove those persons from danger as quickly as possible. Training in this type of evacuation is usually available from police, fire or other units within the community.

You may also train the evacuation unit in search techniques, or you may prefer a separate search unit. Volunteer personnel should be solicited for this function. Assignment of search wardens, team leaders, etc., can be employed. To be proficient in searching the building, search personnel must be thoroughly familiar with all hallways, rest rooms, false ceiling areas, and every location in the building where an explosive or incendiary device may be concealed. When police officers or firefighters arrive at the building, the contents and the floor plan will be unfamiliar to them if they have not previously reconnoitered the facility. Thus, it is extremely important that the evacuation or search unit be thoroughly trained and familiar with the floor plan of the building and immediate outside areas. When a room or particular area is searched, it should be marked or sealed with a piece of tape and reported to the supervisor of that area.

The evacuation or search unit should be trained only in evacuation and search techniques and not in the techniques of neutralizing, removing or otherwise having contact with the device. If a device is located, it should not be disturbed. However, its location should be well marked and a route back to the device noted.

Search Teams

It is advisable to use more than one individual to search any area or room, no matter how small. Searches can be conducted by supervisory personnel, area occupants or trained explosive search teams. There are advantages and disadvantages to each method of staffing the search teams.

Using supervisory personnel to search is a rapid approach and causes little disturbance. There will be little loss of employee working time, but a morale problem may develop if it is discovered that a bomb threat has been received and workers were left unaware. Using a supervisor to search will usually not be as thorough because of his/her unfamiliarity with many areas and his/her desire to get on with business.

Using area occupants to search their own areas is the best method for a rapid search. The occupants' concern for their own safety will contribute toward a more thorough search. Furthermore, the personnel conducting the search are familiar with what does or does not belong in a particular area. Using occupants to search will result in a shorter loss of worktime than if all were evacuated prior to search by trained teams. Using the occupants to search can have a positive effect on morale, given a good training program to develop confidence. Of course, this would require the training of an entire work force, and ideally the performance of several practical training exercises. One drawback of this search method is the increased danger to unevacuated workers.

The search conducted by a trained team is the best for safety, morale and thoroughness, though it does take the most time. Using a trained team will result in a significant loss of production time. It is a slow operation that requires comprehensive training and practice.

The decision as to who should conduct searches lies with management, and should be considered and incorporated into the bomb incident plan.

Search Techniques

The following room search technique is based on the use of a two-person searching team. There are many minor variations possible in searching a room. The following contains only the basic techniques.

When the two-person search team enters the room to be searched, they should first move to various parts of the room and stand quietly with their eyes closed and listen for a clockwork device. Frequently, a clockwork mechanism can be quickly detected without use of special equipment. Even if no clockwork mechanism is detected, the team is now aware of the background noise level within the room itself.

Background noise or transferred sound is always disturbing during a building search. If a ticking sound is heard but cannot be located, one might become unnerved. The ticking sound may come from an unbalanced air-conditioner fan several floors away or from a dripping sink down the hall. Sound will transfer through air-conditioning ducts, along water pipes, and through walls. One of the most difficult buildings to search is one that has steam or hot water heat. This type of building will constantly thump, crack, chatter, and tick due to the movement of the steam or hot water through the pipes and the expansion and contraction of the pipes. Background noise may also include outside traffic sounds, rain, and wind.

The individual in charge of the room searching team should look around the room and determine how the room is to be divided for searching and to what height the first searching sweep should extend. The first searching sweep will cover all items resting on the floor up to the selected height.

You should divide the room into two virtually equal parts. This equal division should be based on the number and type of objects in the room to be searched and not on the size of the room. An imaginary line is then drawn between two objects in the room; e.g., the edge of the window on the north wall to the floor lamp on the south wall.

First Room-Searching Sweep

Look at the furniture or objects in the room and determine the average height of the majority of items resting on the floor. In an average room, this height usually includes table or desk tops and chair backs. The first searching height usually covers the items in the room up to hip height.

After the room has been divided and a searching height has been selected, both individuals go to one end of the room division line and start from a back-to-back position. This is the starting point, and the same point will be used on each successive searching sweep. Each person now starts searching his/her way around the room, working toward the other person, checking all items resting on the floor around the wall area of the room. When the two individuals meet, they will have completed a "wall sweep." They should then work together and check all items in the middle of the room up to the selected hip height, including the floor under the rugs. This first searching sweep should also include those items which may be mounted on or in the walls, such as air-conditioning ducts, baseboard heaters, and built-in wall cupboards, if these fixtures are below hip height.

The first searching sweep usually consumes the most time and effort. During all the searching sweeps, use the electronic or medical stethoscope on walls, furniture items, and floors.

Second Room-Searching Sweep

The individual in charge again looks at the furniture or objects in the room and determines the height of the second searching sweep. This height is usually from the hip to the chin or top of the head. The two persons return to the starting point and repeat the searching technique at the second selected searching height. This sweep usually covers pictures hanging on the walls, built bookcases, and tall table lamps.

Third Room-Searching Sweep

When the second searching sweep is completed, the person in charge again determines the next searching height, usually from the chin or the top of the head up to the ceiling. The third sweep is then made. This sweep usually covers high mounted air-conditioning ducts and hanging light fixtures.

Fourth Room-Searching Sweep

If the room has a false or suspended ceiling, the fourth sweep involves investigation of this area. Check flush or ceiling-mounted light fixtures, air conditioning or ventilation ducts, sound or speaker systems, electrical wiring, and structural frame members.

Have a sign or marker indicating "Search Completed" conspicuously posted in the area. Place a piece of colored Scotch tape across the door and door jamb approximately 2 feet above floor level if the use of signs is not practical.

The room searching technique can be expanded. The same basic technique can be applied to search any enclosed area. Encourage the use of common sense or logic in searching. If a guest speaker at a convention has been threatened, common sense would indicate searching the speakers platform and microphones first, but always return to the searching technique. Do not rely on random or spot checking of only logical target areas. The bomber may not be a logical person.

In conclusion, the following steps should be taken in order to search a room:

1. Divide the area and select a search height.

2. Start from the bottom and work up.

3. Start back-to-back and work toward each other.

4. Go around the wails and proceed toward the center of the room.

Suspicions Object Located

It is imperative that personnel involved in a search be instructed that their only mission is to search for and report suspicious objects. Under no circumstances should anyone move, jar or touch a suspicious object or anything attached to it. The removal or disarming of a bomb must be left to the professionals in explosive ordnance disposal. When a suspicious object is discovered, the following procedures are recommended:

1. Report the location and an accurate description of the object to the appropriate warden. This information should be relayed immediately to the command center, which will, notify the police and fire departments, and rescue squad. These officers should be met and escorted to the scene.

2. If absolutely necessary, place sandbags or mattresses, never metal shields, around the suspicious object. Do not attempt to cover the object.

3. Identify the danger area, and block it off with a clear zone of at least 300 feet, including floors below and above the object.

4. Check to see that all doors and windows are open to minimize primary damage from blast and secondary damage from fragmentation.

5. Evacuate the building. 6.Do not permit re-entry into the building until the device has been removed/disarmed, and the building declared safe for re-entry.

Handling the News Media

It is of paramount importance that all inquiries from the news media be directed to one individual appointed as spokesperson. All other persons should be instructed not to discuss the situation with outsiders, especially the news media.

The purpose of this provision is to furnish the news media with accurate information and to see that additional bomb threat calls are not precipitated by irresponsible statements from uninformed sources.

Summary

This information serves only as a guide and is not intended to be anything more. The ultimate determination of how to handle a bomb threat must be made by the individual responsible for the threatened facility.

Develop a bomb incident plan. Draw upon any expertise that is available to you from police departments, government agencies, and security specialists. Don't leave anything to chance. Be prepared!

Bomb Incident Plan

1. Designate a chain of command.

2. Establish a command center.

3. Decide what primary and alternate communications will be used.

4. Establish clearly how and by whom a bomb threat will be evaluated.

5. Decide what procedures will be followed when a bomb threat is received or device discovered.

6. Determine to what extent the available bomb squad will assist and at what point the squad will respond.

7. Provide an evacuation plan with enough flexibility to avoid a suspected danger area.

8. Designate search teams.

9. Designate areas to be searched.

10. Establish techniques to be utilized during search.

11. Establish a procedure to report and track progress of the search and a method to lead qualified bomb technicians to a suspicious package.

12. Have a contingency plan available if a bomb should go off.

13. Establish a simple-to-follow procedure for the person receiving the bomb threat.

14. Review your physical security plan in conjunction with the development of your bomb incident plan.

Command Center

1. Designate a primary location and an alternate location.

2. Assign personnel and designate decisionmaking authority.

3. Establish a method for tracking search teams.

4. Maintain a list of likely target areas.

5. Maintain a blueprint of floor diagrams in the center.

6. Establish primary and secondary methods of communication. (Caution-the use of two-way radios during a search can cause premature detonation of an electric blasting cap.)

7. Formulate a plan for establishing a command center, if a threat is received after normal work hours.

8. Maintain a roster of all necessary telephone numbers.

ATF BOMB THREAT CHECKLIST

Exact time of call:

Exact words of caller:

QUESTIONS TO ASK

  1. When is bomb going to explode?

  2. Where is the bomb?

  3. What does it look like?

  4. What kind of bomb is it?

  5. What will cause it to explode?

  6. Did you place the bomb?

  7. Why?

  8. Where are you calling from?

  9. What is your address?

10. What is your name?

CALLER'S VOICE (circle)

      Calm   Slow   Crying   Slurred   Stutter   Deep   Loud   Broken

      Giggling   Accent   Angry   Rapid   Stressed   Nasal   Lisp

      Excited   Disguised   Sincere   Squeaky   Normal

If voice is familiar, whom did it sound like?

Were there any background noises?

Remarks:

Person receiving call:

Telephone number call received at:

Date:

Report call immediately to: (Refer to bomb incident plan)

Detecting Suspicious Packages/ Letters

REMEMBER

The item does not have to be delivered by a carrier.
Most bombers set up and deliver the bomb themselves.

1. If delivered by carrier, inspect for lumps, bulges, or protrusions, without applying pressure.

2. If delivered by carrier, balance check if lopsided or heavy sided.

3. Handwritten addresses or labels from companies are improper. Check to see if the company exists and if they sent a package or letter.

4. Packages wrapped in string are automatically suspicious, as modern packaging materials have eliminated the need for twine or string.

5. Excess postage on small packages or letters indicates that the object was not weighed by the Post Office.

6. No postage or non-canceled postage.

7. Any foreign writing, addresses, or postage.

8. Handwritten notes, such as: "To Be Opened in the Privacy of" "CONFIDENTIAL" - "Your Lucky Day is Here" - "Prize Enclosed".

9. Improper spelling of common names, places, or titles.

10. Generic or incorrect titles.

11. Leaks, stains, or protruding wires, string, tape, etc.

12. Hand delivered or dropped off for a friend packages or letters.

13. No return address or nonsensical return address.

14. Any letters or packages arriving before or after a phone call from an unknown person asking if the item was received.

15. If you have a suspicious letter or package,

Call: 911-ISOLATE-EVACUATE

Bombs can be constructed to look like almost anything and can be placed or delivered in any number of ways. The probability of finding a bomb that looks like the stereotypical bomb is almost nonexistent. The only common denominator that exists among bombs is that they are designed or intended to explode.

Most bombs are homemade and are limited in their design only by the imagination of, and resources available to, the bomber. Remember, when searching for a bomb, suspect anything that looks unusual. Let the trained bomb technician determine what is or is not a bomb.

D-1